Inventing the Language to Tell It

Robinson Jeffers and the Biology
of Consciousness

GEORGE HART

Fordham University Press

NEW YORK   2013

Library of Congress Cataloging-in-Publication Data

Hart, George Leslie.
    Inventing the language to tell it : Robinson Jeffers and the biology of
consciousness / George Hart. — First edition.
        pages cm
    Includes bibliographical references and index.
    ISBN 978-0-8232-5489-7 (cloth : alk. paper)
    1. Jeffers, Robinson, 1887–1962—Criticism and interpretation. I. Title.
PS3519.E27Z634 2013
811'.52—dc23

                                                        2013009215

15 14 13   5 4 3 2 1

First edition

THE
AMERICAN
LITERATURES
INITIATIVE
A book in the American Literatures Initiative (ALI), a collaborative
publishing project of NYU Press, Fordham University Press, Rutgers
University Press, Temple University Press, and the University of Virginia
Press. The Initiative is supported by The Andrew W. Mellon Foundation.
For more information, please visit www.americanliteratures.org.

To the memory of my parents

Culture's outlived, art's root-cut, discovery's
The way to walk in. Only remains to invent the language to tell it.
—ROBINSON JEFFERS, "PRELUDE"

The land and sea, the animals fishes and birds, the sky of heaven and the orbs, the forests mountains and rivers, are not small themes . . . but folks expect of the poet to indicate more than the beauty and dignity which always attach to dumb real objects . . . they expect him to indicate the path between reality and their souls.
—WALT WHITMAN, PREFACE TO THE 1855 *LEAVES OF GRASS*

The stars, the dark depths of space beyond, and the light streaming from the sun, speak to us; the earth, the waves and winds, the twittering of birds and the glances of animals, speak to us. The fall of a rock, the shifting of the sands can be read and, in one way of reading, the story of the earth is revealed, in another way of reading, elusive apprehensions of our own inner fate or identity in process emerge. We are creatures of language and invent in turn with the sounds of our mouths, or hands beating surfaces, or with marks upon a stone or arrangements of sticks, an other speech, a speech "for its own sake" in answer to the World Order which was a language before ours.
—ROBERT DUNCAN, *FICTIVE CERTAINTIES*

Contents

Acknowledgments

It has been my good fortune to have great teachers and mentors through-out my education—I hope that this book is adequate thanks to all of them. Those who initiated, supported, and encouraged my interest in Robin-son Jeffers, from high school through college to graduate school, deserve special thanks: Nick Bozanic, Sanford Marovitz, and Albert Gelpi. Tim Hunt took an early interest in my work on Jeffers, and this book is the better for his encouragement and wise counsel. The annual meetings of the Robinson Jeffers Association provided the forum in which most of these readings were first presented, and I am grateful to its members—especially Rob Kafka, Robert Brophy, James Karman, Robert Zaller, Peter Quigley, David Rothman, and ShaunAnne Tangney—for their always thoughtful and helpful responses to my arguments. Colleagues who provided the intellectual community and institutional support that nourished my work also deserve many thanks, especially Scott Slovic, Cheryll Glotfelty, and Michael Cohen at the University of Nevada, Reno, and Eileen Klink, Tim Caron, Paul Gilmore, and Bill Mohr at California State University, Long Beach. My parents, Jay and Sally Hart, did not live to see this book finished, but they raised me to finish what I started, so it is dedicated to them. I also had help finishing it from my wife, Susan Wiggins—my best reader and my favorite person.

Introduction: Robinson Jeffers's Sacramental Poetics

In 1928, Robinson Jeffers received a questionnaire from a local newspaper that was preparing a special feature on him as Carmel, California's most famous literary resident at the time. From the draft response that remains in his papers, it apparently inquired about his current projects, favorite themes, and daily routine, as well as the books, experiences, people, and ideas that influenced him. Under the heading of "ideas," Jeffers wrote: "Mechanistic anti-spiritual point of view from medical school, running in harness with a mysticism that seems almost instinctive."[1] The tension between materialism and mysticism, oppositional powers harnessed together to achieve a unitary purpose, is the cardinal indicator of Jeffers's sacramental poetics. The harness itself is the biology of consciousness. That is, since he is committed to a thoroughly materialist view of reality, which is also at the same time a source of spiritual value, he cannot uncouple the horses and travel on one alone. The biology of consciousness is the idea that the seemingly immaterial epiphenomenon of mind is based materially in the brain. If spirit is immanent in matter, if mind is based in the brain, then the mystical must run in harness with the antispiritual, and a sacramental poetics must accommodate this apparent dualism. In an early poem, Jeffers poses this as a question that he will spend his career trying to answer: "Then what is this unreasonable excess, / Our needless quality, this unrequired / Exception in the world, this consciousness?" (*CP* 1:7).

Albert Gelpi writes that "the drama of Jeffers' writings stems from his fixation on the fact that our species' unique evolution of consciousness has endowed us with mind and will, but mind and will are depraved by the egotism which is a condition and consequence of consciousness."[2] We should hear a Calvinist inflection in the word *depraved*. Jeffers considered consciousness a sort of original sin, the blot on the race that divorces it from nature, absorbing these terms from his father, William Hamilton Jeffers, a Presbyterian minister and professor of theology. At times in his poems, Jeffers finds peace with consciousness, going so far as to consider it the raison d'être for humanity—we are here to witness and praise the "divinely superfluously beauty" and the "excesses of God." But more often, consciousness is the trigger for the depravity of the race, and the poet struggles to integrate it into his religious vision. Consciousness is the Fortunate Fall in evolution—without it we would not know that we are a part of the universe, but with it we are apart from the universe.

I will draw on contemporary neuroscience to understand and assess Jeffers's interest in consciousness, but this book does not take a cognitive studies approach to his work. It is not a reading of Jeffers's poetry to demonstrate how the mind works; neither does it argue that literary art is bound by science or evolutionary processes. I take it as a given that literature is a distinctive activity of our species and that it coevolved with our language and our brains. That it takes Jeffers himself a considerable amount of time to arrive at this same conclusion is part of the interest that I have in his work. It is my intention to use neuroscience and the philosophy of the embodied mind to clarify Jeffers's struggle with the biology of consciousness, as Mark Edmundson admonishes historical critics to "use the past to clarify, but not to contextualize, the work at hand."[3] As we will see, Jeffers himself proposed that science and poetry operate on parallel tracks but by different means, and he insisted that poetry's discoveries are as equally valid as science's. I hope to use the science to clarify the significance of the poetry's discoveries. What is more, the biology of consciousness is at the core of Jeffers's poetry, but it is not all of it. Getting a better sense of why it was so important to Jeffers will allow us to see better the total achievement of his work, the development of a sacramental poetics that expresses a holistic vision of a divine cosmos.

Jeffers is the only major twentieth-century American poet who attempted such a thing, and for this reason he stands apart from the poets who would otherwise constitute his cohort—the modernist generation that includes T. S. Eliot, Ezra Pound, William Carlos Williams, H.D., and Marianne Moore. Also, he is the only modern American poet to be consistently associated with the environmental movement, which embraces and appropriates his work for its intense association with a place of stunning natural beauty and its expression of a nonanthropocentric environmental ethic. The remainder of this introduction will place Jeffers in these two traditions of literary and environmental history, and the first chapter will develop a reading of his sacramental poetics in more detail before I return to the biology of consciousness as the central motivating force in his work. Chapters 2 through 5 trace the consequences of his fixation on consciousness through his poetry chronologically, examining its emergence in the 1920s, his development of new modes of approaching it in the 1930s, the crisis that the Second World War created in his holistic worldview, and the final resolutions he reached in his poetry of the late 1950s. In the Conclusion, I return to the question of Jeffers's place in literary tradition by looking at the quarrel between Kenneth Rexroth and William Everson over his status as a precursor in California poetry.

* * *

Albert Gelpi also notes, "For if there is no Jeffers tradition in American poetry, he clearly belongs to the autochthonous tradition that gives our expression its original and dominant character," which is "a very American sense of location, an equally American commitment to organic nature as the energized ground of a revelation at once erotic and spiritual, and a consequent suspicion of ego-goals and civilization as subversive to the field of revelation."[4] William Everson concurs, arguing that Jeffers is in fact "a transcendentalist gone West and turned inside out" and that in this sense he is vitally connected to Whitman, "each poet present[ing] a distinct facet of what might be called our fundamental native pantheism."[5] Such coordinates, "the autochthonous tradition" and "our fundamental native pantheism," place Jeffers in the broad mainstream of a literary-cultural tradition that is best called sacramental. Two of this book's epigraphs chart the romantic and the postmodern versions of this sacramental tendency in American poetry. Both Walt Whitman and Robert Duncan acknowledge the material existence of the world "out there," and both emphasize the need for our connection with it through language. Whitman's romanticism posits the poet as mediator, Emerson's "liberating god," connecting the soul of the reader to the "dumb real objects" that would otherwise fail to achieve meaning. Duncan's postmodernism makes the universe itself a language system, and we read "elusive apprehensions of our own inner fate or identity" in it. To grasp what eludes us, we create our own language and meaning, distinct from the world but in response to it. Spirit and matter, mediated by and discovered in language—this is the essence of a sacramental poetics. Jeffers occupies the modernist position between Whitman and Duncan, and it is in terms of modernism that he is most often misunderstood.[6]

In a significant sense, the idea of a literary tradition is a modernist invention, propounded by T. S. Eliot in his 1919 essay "Tradition and the Individual Talent." Although the "autochthonous tradition" is antimodernist in many ways, Eliot's version of the concept offers some key ideas for our consideration of it. In her reassessment of Eliot's essay, Aleida Assmann asserts that Eliot's "strong concept of tradition" is normative and that "in this sense [it] is usually seen from the inside, denoting the construction of a continuity that is established through cultural practices, rites and symbols, designed to counter change, decay and forgetting."[7] In its normative sense, Eliot's tradition is a response to historicism's relentless temporalization of artistic works and human experience. The sacramental nature poetry on which this study focuses is also unified in its response to modernity's historicist relativism.

Furthermore, Assmann associate's Eliot's sense of tradition with the disruptions and upheavals of the First World War. Tracing the essay's dialectic between "whole" and "fragment," she offers an insight that can help us see Jeffers's sacramental poetics as a shadow version of modernism:

> Nearly ninety years after the publication of "Tradition and the Individual Talent," we are becoming aware of the fact that the normative quality of the terms "whole" and "fragment" have been inverted. Separated from Eliot's essay by a yet more destructive war, we notice that the term "whole" has now lost nearly all of its positive and beneficial flavour. It has become a problematic term that we have learned to mistrust, to shun, to deconstruct. The term "whole" smacks of false hopes, of misguided idealism, perhaps even of a menacing totalitarianism. While "whole" has come to be linked with a modern "unity" that may be imposed by force and repression, the term "fragment" has come to be linked with a postmodern "diversity" that has now, after we have come to suspect the ambitious visions of modernity, gained the status of a positive and salvaging term.[8]

The fragmentation of culture and consciousness precipitated by the Great War affected Jeffers, a year and half older than Eliot, nearly as deeply as it did the expatriate Eliot, and the Second World War had the same effect on him and the next two generations, as we will seen in chapter 4.

Inasmuch as Eliot's tradition attempted to escape time and history to reestablish continuity and wholeness by integrating the individual artist and his or her work into a living system of great works, Jeffers attempted to integrate the individual into the living, and divine, system of nature in order to recover the whole. Whereas Eliot deliberately constructed his tradition to preserve and restore culture, thereby liberating the individual from the wreck of history, sacramental poetics offers restoration by discovering the spiritual in the material, by finding the whole outside culture and history, and Jeffers's "invention of a language to tell it" thereby liberates the individual from the wreck of civilization.[9]

Another way in which Jeffers's sacramental poetics shadows modernism is this fusion of the spiritual and the material. While Eliot turned away from his modernist version of tradition to find a sense of the whole in Anglo-Catholicism and British citizenship, many of his fellow modernists pursued alternative forms of spiritual practice and belief as a response to materialism. As scholars such as Timothy Materer and Leon Surette have demonstrated, modernism's dominant spiritual interest was in occult religions and practices. Surette posits the occult's constitutive role in the "birth" of modernism and argues that "modernism continued the Romantic celebration of passion, revelation, and revolution, and found much of its inspiration in many of the same sources as the Romantics—in Neoplatonism, Gnosticism, the Kabbala, and Swedenborg. These sources have been obscured by modernist scholarship's fixation on nineteenth- and twentieth-century archaeology, anthropology, and comparative religion."[10] Although sacramental poetics does draw from similar alternative systems of belief, as well as from those of the mainstream, and Jeffers himself incorporates occult rituals into his verse on occasion, his sacramentalism is distinctly different from modernism's occult.[11]

Surette makes this observation about the occult's worldview: "A ... fundamental feature of Western religions is a dualistic ontology—that is, the postulation of a spiritual and a material realm. The occult is almost invariably monist, assuming a single realm modulating from material or 'hylic' thickness through mental or psychic attenuation to spiritual or noumenal reality. Because of this monism, the modern occult thought it had found an ally in materialist science's discovery of radiation and the nonparticulate nature of quantum physics."[12] Jeffers's sacramentalism also rejects Western religions' ontological dualism, and it also finds an ally in scientific materialism, but it does not follow the occult's lead into monism. A practicing occultist can claim the authority of his or her experience of the continuum between matter and spirit, but a poet, whether sacramental or occultist, must present that experience in poetic language, which presents a dualistic break from the monist ontology. According to Materer, irony is the solution for the occult modernist, who "deal[s] with the problem of belief and disbelief with a modernist sophistication and self-consciousness that is neither merely credulous nor merely skeptical." Occult modernists take an "ironic stance" to negotiate between skepticism and belief, and therefore they can both entertain their visions of the "uncanny world" and distance themselves from it.[13] This ironic stance is perhaps the most significant distinction between modernist occultism and sacramental materialism. Whereas both modes refuse the "merely credulous" and the "merely skeptical," seeking to accommodate both to the monism of spirit and matter, Jeffers's sacramental poetics does not turn to irony to resolve this dilemma.

While occult modernism is a shadow-twin of a sacramental poetics, the dominant modes of modernism displaced both. Materer observes that for Eliot "skepticism is dialectically in relation with belief," and he points out that Wallace Stevens's "modernism is characterized by his skeptical and ironic sensibility," which, for many critics, "expresses the true spirit of modern poetry."[14] In 1959, Robert Langbaum argued that modernism of this sort produces a "new nature poetry," the exemplars of which are Stevens and Marianne Moore. Both poets "convey in their sense of nature their sense of the age," and their sense of nature is the modern view of "the mindlessness of nature, its nonhuman otherness."[15] Langbaum admits that "the ultimate subject of nature poetry [is] the divinity in nature," but the conditions of modernity leave us in a state of doubt about what that divinity is, uncertain if it is a human construct imposed on nature or if it is completely other and thus unknowable. In short, Langbaum's "new nature poetry" has a religious valence, but it is not sacramental; it makes divinity in nature an epistemological dilemma, not an ontological one. It is what Guy Rotella, in *Reading and Writing Nature*, calls epistemological nature poetry, and its motivating force is skepticism rather than faith.

Thus, according to Surette, modernism suppressed the occult roots of its own tradition and dismissed the sacramental materialism of Jeffers's West Coast ethos. It made a strong enough impact that one critic, Nathan A. Scott, in search of a sacramental tradition, failed to find it in the modernist period at all. In *The Wild Prayer of Longing*, Scott explains the post–World War II emergence of a new sacramentalism as the response to modernity and its rejection of the "figural imagination." According to Scott, "the traditional or premodern imagination" interpreted reality as a figure of God—"the world [was] considered to be but a shadow of the Eternal . . . itself . . . essentially a *figura* of an occult reality."[16] Modern science brought an end to the figural imagination, and for Scott modern literature takes place under the sign of either realism or symbolism, embodied in what he calls the realistic or angelic fallacies. For the modern writer, the choice was either brute fact, only to be represented as accurately as possible, or pure poetry, with no reference at all to the world "out there." The figural imagination, which is essentially dualistic, was polarized into a choice between two different monisms. Scott writes, "A literature under the dominance of either [fallacy] . . . is one which has been evacuated of anything resembling a sacramental vision of existence."[17] This division can be seen as one between epistemological nature poetry and occult modernism.

Jeffers's sacramental poetics locates itself at the divide between the angelic and realistic fallacies, rejecting the necessary decision between them as monisms and reasserting the dilemma of the figural imagination's dualism. However, the objective of the poetry it produces is the reinstatement of a sense of the divine inherent in nature without erasing the fact of nature's materiality. It rejects skepticism's epistemological dilemma, taking the divinity of nature on faith, but this choice is not a regression to the premodern imagination. Such poetry still addresses issues crucial to the modern world and offers self-aware instances of the difficulty of maintaining an ontological stance toward sacramental reality. For example, Scott points out that the implication of the Christian sacrament is twofold and that this implication holds for all sacramental poets, Christian or not. The common objects of bread and wine indicate the holy in the most mundane, and thereby the Christian sacrament touches an ontological condition that creates an ethical obligation. Scott writes: "And thus one of the most searching questions posed by the sacramental principle concerns what general perspective on reality it may be under which the world, in its every aspect, can be found to be itself something essentially sacramental."[18] For Scott, this sacramental perspective is a postwar phenomenon, a reaction to the diminished thing of nature in modernity. Jeffers does not figure into his argument because his influence is invisible in the glare of mainstream modernism.

Scott's nominee for preeminent postwar nature poet is Theodore Roethke, who comes closest to achieving a "logic of 'sacramentation'" in his estimation.[19] Certainly, other postwar poets have devised various strategies for presenting a sacramental vision of reality in nature poetry, yet it is remarkable that Jeffers, whose work Robert Brophy describes as "the record of a fervent quest for a sacramental view of reality," always falls outside discussions of this literary history.[20] One reason for this is the isolation of the West Coast writer in the early part of the twentieth century. West Coast poets produced a renewed tradition of sacramental nature poetry unlike that of any other literary region or movement, but even in studies of West Coast poetics Jeffers is denied standing because postwar poets are always discussed in regard to modernism. Michael Davidson identifies "an impulse toward the sacramental" in the work of Kenneth Rexroth, William Everson, and Robert Duncan in the 1940s, and Charles Altieri, in his study of poetry of the 1960s, *Enlarging the Temple*, discusses the "postmodern religious nature lyric" using the examples of two West Coast poets, Duncan and Gary Snyder. Neither Davidson nor Altieri looks back to Jeffers as the nearest conduit for this "sacramental impulse."[21]

* * *

Although Jeffers is often left out of the literary histories that document twentieth-century American poetry, he has found a prominent place in environmental histories concerned with nature and religion.[22] Environmental history offers the cultural context for Jeffers, but the problem with this approach is that it tends to read him as a prophet or a philosopher. The poetry is treated as statement, as a transparent record of his evolution as an environmental thinker. A good example is Thomas R. Dunlap's *Faith in Nature: Environmentalism as Religious Quest*. Dunlap places Jeffers in the history of environmentalism as a religious perspective in two significant ways—locating him in the midcentury as one of "Emerson's Children" along with Aldo Leopold, and commenting on his appropriation by activist groups such as the Sierra Club. However, it is Dunlap's explanation of environmentalism as a secular faith that offers more for our consideration of Jeffers's sacramental poetics: "Environmentalism's future seems to lie in the possibilities offered by its situation as a secular faith, searching for a transcendent within this world, building a morality on our scientific understanding of our place in it, and using science, which refuses to ask about purpose, to search for ultimate meanings. Facing that paradox, solving or embracing it, remains environmentalism's central task."[23] This paradox is the same one that sacramental nature poetry confronts, and it is the motivation behind Jeffers's work as a whole. It is the tension inherent in harnessing a "mechanistic anti-spiritual point of view" with an instinctive mysticism.

Perhaps the grandest claim for Jeffers's prominence in environmental history has been made by Max Oelschlaeger in his massive *The Idea of Wilderness: From Prehistory to the Age of Ecology*. Oelschlaeger pairs

Jeffers and Snyder and places them in a line of American writers that includes the "giant[s] of wilderness philosophy": Thoreau, Muir, and Leopold. Although he reads and quotes the poetry extensively, Oelschlaeger is mainly concerned with the expression of "the idea of wilderness" as he finds it there. For him, Jeffers is a "wilderness poet" because his "premodern" sensibility leads him to the "postmodern perspective" of inhumanism, which rejects the modernist view of nature as mechanism. Inhumanism, for Oelschlaeger, is a version of phenomenological bracketing that suspends modernity and allows an experience of the Paleolithic condition of oneness with nature that is the basis of the wilderness idea. As a wilderness poet, Jeffers locates sacramental value in the material world: "Jeffers's religious vision reflects . . . the inhumanist bracketing of conventional wisdom and turning away from the merely human. The poetry recognizes that the modern person—the humanist of modern culture—has become Homo oeconomicus, and the world in which life plays out its course merely profane. The inhumanist, however, is a specimen of Homo religious, and celebrates an eternal mythical present: a living-God in the world."[24] In this way, for Oelschlaeger, Jeffers stands as the twentieth-century Thoreau, expressing a vision of humanity's relation to nature that his contemporaries were not ready to embrace, and Snyder is the century's Muir figure, finding a ready and willing audience for his "wilderness poetry."[25]

Oelschlaeger's intellectual history is relevant to the history of sacramental nature poetry because he acknowledges the importance of language, but he fails to account for the motivating tension of sacramental poetics in its struggle with language. Drawing his terms from Heidegger, Oelschlaeger claims that poets such as Jeffers and Snyder "dwell poetically" in language. "Language is ontogenetic, world making," and it "is the house of being," yet it is also the screen of convention that the poet must pierce through to make contact with being: "The thinking poet reaches toward a presence obscured by the obvious, toward what is absent because of its concealment behind language, behind opinion, behind ideology: *the wilderness poet calls forth being.*"[26] Oelschlaeger, citing Gadamer, grants the poet's words (the poem itself) ontological status and thereby absolves himself of the necessity to account for his reading—for the explanation of how that being, which is beyond language, is called forth in language.

Thus language is the fall into consciousness from an Edenic state of unity that is the Paleolithic mind, and, paradoxically, language is the only way out of modernist dualism. "Language deceives us," Oelschlaeger writes, "for its implicit teleological structure is confused with . . . the constitution of the world. . . . We must refocus attention on language in its symbolizing function, for with the Paleolithic mind's coming to self-consciousness, humankind unknowingly severed the organic link with the Magna Mater, with the cosmic womb that gave us birth." However, he fails to investigate how poetry itself negotiates this contradictory terrain: "By standing within the hermeneutic circle we somehow engage ourselves in a self-conscious quest to escape the strictures of language (and therefore culture) and reestablish contact with the ground (bios, Ursprung) that lies beneath our feet." But *how* do we engage in this process? He goes on, "The thinking poets and poetic thinkers . . . . have stood within the hermeneutic circle, and then passed through environment (the ecomachine) to the green world on its other side," but we must take their word for it.[27] Without an account of the "somehow," without an interpretation of how the poet attempts this escape, we have no way of understanding what has happened. Oelschlaeger transforms Heidegger's hermeneutical circle from an epistemological theory of interpretation into an ontological category. Yet it might be best to think of the circle as temporal rather than spatial, not a radical bracket that can open space and make a past state of mind available again but a process of interpretation that moves in a circle because it adds nothing new to what is already there, only arriving at an understanding of it. Paul de Man pointed out a similar slippage between a spatialized hermeneutical circle and a temporal process of reading that moved in a circle in his critique of American New Criticism, observing that the New Critics "pragmatically entered into the hermeneutic circle of interpretation, mistaking it for the organic circularity of natural processes."[28] Jeffers's vision may indeed be a version of the Paleolithic mind, a sense of oneness with natural process that is beyond language, but that is not what is important about his contribution to sacramental nature poetry. When we read his poetry we are participating in the hermeneutical circle that allows the poem to exist, and the recapitulation of that process sacramentalizes both poet and reader. To claim to step out of it is to leave the poetry altogether, a negation of the need for sacramentality at all. Robert Pogue Harrison offers a more subtle version of an ecologically informed poetic dwelling. The discontinuity between human and nature, he writes, "manifests itself in the phenomenon of language, which does not belong to the order of nature. Language is a differential, a standing-outside of nature, an *ecstasis* that opens a space of intelligibility within nature's closure. Understood not merely as the linguistic capacity of our superior intelligence but as the transcendence of our manner of being, language is the ultimate 'place' of human habitation. Before we dwell in this or that locale, or in this or that province, or in this or that city or nation, we dwell in the *logos*."²⁹ The hermeneutical circle, in this sense, is not something that can be stepped through, a portal into a nonlinguistic realm of pure being. The ontology of the work of art made out of language is its existence in the symbolic realm; transposed to the nonsymbolic, it ceases to exist.

In *The Rhetoric of Religion*, Kenneth Burke observes, "The supernatural is by definition the realm of the 'ineffable.' And language by definition is not suited to the expression of the 'ineffable'"; therefore our words about the divine are by necessity borrowed from our words that refer to things. He continues, "If the symbol-using animal approaches nature in terms of symbol-systems (as he inevitably does), then he will inevitably 'transcend' nature to the extent that symbol-systems are essentially different from the realms they symbolize. And these realms will be *necessarily* different, inasmuch as the translation of the *extra-symbolic* into *symbols* is a translation of something into terms of what it is not."³⁰ A sacramental poet is confronted with this paradox, and Jeffers is sensitive to it time and again, explicitly commenting on it in poems such as "Love the Wild Swan" (*CP* 2:410). Without the poet's struggle with his medium, a sacramental poetics would be liable to violations and dangers that critics have accused it of. A self-consciousness about language saves sacramental nature poetry from easy New Age spirituality, political demagoguery, and mere sloganeering. Though prophetic in tone and stance, Jeffers is not a prophet; though philosophical in attitude and worldview, he is not a philosopher. He is a poet, and we will find more value in his poetry if we read it as such.

* * *

This linguistic dilemma brings me to the lines from Jeffers's "Prelude" that provide this book's title. The tension in these lines resides in the distinction between invention and discovery. This statement has always seemed paradoxical to me, if not outright contradictory. In the exhaustion of culture and art we arrive at discovery, but discovery is meaningless unless we invent culture and art (language) to explain it. Discovery implies an ontological status (the thing exists in and of itself), and invention produces an epistemological dilemma (how do we know that our invention has not in fact produced the thing itself in the telling). The tension can be between mysticism and materialism, or invention and discovery, but it comes down to word and thing. We invent the language to tell the experience of discovery and thereby create another layer of culture or art that in turn needs to be outlived or cut through.

"Prelude" itself embodies the tension in this conflict, and chapter 2 provides an extended discussion of it. For now, a brief look at a more familiar and simple poem will suffice. In "Rock and Hawk" (*CP* 2:416), Jeffers presents an emblem of his sacramental poetics:

> Here is a symbol in which
> Many high tragic thoughts
> Watch their own eyes.
>
> This gray rock, standing tall
> On the headland, where the sea-wind
> Lets no tree grow,
>
> Earthquake-proved, and signatured
> By ages of storms: on its peak
> A falcon has perched.
>
> I think, here is your emblem
> To hang in the future sky;
> Not the cross, not the hive,
>
> But this; bright power, dark peace;
> Fierce consciousness joined with final
> Disinterestedness;
>
> Life with calm death; the falcon's
> Realist eyes and act
> Married to the massive
>
> Mysticism of stone,
> Which failure cannot cast down
> Nor success make proud.

The speaker invents and then interprets the image for us, explaining that the falcon perched on the rock symbolizes "Fierce consciousness joined with final / Disinterestedness." The hawk's consciousness is described as "realist," and the rock's presence is associated with mysticism. As an emblematic image, rock and hawk works well enough, but it also holds in abeyance the inherent tension between materialism and mysticism, discovery and invention, that Jeffers more fully engages in his experimental narratives. Nonetheless, the first tercet gestures toward this tension in its evocation of self-consciousness: the "tragic thoughts" of the human mind watch themselves in this reflection on the falcon's "realist eyes." However, in turning this vision outward the poem escapes the torsion of self-reflexive consciousness that twists and breaks forth in poems such as "Tamar," "Prelude," and "The Women at Point Sur."

In 1941, Jeffers concluded a talk called "Themes in My Poems" with a reading of this "little poem about a hawk" (*CP* 4:415), and he closed with a few comments on poetry as a means of discovery: "Science usually takes things to pieces in order to discover them; it dissects and analyzes; poetry puts things together, producing equally valid discovery, and actual creation. Something new is found out, something that the author himself did not know before he wrote it; and something new is made" (*CP* 4:416). Here the discoveries of science and the discoveries of poetry accommodate one another comfortably—much like the hawk perched upon the rock. However, the sacramental qualities of poetry come into effect when the two modes of knowing come into conflict. For if both are seen as modes of discovery, they may lead to versions of the same truth, but they also produce different ethical obligations in regard to that truth. The task of Jeffers's poetry, I think, is to bring together the analytic and synthetic ways of knowing without allowing them to cancel each other out, but also without merging them into an indistinct unity. In a significant sense, this is a task always doomed to failure because it happens in language, and, as readers such as Jacques Derrida and Paul de Man have shown, analysis and synthesis deconstruct in the process of interpretation.[31] The question is really about what might constitute "equally valid" discovery, because in one sense poetry invents what it discovers; as Jeffers puts it, "something new is made."

This sacramental poetry is important because it refuses to choose one monism over the other—the angelic over the realistic, or the spiritual over the material, or synthesis over analysis—and, in Jeffers's case, the strain between these forces that can be only temporarily resolved is the source of his power. In "Experience," Ralph Waldo Emerson says, "Spirit is matter reduced to an extreme thinness," and Gary Snyder, according to Jack Kerouac's *The Dharma Bums*, proclaimed a hundred or so years later: "The closer you get to real matter . . . the more spiritual the world is."[32] The acknowledgment of the inherent tension of putting this discovery into words is Jeffers's major contribution to sacramental nature poetry. Edward Abbey, who is perhaps Jeffers's foremost disciple after William Everson, begins and ends his book *Desert Solitaire* under the sign of bedrock and paradox, another figure of sacramentality. In the emblematic formulation of "Rock and Hawk," the "massive mysticism of stone" is sacramentality's bedrock. Consciousness, the hawk's "realist eyes and act," is its paradox. Echoing Jeffers, Abbey writes, "I dream of a hard and brutal mysticism in which the naked self merges with a non-human world and yet somehow survives still intact, individual, separate. Paradox and bedrock."[33] This is the dream of a sacramental poetics. It takes consciousness to recognize our oneness with nature, yet that consciousness, especially when it is manifest in language, is precisely what separates us from nature. Abbey, like Kenneth Burke, realized that the more firmly one grounds oneself in bedrock by means of words, the more paradoxical one's grasp on reality becomes. As he admits, language can never accommodate the facts in their totality, so a writer must "create a world of words" parallel to the real one.[34] Jeffers's sacramental nature poetry is the story of this invention, his world of words parallel to science's unfolding discovery of the materiality of nature, and his own equally valid discoveries of its divinity.

1 / Rock, Bark, and Blood: Sacramental Poetics and West Coast Nature Poetry

At a "Reinhabitation Conference" in 1976, Gary Snyder remarked: "The biological-ecological sciences have been laying out (implicitly) a spiritual dimension. We must find our way to seeing the mineral cycles, the water cycles, air cycles, nutrient cycles as sacramental."[1] Poets deal in metaphors and paradoxes, the tensions between image and reality, mind and nature, word and thing. Snyder deftly handles a central paradox of environmental thinking—the idea that material facts contain essential values—making a case (implicitly) for the function of poetry in matters of ecological concern. Environmentalists are committed to preserving the material world, and popular ecology supplies them with concepts such as ecotones, interdependence, biophilia, and biocentrism, concepts that they use to ascribe moral and purposive value to the natural world. Yet such terms alone cannot account for the sacramentality of natural process. Based solely on materialism, environmentalism would be no more than enlightened resource management. Snyder calls for a manifold relationship to the material cycles that sustain life, a relationship informed by science, bound by ethics, and animated by spirit. The physical acts of eating, breathing, walking, building, and so on imply a spiritual dimension that he calls "sacramental."

How can poetry negotiate the rift between fact and value and bring about an awareness of or attitude toward reality that may be legitimately called sacramental? Snyder's answer to this question would be "ritual." Poetry's basis in song, chant, litany, for a practitioner of "ethnopoetics" such as Snyder, enables it to function in a ritualistic mode that discovers sacramentality in nature. Recently, ritual studies scholar Ronald L.

Grimes has followed Snyder's lead, finding in it an opening to synthesize current ritual theory's emphasis on performance with environmentalism.[2] For both Grimes and Snyder, ritual/performance is the means by which material facts can blossom into sacramental value. In our consideration of the sacramental poetics of Robinson Jeffers, an additional element is required to understand the connection between ritual and sacramentality: rhetoric.

Ritual, Rhetoric, and Sacramentality

Grimes and Snyder are thinking of actual ritual, hence the necessity of performance. Performance theory has its roots in poststructuralism, so language—as a performance itself but also as a theoretical framework for understanding performance—is central. Contra strictly materialist approaches to environmentalism, ritual/performance makes a case for the importance of language not only as the means by which we express feeling for nature but also as constitutive of those feelings or attitudes. The standard liberal-Protestant response to the environmental crisis, according to Grimes, is simply to align one's beliefs and moral codes with "green" politics and ethics, and the only role for ritual is to illustrate this alignment. Performance as action or activism is left to the realm of politics and policy. "This strategy," Grimes writes, "is necessary but insufficient, because moral principles and legislation do not by themselves ground worldviews or form attitudes. Attitudes are not merely emotional, nor worldviews merely intellectual. Each collaborates with the other in determining how people act, what they perform, and therefore how they behave."[3] Grimes offers a preliminary account of the theories that ritual studies might put into practice in order to cultivate environmental attitudes, including Victor Turner's performativity, Charles Laughlin's and Eugene d'Aquili's biogenetic structuralism, and Roy Rappaport's ecological anthropology.[4] Underlying this interdisciplinarity is the linguistic turn of poststructuralism, and it provides the tension between word and action that motivates ritual theory. Language, as a differential system of signification, allows for performance and ritual to be equal: ritual is no longer the privileged term but another form of performance; meaning is produced not by reference—ritualized actions pointing to or mimicking divine actions—but by difference. Yet ritual returns language to the realm of action in order to take effect. Grimes writes, "For me, religious ritual is the predication of identities and differences (metaphors) so profoundly enacted that they suffuse bone and blood, thereby generating a cosmos, an oriented habitat. In such rites people enact a momentary cosmos of metaphor. Ritually, people do not dance merely to exercise limbs or to impress ticket buyers with their skills or even to illustrate sacredly held beliefs. Ritualists dance, rather, to discover ways of inhabiting a place. This is the noetic, or the divinatory, function of ritual; ritual helps people figure out, divine, even construct a cosmos."[5] Grimes's sophisticated ritual theory offers a new way of reading ritual as it structures Jeffers's poetry. This way of reading will show how his poetics achieves sacramentality and, in turn, how his use of rhetoric and ritual is revised and extended by Kenneth Rexroth and then by Snyder. Such an interpretation is necessary because ritual has been one of the major devices by which Jeffers's sacramentality is gauged, and a one-to-one correlation of his use of ritual has often been cited as his form of cosmogony. It is time to assess more accurately language's role in this process, and ritual theory helps bring about this clearer view. In a moment, I will turn to a close reading of a short poem that exemplifies Jeffers's sacramental poetics, but any discussion of ritual and sacrament in Jeffers must begin with his poem "Tamar."

"Tamar" has received its most thorough treatment as a ritualized narrative in Robert J. Brophy's *Robinson Jeffers: Myth, Ritual, and Symbol in His Narrative Poems*. Brophy's readings in this seminal study outline and elaborate the myth-ritual structure of five of Jeffers's long poems from the crucial period in which he discovered and perfected his mature voice, 1921 to 1928. His reading is detailed and exhaustive, and it shows how elaborately structured and finely written this poem is. Without reference to the mythical, biblical, and classical sources and structures so completely analyzed by Brophy, the poem can be briefly summed up: the character Tamar Cauldwell lives on Point Lobos with her father, brother, and two aunts. She commits incest with her brother, becomes pregnant, takes one of his friends as a lover, and then burns down the family farmhouse to purify it of the sins she and her father, who also had an incestuous relationship with his sister, have committed. As we will see, Jeffers gave various accounts of this strange and melodramatic poem's origins. In a well-known comment in the foreword to his *Selected Poetry*, he described its genesis: "'Tamar' grew up from the biblical story, mixed with a reminiscence of Shelley's *Cenci*, and from the strange, introverted and storm-twisted beauty of Point Lobos" (*CP* 4:393). He makes no direct reference to its ritualistic element here, offering only his version of its literary and place-based influences.

In the conclusion of his argument on the themes and sources of "Tamar," Brophy summarizes the myth-ritual aspect of the poem: "This is the action of the poem . . . simply stated: corruption, descent to death, and anticipated rebirth. In these cyclic terms and this movement, one can discover Jeffers' cosmogonic vision, his psychology of peace, and his metaphysics of value."[6] Indeed, Jeffers's first major poem outlines the contours of his worldview, and such a totality of vision is at once his power and his fatal flaw. The determinism inherent in it leaves little room for inventing new stories and developing new themes, and with such slight concern in the narratives for the intimacies and complexities of human interaction there are only large patterns of action for his characters to engage in. Nonetheless, as Brophy contends, the intention behind Jeffers's narrative poems is a presentation of a sacramental worldview through dramatized and narrated ritual.

Whereas Brophy treats "Tamar" as an index to Jeffers's religious themes in a literary-critical context, grafting Northrop Frye's archetypal myth criticism onto new critical formalism, William Everson, in *The Excesses of God: Robinson Jeffers as a Religious Figure*, reads the poet himself, as the subtitle has it, as "a religious figure."[7] Juxtaposing quotations from the poetry with excerpts from archetypal theologians such as Rudolph Otto, Everson demonstrates the mystical cast of Jeffers's mind as well as his themes and subjects. Rather than incorporating archetypal motifs into modern poetry by reduction and repetition, as Brophy would have it, Jeffers, according to Everson, actually ritualizes the writing process.[8] In his own ecstatic prose, Everson argues that "Tamar" was the poem by which Jeffers discovered this ritualizing process. Linking the conception of the narrative with the death of the poet's mother, Everson writes, "Writing her poem was his first efficacious ritual of the spirit. . . . his first sacrificial attempts—the creation of poems—had been inefficacious. His materials, his words, had lain damp within the body of her womb and he could not ignite them. When she died, he stepped forth fully blown, invincible, and uttered the name of the secret, incestuous Yin, whose offering to life he was—'Tamar'!"[9]

For the poet himself, Tamar embodies the spirit of place, "the wild rock coast / Of her breeding" (*CP* 1:25). Tamar's ritualistic value is presented in two poems. In her namesake poem, a climactic scene involves Tamar's dance and descent to the dead in a séance on the beach with her Aunt Jenny. Brophy reads the scene as a rite that follows Eliade's plan for seasonal, death-rebirth rituals.[10] Tamar enacts a ritualized dance in a trance—she "slip[s] every sheath down to her feet, the spirit of the place / Ruling her . . . / And dance[s] on the naked shore" (*CP* 1:44)—and her subconscious is linked to the spirit presences in the landscape: she dreams "two layers of dream," the "undercurrent layer" tapping into a collective unconsciousness that images the autochthonous presence of Indian tribes and the arrival of Spanish conquistadors (*CP* 1:34). By inventing such characters to be "vessels," as he calls them, to be filled with the spirit of a place, Jeffers creates a sort of objective correlative. Rather than being an allusion that objectifies the poet's subjective emotions, Tamar subjectifies the poet's intuition of the spirit of place.

Tamar is an unusual character in that her "spirit" seemed to haunt Jeffers's imagination, and in his mind she continued to haunt Point Lobos as its genius loci. She participates in another aspect of ritual in her appearance in the poem "Come Little Birds." This uncanny lyric, written fifteen years after "Tamar" and first published in *Poetry* in October 1939, matter-of-factly describes Jeffers's visit to a medium for the purpose of contacting his dead father. At the mouth of the Sur River, the old woman goes into a trance as her two sons ritually slaughter a calf and pour its blood into a trench. Drawn by the fresh blood, the dead appear, and after the poet speaks to the ghosts of some soldiers killed in the First World War (the speaker says that the year is 1920), the poet's father appears. Driven by a filial impulse, the speaker attempts to apologize to his father for some vague failure on his part, but the spirit seems to be unconcerned with news from the living. Then the medium begins to tire and spasms, and the boys prop her up and stoke the fire that has died down. The spell seems broken, and the dead fade away, "but," the speaker says, "a certain one of them came running toward me, slender and naked, I saw the firelight / Glitter on her bare thighs; she said 'I am Tamar Cauldwell from Lobos: write my story. Tell them / I have my desire.' She passed me and went like a lamp through the dark wood" (*CP* 3:9). The speaker is left on the beach alone to ponder these supernatural phenomena, and he concludes:

> I thought these decaying shadows and echoes of personality
>   are only a by-play; they are not the spirit
> That we see in one loved, or in saint or hero
> Shining through flesh. And I have seen it shine from a
>   mountain through rock, and even from an old tree
> Through the tough bark. The spirit (to call it so: what else
>   could I call it?) is not a personal quality, and not
> Mortal; it comes and goes, never dies. (*CP* 3:9)

Everson calls the séance in "Come Little Birds" "a primitive sacrificial liturgy," and he argues that such representations of ritual mirror Jeffers's own ritualizing, which takes the form of "a direct ceremonial utilization toward a method in poetic composition."[11] The compositional act, for Everson, is a form of "ritual propitiation." Jeffers presents the formula in "Apology for Bad Dreams" as the imagining of victims in order to pro-pitiate evil spirits, thereby protecting himself, his family, and his home. In the narratives, these fictional constructs are reified into idols and ves-sels. Everson, in turn, literalizes these objects in his account of Jeffers's method: "Thus Jeffers, priest of the word, victimizes the imagination in order to purge the proud flesh of man's primordial wound. . . . When the liturgy is completed and they disappear into time, he rouses from birth-trance and, peering about him, discovers their words in his book."[12] In his rhapsodic prose, Everson completes the process for Jeffers. Perhaps, we might say, he invents it. Whereas Brophy approaches Jeffers's ritual-izing from a sympathetic though critical perspective, Everson uses the textual evidence of ritual patterns in the poetry to create a sympathetic response to the tone and mood of the poetry that allows him access to the poet's subjectivity. Brophy matches the patterns of the poetry to pat-terns in comparative accounts of myth and ritual, thereby establishing Jeffers's credentials as a ritualistic poet. Everson attempts, not to deter-mine the accuracy of Jeffers's representations of ritual, but rather "to sense in his use of them that quality corresponding to the part of the soul from which they originated, to use them as gauges of his authentic religious disposition."[13] In both cases, language, through a system of pos-itive identifications, is reified into ritual process. Metaphors transform into action, reversing Grimes's sense that ritual enacts metaphor, not the other way round.

This inversion is the crux for my discussion of Jeffers and sacramen-tality. Jeffers knows as a poet he only has language's signifying capacity at his disposal. He enacted ritual "to discover ways of inhabiting a place,"[14] not least of which, of course, was building Hawk Tower and additions to Tor House. But stonemasonry and writing are different processes, so their productions are ontologically different. One could imitate Jeffers's rituals of inhabitation and endow a home with sacred significance, and such a practice would differ greatly from visiting Hawk Tower as a fetish, which would lack any ritualistic value. Reading his poetry offers a differ-ent ritual process—to locate meaning in the texts themselves abrogates Brophy's and Everson's methods, which locate meaning outside the text, yet it offers other prospects for sacramentality. Grimes's precursor in rit-ual theory, Jonathan Z. Smith, contends that ritual and sacramentality, like language, produce difference rather than identity, and that linguistic difference takes on meaning only through an abstract system of social hierarchy. In other words, ritual functions arbitrarily and convention-ally. Jeffers can neither find the sacred through language nor point us toward it, though he might try. However, he can engage in the process of sacramentation in language, and readers, in the process of interpreting to make meaning, can too. Smith writes, "We do well to remember that long before 'the Sacred' appeared in discourse as a substantive (a usage that does not antedate Durkheim), it was primarily employed in verbal forms, most especially with the sense of making an individual a king or bishop (as in the obsolete English verbs to sacrate or to sacre), or in adjectival forms denoting the result of the process of sacration. Ritual is not an expression of or a response to 'the Sacred'; rather, something or someone is made sacred by ritual (the primary sense of sacrificium)."[15] Smith's poststructuralist approach to ritual has deep implications for sacramental-materialist poetry. Ritual enacted through performance, as Grimes argues, balances the bipolar aspect of language, allowing metaphor to produce both difference and identity. However, like ritual, language itself, decoupled from physical performance, does not point to the sacred but rather produces it. Sacramentation happens in language as process—there is no transcendent divinity outside language (or consciousness) to which to point.

Through the conventions of story and character, narrative poems such as "Tamar" offer the most apparent analogues for ritual in Jeffers's poetry. They provide the large-scale means by which he reveals the spirit "shining through flesh"; his lyric poems, on the other hand, deploy different strategies by which that spirit can be seen shining "from a mountain through rock" or "from an old tree / Through the tough bark." Brophy's account of the narratives is a case in point. Viewed through the lens of archetypal myth criticism, the abstract patterns of ritual action are clearly seen. Most interesting, such structural designs are most readily apparent in Jeffers's more controlled narratives. Of the poems written in the 1921–28 period, Brophy omits "The Women at Point Sur," the most troublesome in terms of structure and purpose. The distancing effects of the myth-ritual system did indeed allow Jeffers to "magic" horror away from himself, as he puts it in "Apology for Bad Dreams." When he approached his sacramental vision more closely, and there is sufficient evidence to indicate that the conception of "The Women at Point Sur" is closely related to his "discovery" of what he later called Inhumanism, the sacramentality of myth did not suffice.[16] To see the significance of Jeffers's sacramental poetics in environmental terms, we need to consider his lyric poems. Rather than imposing classical and ancient myth onto his contemporary characters and Californian locale, the shorter poems sacramentalize natural history. His lyric strategy maintains a dual focus on the material and the mystical by means of the rhetorical. Language serves, not as a pointing device, but as a mediating ground on which the sacred and the profane coexist. "Oh Lovely Rock," from *Such Counsels You Gave to Me* (1937), and "The Summit Redwood," from *Cawdor* (1928), if not the actual accounts of the experiences mentioned in "Come Little Birds," are direct parallels; respectively, they are the rock and the bark evoked in this chapter's title. In "Oh Lovely Rock," as we will see later in this chapter, Jeffers deploys the so-called pathetic fallacy to reveal the spirit shining through the rock; in "The Summit Redwood," anecdotal narrative and descriptive technique produce the sacramental connection.

The Sacramental Natural History of Bark and Blood

"The Summit Redwood" provides an excellent example of the distinction between my approach to sacramentality in Jeffers's poetry and Brophy's and Everson's. These two books, as we have seen, read Jeffers through a myth-ritual lens that in Brophy's account draws on comparative anthropology's account of myth, especially Joseph Campbell and Mircea Eliade, and in Everson's draws on an archetypal psychology, informed by Jung, of course, as well as Rudolph Otto and Eliade. While building on these seminal works of Jeffers criticism, I want to critique their interpretation by adding an ecologically informed approach to the sacramentality of natural process. From an ecocritical perspective, the archetypal patterning privileged by Brophy and Everson interferes with the rendering of accurate natural history. For a religious nature poetry to be relevant to the environmental imagination, sacramental value must arise from natural process; it must be a part of that process, not an interruption or violation of it. "The Summit Redwood" (*CP* 1:389), which is distinctly grounded in the redwood ecology of the fog belt of maritime central California, offers an excellent example of the fusion of natural history and mysticism by means of sacramental poetics. Here is the poem:

> Only stand high a long enough time your lightning will
>   come; that is what blunts the peaks of redwoods;
> But this old tower of life on the hilltop has taken it more
>   than twice a century, this knows in every
> Cell the salty and the burning taste, the shudder and the
>   voice.
>
>   The fire from heaven; it has felt earth's too
> Roaring up hill in autumn, thorned oak-leaves tossing their
>   bright ruin to the bitter laurel-leaves, and all

Its under-forest has died and died, and lives to be burnt; the
    redwood has lived. Though the fire entered,
It cored the trunk while the sapwood increased. The trunk is
    a tower, the bole of the trunk is a black cavern,
The mast of the trunk with its green boughs the mountain
    stars are strained through
Is like the helmet-spike on the highest head of an army;
    black on lit blue or hidden in cloud
It is like the hill's finger in heaven. And when the cloud
    hides it, though in barren summer, the boughs
Make their own rain.

                    Old Escobar had a cunning trick when he stole
    beef. He and his grandsons
Would drive the cow up here to a starlight death and hoist
    the carcass into the tree's hollow,
Then let them search his cabin he could smile for pleasure,
    to think of his meat hanging secure
Exalted over the earth and the ocean, a theft like a star,
    secret against the supreme sky.

At the beginning of my course on literature and environment, I present
students with this poem and ask them if it meets Lawrence Buell's four
criteria of the environmental text:

1. The nonhuman environment is represented in a way that suggests
   human history is implicated in natural history.
2. Human interest is not understood to be the only legitimate
   interest.
3. Human accountability to the environment is part of the text's
   ethical orientation.
4. Some sense of the environment as a process rather than a constant or a given is at least implicit in the text.[17]

Students have little difficulty in checking off the first two and the last
items on Buell's list. The fourth criterion is most easily identified: Jeffers
explicitly describes the distinctive fire ecology that allows redwoods to
thrive on the central coast. Despite the personification (the tree "knows"
the divinity transferred to its cells in the lightning strike) and the imagery that transfers cultural values onto the redwood (it is a tower, a helmet-
spike), students, especially if they are biology or environmental studies
majors, can point out that the tree is part of the process of what natural

historian Elna Bakker calls "disaster climax forests." The phrase "lives to be burnt" emphasizes the cyclical, natural process and also underscores the legacy of this particular redwood as a survivor. Bakker explains that "that if totally protected from the rejuvenating effects of near calamity the species would sooner or later suffer the consequences of its vigorous nature and degenerate under the decadence of soft living."[18] What's more, the tree itself has literal self-sustaining and life-giving power—it makes rain. Alfred Powers, author of the American Folkways *Redwood Country*, points out: "Fog is the *sine qua non* of the redwoods. Without it they would not grow; with it they are radiant, still youthful-looking at the age of a thousand years. . . . Some early inhabitants thought that redwoods caused fog, instead of the other way around."[19] The description of ecological process places the tree firmly in the context of its natural history.

All of these details fulfill Buell's requirement for environment as process, and then the account of Escobar and his use of the tree introduce a human implication in natural history, and the figurative treatment of the tree—its participation in both atmospheric and earthly process and its concomitant significance because of that participation—indicate its legitimate interest in the natural history as it unfolds. What usually causes students the most difficulty is number three—what is the human accountability here? There is a human in the text, but Old Escobar complicates matters because his behavior, at first, is seen as distinctly "unaccountable" because it is criminal.[20] Escobar extends the poem's connections with the local history of the redwoods. Describing the uses of the enormous, hollowed-out stumps of redwoods, Powers recounts tales of packers corralling their mule teams in them, farmers using them as chicken coops, and bootleggers hiding their stills in them. "In a few instances," he concludes, "suicides, instead of using gas or jumping off a height, sought out in some final fascination these remote charred chambers in which by their own hands to give up the ghost."[21] Escobar surely is of this company, and his "cunning trick" combines the pragmatism of ranchers and bootleggers with the sacrificial quality of the suicides. Then, as we look at the language and the story more closely, a student (this time, usually an English major) will, if I'm lucky, point out the religious diction in the last line.

Once the ritual value of the slaughter is identified, the poem's ethical dimension comes into focus. At the beginning of his classic study *Violence and the Sacred*, René Girard points out that the inherent contradiction of sacrifice is that it is at once a sacred obligation and a criminal activity, and the anecdotal narrative allows Jeffers to present this paradox.[22] The meat is "exalted," raised up physically by the thieves but elevated symbolically by the poet—it confers the secret meaning of blood sacrifice on the redwood. In Eliade's myth-ritual terms, the redwood is an *axis mundi*. In his account, the *axis mundi* is a hierophany, a manifestation of the sacred that makes a place or thing holy: "Every sacred space implies a hierophany, an irruption of the sacred that results in detaching a territory from the surrounding cosmic milieu and making it qualitatively different."[23] Eliade's main example of the *axis mundi* is drawn from an aboriginal Australian myth in which the creator god, after establishing earthly institutions, anoints a pole made from a gum tree with blood and ascends into the sky. This myth is Eliade's cosmogony: "This pole represented a cosmic axis, for it is around the sacred pole that territory becomes habitable, hence transformed into a world."[24]

However, locating the redwood in a myth-ritual context misses the power of Jeffers's sacramental poetics. Ritual studies can revise a reading of Jeffers's sacramentalism in significant ways, and it supplies the textual and rhetorical element that completes my students' reading of it as an environmental text. Jonathan Z. Smith has presented a series of provocative critiques of Eliade's concept of sacred space. Finding a sacred space, for Eliade, represents the founding of the world—it is a recapitulation of cosmogony. Discussing Eliade's cosmogony, Smith observes that creation/founding, for Eliade, is not an anthropological but an ontological category. Smith writes, "Man's fundamental mode is not freedom and creativity but rather repetition. Or, perhaps more accurately, man's creativity is repetition."[25] As such, Eliade's cosmogony limits human action to mere repetition, a condition for Jeffers's work in Brophy's reading of it. For Brophy, ritual means repetitive, formal patterns of action, and Jeffers's method as an artist is a reduction of an evolutionary sequence— from primitive ritual to primitive myth, from myth to drama and narrative; in short, from enacted rite to an aesthetic reenactment. Because Jeffers's worldview is "sacramental-ritualistic," in Brophy's terms, myth is his primary "literary vehicle."[26] This method of interpretation relies on anthropologists' and mythographers' interpretations of anthropological and ethnographic evidence of primitive rites and beliefs. Myth-ritual interpretation moves from the literary to the metaphysical by means of an author's deployment of a mythic theme or device. One way of putting it might be that ritual (action) turns into myth (narrative), which creates symbol (meaning). Ritual studies problematizes this sequence by unsettling distinctions between myth and ritual, by questioning evidence and warrants of earlier scholars. What happens, then, is an opening of the text, a rending of a seam in what has been assumed to be seamless. For all his attention to "irruptions," one of his favorite terms according to Smith, Eliade's interpretations often seal and close the opportunities for meaning.[27]

For example, according to Smith the *axis mundi* as a cosmogonic motif is in fact Eliade's misreading of certain Australian aboriginal myths. The main example of a sacred pole connecting heaven and earth, according to Smith, inserts a Christianized sky-god where there was none in the original. The Tjilpa texts on which Eliade bases his account are not about the creation of a vertical connection between heaven and earth and subsequently the loss of that connection; rather, they record a series of events in the tribe's wanderings and the memorialization of those events. Smith writes, "The horizon of the Tjilpa myth is not celestial, it is relentlessly terrestrial and chthonic. The emphasis is not on the dramatic creation of the world out of chaos by transcendent figures, or the 'rupture' between these figures and men. Rather, the emphasis is on transformation and continuity, on a world fashioned by ancestral wanderings across the featureless, primeval surface of the earth." What this means for Smith is that "anthropology, not cosmology, [comes] to the fore," and he cites Géza Róheim's interpretation of these myths: "*Environment is made out of man's activity.*"[28] These revisions of Eliade have serious implications for a myth-ritual reading of Jeffers. To read his figures in Eliade's terms gives us a convincing misreading of them. Certainly, from a comparative perspective, the summit redwood is an *axis mundi*, but what, in a pantheistic materialism, can that be? To remove the tree from its ecosystem, to make it a sacred pole, severs it from the material process that makes it sacramental in a pantheistic system. In such a system, there is no transcendent divinity to lose connection with. What has been lost is the awareness that we are enmeshed in natural process, and Jeffers's poetry assumes the paradoxical task of pointing this out by means of the very mechanisms that have effected that separation, language and consciousness. Smith's sense of the function of ritual quoted earlier indicates this shift that we might make in reading Jeffers: "Ritual is not an expression of or a response to 'the Sacred'; rather, something or someone is made sacred by ritual (the primary sense of *sacrificium*)."[29] Escobar's crime and the poet's recognition of it, and its integration in natural history, sacramentalize the summit redwood.

Jeffers's redwood is homologous with Eliade's *axis mundi*, but to rely on that homology to determine meaning closes the opportunity for a reader to find meaning in Jeffers's language. Jeffers's poetics is sacramental because it deploys language to create sacramentality. Its intended rhetorical effect is the sacramentation of consciousness. Jeffers may have wanted it to be a pointing system—a deictic gesture that directs readers' attention outward to a transhuman beauty—but he also knows that it cannot be, to his great regret. What is most compelling about Jeffers's sacramental poetics is that it refuses the modernist solution of linguistic materialism. Written language remains a sign system parallel to the world, not a material part of it, and it is his strategies of narrative, rhetoric, and oratory that in the end he relies on to present sacramental process. Symbols that are drawn from religious traditions appear in the poetry, certainly, and ancient and classical myths supply plots, characters, and stories, but these features are not what make the poetry sacramental. These are sacramental themes and images, but it is the relentless questioning and testing of language that makes the poetry sacramental. In many of his shorter poems, such as "The Summit Redwood" and, as we are about to see, especially "Oh Lovely Rock," Jeffers anticipates Snyder's sacramental materialism; perhaps, we might say that he invents it. He "lays out" (explicitly) the sacramental reality of natural history as it is manifest in rock, bark, and blood.

Varieties of Geological Experience: Jeffers, Rexroth, and Snyder

One indicator of the vitality of Jeffers's sacramental poetics is his proleptic answer to Snyder's call for a sacramental approach to the "mineral cycles" that opened this chapter. Jeffers looked to geological processes for one of the profoundest expressions of his pantheism, and throughout his work he developed various strategies for incorporating rocks and stones into his religious view of nature, a practice that James Karman calls his "phenomenology of stone" and Kirk Glaser dubs "the geologic sublime."[30] Variously, Jeffers renders rocks emblematically or symbolically, as in "Rock and Hawk," where he presents the emblem of a hawk's "fierce consciousness" "Married to the massive / Mysticism of stone" (*CP* 2:416). By apostrophizing a particular stone, as in "To the Rock That Will Be a Cornerstone of the House," he evokes the latent power in geological endurance, ritualistically tapping into it as well as contributing to it: "Lend me the stone strength of the past and I will lend you / The wings of the future, for I have them. / How dear you will be to me when I too grow old, old comrade" (*CP* 1:11). As a stonemason himself, he was also able to portray a physical intimacy with rock gained from daily labor extracting boulders from "the wet / Quarry under the shadow of the waves" to build additions to his house and three-story Hawk Tower ("To the House," *CP* 1:5). However, Jeffers's most significant lyric strategy for representing the intuition of spirit immanent in stone is the revalidation of the pathetic fallacy in a touchstone poem written in the mid-1930s. "Oh Lovely Rock" is one of the central poems of the sacramental tradition because its "geological mysticism" sets the pattern for the camping and mountaineering poems that are Rexroth's and Snyder's definitive contribution to midcentury nature poetry.

"Oh Lovely Rock," first published in *Such Counsels You Gave to Me* (1937), develops a lyric strategy that is a hallmark of West Coast nature poetry. The poem operates on three levels, the material, the mystical, and the rhetorical, which combine to manifest a sacramental reality. The lyric strategy represents these three levels through precise, naturalistic description that emphasizes nonhuman nature, a religious or mystical awareness triggered by the natural setting, and an elaborate version of the pathetic fallacy that jumps the gap between material substance and spiritual essence and thus completes the circuit between mind and nature. The poem describes an overnight hike in the wilderness of the Coast Range:

> We stayed the night in the pathless gorge of Ventana Creek,
>   up the east fork.
> The rock walls and the mountain ridges hung forest on
>   forest above our heads, maple and redwood,
> Laurel, oak, madrone, up to the high and slender Santa
>   Lucian firs that stare up the cataracts
> Of slide-rock to the star-color precipices.
>
>   We lay on gravel
>   and kept a little camp-fire for warmth.
> Past midnight only two or three coals glowed red in the
>   cooling darkness; I laid a clutch of dead bay-leaves
> On the ember ends and felted dry sticks across them and lay
>   down again. The revived flame
> Lighted my sleeping son's face and his companion's, and the
>   vertical face of the great gorge-wall
> Across the stream. Light leaves overhead danced in the fire's
>   breath, tree-trunks were seen: it was the rock wall
> That fascinated my eyes and mind. Nothing strange: light-
>   gray diorite with two or three slanting seams in it,
> Smooth-polished by the endless attrition of slides and
>   floods; no fern nor lichen, pure naked rock . . . as if I were
> Seeing rock for the first time. As if I were seeing through the
>   flame-lit surface into the real and bodily
> And living rock. Nothing strange . . . I cannot

Tell you how strange: the silent passion, the deep nobility
    and childlike loveliness: this fate going on
Outside our fates. It is here in the mountain like a grave
    smiling child. I shall die, and my boys
Will live and die, our world will go on through its rapid
    agonies of change and discovery; this age will die
And wolves have howled in the snow around a new
    Bethlehem: this rock will be here, grave, earnest, not
    passive: the energies
That are its atoms will still be bearing the whole mountain
    above: and I many packed centuries ago
Felt its intense reality with love and wonder, this lonely rock.
    (CP 2:546–47)

This poem follows a typical pattern for Jeffers's lyrics: a two-part structure, often signaled by a verse paragraph break, of detailed, naturalistic
description and moral or philosophical observation. Sometimes he starts
with the description and moves into the moral; sometimes he presents
the moral first and uses the description as an example or proof. In "Oh
Lovely Rock," this two-part structure is emphasized by the parallelism
between the opening sentences of each verse paragraph, "We stayed" and
"We lay." The first verse paragraph briefly sets the scene through description, and the second, longer paragraph begins with more description
and then proceeds to the meditative observations of the final lines. The
description is objective, precise, and detailed. The location is specified
by name, and the diction includes common species names of trees. In
turn, such specificity indicates precisely the growth pattern of what the
guidebook *California: A Guide to the Golden State* calls "the transition
zone," which includes the Coast Range forests, where this poem is set.
The *California* guide points out that "the trees most commonly found in
association with the redwood are the broad-leaved maple, madrona, tan-
bark oak, California laurel, and (usually in separate stands) the somber
Douglas fir."[31] In the second section, the rock is identified by its geological type and its surface appearance described precisely. Such description
not only allows readers to see the setting vividly and exactly, especially
if they are familiar with western flora and geology, but also places a distinct emphasis on the material substance of the nonhuman nature being
described. It is not vaguely evoked trees and rocks, but specific trees
growing in a specific pattern, and a certain type of rock that has weath-
ered in a certain type of way. The objective and materialistic description
will ground the subjective and mystical response to come.

The second verse paragraph introduces the dramatic situation, and the antecedent of the previously indefinite first-person plural pronoun is revealed to be the speaker, his son, and his son's friend.[32] The shift from the plural to the singular first-person prepares the way for the shift from the material to the mystical content of the poem. Jeffers would use the term *mysticism* carefully, and I use it here advisedly, but the experience he describes in this poem fulfills William James's four criteria of a mystical state: ineffability, noetic quality, transiency, and passivity.[33] As the point of view becomes singular, the boys themselves become objects in the described scene rather than experiencing subjects. Because of the homonymic denotation of "face," the boys' sleeping countenances and the rock surface are given the same value in their illumination by the "revived flame." This moment is a crux in Jeffers's poetry because he associates love between humans with an incestuous self-love. Here, however, the speaker's love for his son is immediately, or simultaneously, transferred to the rock across the creek. The play of the firelight creates a passive state in the speaker for a moment, revealed by the odd shift to passive voice: "Light leaves overhead danced in the fire's breath, tree-trunks were seen: it was the rock wall / that fascinated my eyes and mind." The speaker's attention is arrested by the rock, the surface of which has been animated by the breathlike light and heat of the fire. It is a moment of noesis, the mind apprehending through the eyes, but the speaker emphasizes the material qualities of that vision: "nothing strange" that is at the same time ineffably strange. Again, the presence of the boys colors the speaker's figurative language: "childlike loveliness," "like a grave smiling child." The speaker experiences a vision of divinity inhabiting material reality—the permanence of the rock both symbolizing and embodying the energy or spirit that inheres even in the inorganic.[34]

Thus the poem moves from the materialistic to the mystical by means of the rhetorical. The speaker twice invokes the pathetic fallacy in his response to the rock, assigning it passion and nobility in his first realization, and projecting a human loneliness onto it in his sympathetic response at the conclusion. In *Pathetic Fallacy in the Nineteenth Century*, Josephine Miles traces the rise and fall of the trope, and she finds that before Ruskin coined the term, which of course carries a negative connotation, a high percentage of poems contained "pathetic fallacies." That percentage dropped after Ruskin branded the device fallacious, and Miles concludes that this decline in usage reflected not only changing poetic conventions but also changing views of the inherent value of nature. In the twentieth century, Miles finds the frequency of the pathetic fallacy to be still diminished from its pre-Ruskin heyday, but she detects a curiously high occurrence of the trope among the Imagists. Her bellwether for the twentieth century is naturally T. S. Eliot, who uses the pathetic fallacy once for every three hundred lines. Most interesting, she pairs Jeffers and Eliot as indicators of the twentieth-century attitude toward the device and the stance toward nature that it implies: "The scantiness in the work of Eliot and Jeffers therefore seems certainly to participate in the fading of a way of thought."[35] Yet in his most public dismissal of Jeffers, a 1957 review of Radcliffe Squires's *The Loyalties of Robinson Jeffers*, Rexroth cites such personification as one of Jeffers's highest offenses: "His lyrics and reveries of the California landscape seem to me to suffer in almost every line from the most childish laboring of the pathetic fallacy, elevated to a very system of response."[36] Indeed, in "Oh Lovely Rock" it is used as a system of response, and Miles's analysis of the trope, which is concerned, not with the validity of attributing human emotion to natural objects, but rather with the view of nature that sanctions such attribution, reveals how the pathetic fallacy works as a viable rhetorical device.

It is worthwhile to pause here and consider the implications of Jeffers's pathetic fallacy. His "elevation" of the trope brings a distinctly romantic lyric strategy into twentieth-century poetics, and thus it has profound meaning for West Coast poetics and sacramentalism in general. Moreover, this is one place where poetry, by its operation in the realm of feeling and affect, contributes a depth to environmental discourse that ecological science itself cannot provide. Environmental philosopher Neil Evernden writes, "Once we engage in the extension of the boundary of the self into the 'environment,' then of course we imbue it with life and can quite properly regard it as animate—it is animate because we are a part of it. And, following from this, all the metaphorical properties so favored by poets make perfect sense: the Pathetic Fallacy is a fallacy only to the ego-clencher. Metaphoric language is an indicator of 'place'—an indication that the speaker has a place, feels part of a place."[37]

In his poem, Jeffers attributes two primary emotions to the rock: love and loneliness. As Ruskin would have it, these are Jeffers's emotions, transferred to the object by a temperament "borne away, or over-clouded, or over-dazzled by emotion," which is "more or less a noble state."[38] Miles uses the term *bestowal* to indicate the pathetic fallacy in its pre-Ruskin, Wordsworthian mode.[39] For Miles, the bestowal of emotion upon an object exhibits three emphases that indicate the relation of speaker to nonhuman object. The pathetic fallacy, defined by Miles as "an object and an attributed feeling," contains a "face," a "breath," and a "pulse," each of which can be found in Jeffers's use of the trope here.[40] "Face" is the object's "outward representative aspect," which in this lyric can be seen in "the flame-lit surface" of the rock. "Breath" is "the shared sympathy of an increasing number of objects, their spirit," which can be found in the analogies between the "childlike" qualities of the sleeping boys and the rock, and then the energy of the rock as it supports the rest of the landscape. And "pulse" is the "power of adjective within noun, its own generation of emotion," which Jeffers's rock doubly signifies in the one-letter difference between the title and the last phrase. Both its "loneliness" and its "loveliness" hold the key to Jeffers's mystical insight. *Lovely* carries a trite connotation in contemporary usage, used to signify that something is pleasant or merely appealing. Jeffers, of course, would be aware of the adjective's more significant denotations (full of love, loving; inspiring love or affection; having beauty that appeals to the emotions as well as to the eye), which inform the multilayered emotional experience of the speaker.[41] He sympathetically identifies with the state of the rock, isolated in the "pathless" canyon, and projects that geographical fact into a historical and geological image. The "power of adjective within noun" is even more profound in the title phrase, "lovely rock." The "intense reality" of the rock calls forth love from the speaker. The efficacy of the rhetorical device of the pathetic fallacy completes the ego-negating mystical experience.

"Oh Lovely Rock" is the definitive example of a West Coast "geological mysticism," in which the mineral cycles are taken for analogues of spirit in various ways. In this camping poem, as well as in his more numerous stonemasonry poems, the human is subsumed in the vastness of geological time, yet human and rock mutually enhance each other's existence. Moreover, I'd like to pun on "geological" explicitly—this is Jeffers's "hard" mystical mode. (In an earlier poem he calls it his "harder mysticism" ["Credo," *CP* 1:239].) In the development of their sacramental poetics, Rexroth and Snyder exhibit the qualities of this geological mysticism, albeit in reduced and adapted tropes. Although this is Jeffers in a "rationalist" mode, the pathetic fallacy is still too much for Rexroth, as a second-generation modernist, and Snyder, as a postwar poet. However, they both adapt the trope following modernist imperatives against rhetoric and "smuggle" in its effect, the intuited connection between essence and matter, mind and nature.

Rexroth's "Lyell's Hypothesis Again," written in the mid-1940s, describes another "geological" experience that is at once material and spiritual.[42] Like Jeffers's lyric, this poem employs a two-part structure, indicated by a ruler line inserted between the first and second verse paragraphs. Although Rexroth's scene occurs during the day, the setting resembles Jeffers's: a coastal mountain location with a creek, waterfall, cliffs, and vegetation. The poem begins with detailed description of the locale: "The mountain road ends here, / Broken away in the chasm where / The bridge washed out years ago. / The first scarlet larkspur glitters / In the first patch of April / Morning sunlight." The description shifts into a meditation on the general theme of the poem, the conflict between the "me" of the soul or ego and the "not me" of the body and the material universe. The pull of the dual forces of "sympathy and agony" is momentarily relieved as the speaker projects his concerns onto the landscape. As the vernal life of the natural setting flows down the creek "to the sea and death," the speaker enacts a kind of combination molting and scourging, experiencing a moment of immortality. The larkspur blossoms become "flecks" of "flagellant blood" in the sun, and the mist of the falls images the evaporation of ego. Against these images of metamorphosis and mutability, the speaker finds a symbol for endurance in the geological strata surrounding him. The ego is "As passionate, as apathetic, / As the lava flow that burned here once; / And stopped here; and said, 'This far / And no further.' And spoke thereafter / In the simple diction of stone." As opposed to Jeffers's granite, Rexroth's rock is extrusive igneous rock—lava that cooled on the surface—and it becomes a correlative for the personal ego torn between sympathy and detachment.

It is important to note how Rexroth produces the effect of the pathetic fallacy without the trope itself, as he does in a couple of ways. First, the personification of the lava flow and its metamorphosis into rock are distanced from the pathetic fallacy by the use of a "lesser" figure of speech, the simile. By comparing the personal ego to the lava with the preposition *as*, the speaker reduces the prominence of the fact that he is attributing feeling to an inanimate object. Second, the personification itself is almost immediately made self-reflexive—that is, the molten rock "speaks" but then is metamorphosed into the sign of itself by the metaphor "diction of stone." Analogizing nature to language is one of Rexroth's standard strategies, and it places him more directly than Jeffers in the twentieth-century mode. What's more, Rexroth immunizes his whole poem against Jeffersian excess with the elaborate, but largely implied, scientific metaphor evoked by his title. He is not being obscure—he gives readers a headnote by way of explanation: "An Attempt to Explain the Former Changes of the Earth's Surface by Causes Now in Operation." However, he does not integrate this reference into the body of the poem itself. The scenes described there stand as objective examples of the process, as if he were performing an experiment to prove "Lyell's hypothesis again." Of course, he presents experiences as subjective as Jeffers's intuition, but the metaphor derived from Lyell adds the luster of cool objectivity and disinterestedness. Rather than directly addressing his readers, Rexroth delivers them a deeply personal and subjective experience packaged as verifiable "fact."

In comparison to "Oh Lovely Rock," the key distinction in the second part of Rexroth's poem is that it portrays erotic rather than paternal love; otherwise, other significant similarities become apparent. In both, the speaker and his companion(s) separate themselves from the rest of society, seeking out solitude for recreational purposes. Most important, in both poems geological time and human experience are juxtaposed, mutually informing one another. The first of the two verse paragraphs in the second part reads:

> Naked in the warm April air,
> We lie under the redwoods,
> In the sunny lee of a cliff.
> As you kneel above me I see
> Tiny red marks on your flanks
> Like bites, where the redwood cones
> Have pressed into your flesh.
> You can find just the same marks
> In the lignite in the cliff
> Over our heads. *Sequoia*
> *Langsdorfii* before the ice,
> And *sempervirens* afterwards,
> There is little difference,
> Except for all those years.

Rexroth's explicit eroticism contrasts neatly with Jeffers's implicit Stoicism: Jeffers sees the eternal etched in the rock and human consciousness passing ephemerally over it; Rexroth sees the fossils in the rock mirrored on human flesh, and that moment of erotic intensity achieves immortality by analogy to the rock's sign of geological fortitude. After the speaker again experiences a moment of escape, this time from the complexities of romantic entanglements in his and his wife's past, the poem concludes with an image of the integration of the human and geological: "these ideograms / Printed on the immortal / Hydrocarbons of flesh and stone." Rexroth has imported the same effect that Jeffers achieves with the pathetic fallacy, but he has avoided using the trope. His modernist diction ("ideograms") and textual figuration disguise it well, but it is present nonetheless. The keynote trope of the "hypothesis" sounds again—in reading the surface of his wife's body as evidence of the geological process that inscribed the earth's surface, the speaker invests the rock with love.

Gary Snyder's mystical geological experience is twice removed, filtered through Rexroth's reduction of the Jeffersian stance, but his poems involving rocks and geology depart from and return to many of his precursors' strategies and insights. In 1955, Snyder worked on a trail crew in Yosemite National Park, and the poems that he wrote based on this experience, published in his first book, *Riprap*, are definitive examples of West Coast nature poetry. Snyder's lyric style combines many influences, primarily the modernist poetics of Pound and Williams, the wilderness lyrics of Rexroth, and classical Chinese and Japanese poetry.[43] Based on these elements, Snyder's poetry appears to have little in common with Jeffers's long-lined, oratorical style. However, his hybrid poetics is often built upon, or anchored in, lyric strategies that can be found in Jeffers's work as well. At times, the modernist-derived style obscures the particularly western attributes, but at others it mingles productively, extending Jeffers's legacy into the postwar and contemporary idiom. Of course, Snyder's grounding, as with Rexroth and Jeffers, is always the sacramental connection to nature.

One of Snyder's best-known trail crew poems, "Piute Creek," presents a nighttime meditation on permanence and flux that simultaneously rejects an overt connection to Jeffers's geological mysticism and adopts some of his lyric strategies:[44]

One granite ridge
A tree, would be enough
Or even a rock, a small creek,
A bark shred in a pool.
Hill beyond hill, folded and twisted
Tough trees crammed
In thin stone fractures
A huge moon on it all, is too much.
The mind wanders. A million
Summers, night air still and the rocks
Warm.   Sky over endless mountains.
All the junk that goes with being human
Drops away, hard rock wavers
Even the heavy present seems to fail
This bubble of a heart.
Words and books
Like a small creek off a high ledge
Gone in the dry air.

A clear, attentive mind
Has no meaning but that
Which sees is truly seen.
No one loves rock, yet we are here.
Night chills. A flick
In the moonlight
Slips into Juniper shadow:
Back there unseen
Cold proud eyes
Of Cougar or Coyote
Watch me rise and go.

The poem's syntax and line breaks are more objectivist, or cubist, than even Rexroth's, so its grammar is far from Jeffers's cumulative cadences. Yet it does contain some of the same shifts in perspective, from minute naturalistic description to cosmic vision, that characterize the West Coast stance of Jeffers and Rexroth, and it also follows a two-part structure. What's more, the same passive state is rendered here as in "Oh Lovely Rock," a moment of clarity in which the speaker's response seems beyond his control. Yet because of the Sierra Nevada's vastness, and the speaker's solitude, the effect is somewhat different. Instead of "seeing" into the rock, or seeing geological process mirrored on the body of a beloved, Snyder's speaker *feels* the illusion of meaning based on what we think is certain, on physical mass, the "now." The shift from "mind" to "heart" back to "mind" is telling. Even emotion, the more fundamental response, fails to find correspondence at this moment. The flow of meaning, "like a small creek," evaporates. Unlike Jeffers and Rexroth, who find correlatives for the human in the nonhuman, Snyder, in this instance, finds no such reciprocity. It is not until the paragraph break, when the subject returns to his senses, so to speak, that the poem's "moral" can be drawn, and then a connection to the nonhuman is possible.

Snyder describes a mystical state as does Jeffers, but his syntax and imagery in the first stanza attempt to enact it, whereas Jeffers uses rhetorical language to present it. For the experience to be "processed," Snyder must append an explanatory statement. The "too much" of the mountain range produced a Zen emptiness, the clearness of the mind which is in fact no mind at all—in ineffable state that can be described only indirectly. As Jeffers was "seeing rock for the first time," Snyder's "clear, attentive mind" is seeing by being "truly seen." Empty of thought or emotion, the speaker cannot respond by attributing emotion to the nonhuman; there can be no "bestowal." Thus "No one loves rock," Jeffers and Rexroth notwithstanding. However, unusual for Snyder, a touch of the pathetic fallacy creeps in when the speaker turns from perceiving subject to perceived object. The "proud eyes / Of Cougar or Coyote" serve as the connective presence, the Other, that was lacking in the first stanza. The conclusion is highly literary and allusive—the capitalized animal names, the echo of Yeats's "Lake Isle of Innisfree"—and it is by this "lapse" into the rhetorical that the speaker is naturalized by the beast's watchful presence, making the connection, however fleeting, at last.

A sustained sacramental connection is established when Snyder integrates a Rexrothian eroticism into his poetry. A love poem from *The Back Country*, "Beneath My Hand and Eye the Distant Hills, Your Body," presents a moment in which a lover's body and geological fact correspond under the hand and gaze of the male poet.[45] As in Rexroth's poem, the presence of the beloved allows the speaker to escape the bonds of ego and merge with the Other; as in Jeffers's poem, love extends from the human and is returned by nature.[46] The poem begins:

> What my hand follows on your body
> Is the line. A stream of love
> of heat, of light,   what my
> eye lascivious
> licks
> over, watching
> far snow-dappled Uintah mountains
> Is that stream.

Hand and eye mingle in a synesthesia of touch, taste, and sight, producing a continuum of sense and emotion so that looking with affection at a landscape, as the poet's friend did once, "—Drum Hadley in the Pinacate / took ten minutes more to look again—," becomes an erotic experience that quickens the pulse: "My heart beat faster looking / at the snowy Uintah mountains." Geology incarnates in the beloved,

> As my hand feeds on you runs down your side and curls
> beneath your hip. oil pool; stratum; water—

and love-making mirrors geological cycles, the lovers learning that the "stream of love / of heat, of light, / . . . / Of power" flows from the earth's core and theirs too:

> Beneath this long caress of hand and eye "we" learn the
> flower burning, outward, from "below."

Snyder has said that he considers the West's conjoining of "the Muse and Romantic Love" as a replacement for primitive sacramental rites. He writes, "The lovers [sic] bed was the sole place to enact the dances and ritual dramas that link people to their geology and the Milky Way."[47] Although he is a practitioner of ethnopoetics, which reinscribes ritual directly through performance, Snyder in this case allows for a rhetorical mediation to create sacramentality.

In Rexroth's mountaineering poems, the geological processes that inscribe meaning onto the earth's surface are personalized in the body of the beloved, and the sexual bond between husband and wife is sacramentalized through its participation in and embodiment of the deeper cycles of the earth. In Snyder's backcountry and trail crew poems, rock becomes the means to enlightenment, either by its vastness in the Sierra Nevada range, which pushes the mind to emptiness, or by its capacity to ground the metaphysical in the physical, as in his trail building with "riprap." Moreover, as in "Beneath My Hand and Eye," Snyder's eroticism completes the connection to his precursors. Like Jeffers and Rexroth, he finds love incarnated in material nature through the Other. Snyder successfully melds the West Coast strategy to imagist-objectivist technique, achieving a sacramental connection to nature by adapting the material, mystical, and rhetorical levels of Jeffers's lyric strategy to modernist poetics. Whereas the biology of consciousness, to which we will turn next, is an obsession not shared by Rexroth and Snyder, Jeffers's geological mysticism provides a direct link with his two most prominent successors.

2 / The Strain in the Skull: Biopoetics and the Biology of Consciousness

In the first paragraph of "The Poet," Ralph Waldo Emerson introduces one of the essay's four master metaphors, fire:

> There is no doctrine of forms in our philosophy. We were put into our bodies, as fire is put into a pan, to be carried about; but there is no accurate adjustment between the spirit and the organ, much less is the latter the germination of the former. So in regard to other forms, the intellectual men do not believe in any essential dependence of the material world on thought and volition. . . . We are not pans and barrows, nor even porters of the fire and torch-bearers, but children of the fire, made of it, and only the same divinity transmuted, and at two or three removes, when we know least about it.[1]

"Children of the fire" is the first figure for organic form presented in the essay, but rather than the form of the poem it expresses the form of human consciousness. Fire stands for divinity, spirit, energy, consciousness, and Emerson argues that a proper "doctrine of forms" would account for the relation between the spiritual and the material.[2] Robinson Jeffers inherited Emerson's metaphor but not his organic doctrine. Consciousness is Promethean in Jeffers's poetry of the 1920s, but it does not achieve its metamorphosis into organic form as it does in Emerson's essay. The container/contained dualism that denies the "organic" connection between body and soul, brain and mind, matter and spirit, suffuses Jeffers's most important poetry of this period, and figures of tension and strain—recurring images of vessels shattering, containers overflowing, and force exceeding its bounds—express the dilemma of consciousness at the heart of his sacramental materialism. Lacking an adequate theory of the biology of consciousness, Jeffers embarked on a language experiment as radical as that of any of his modernist contemporaries, and it is his inability to embrace Emerson's organic form that leads him to his greatest discovery. Rather than extending Emerson's organicism to an ideogrammic method, as Ezra Pound did by following Ernest Fenollosa, Jeffers arrives at an incipient biopoetic theory of language. Unlike those who expound romantic and modernist analogy-based theories of natural language, Jeffers anticipates an evolutionary basis for language, one that comports more closely with the current neurobiological understanding of language and its intimate connection with consciousness. He will not fully realize an evolutionary role for language and consciousness until his later poetry, discussed in chapter 5, but the work of the 1920s is his most dramatic attempt at realizing the biology of consciousness.

Tension, strain, shattering, and breaking are not only thematic and figurative in this period—they also manifest at the textual and compositional level of the poetry. Many of his important poems of the 1920s—"The Tower beyond Tragedy," "Roan Stallion," "Apology for Bad Dreams," "Prelude," "The Women at Point Sur"—are related to or emerge from the drafts, notes, and false starts for a long work called "Point Alma Venus," in which Jeffers attempted to articulate a theory of poetry based in his sacramental materialism. In notes apparently related to "Point Alma Venus," Jeffers writes: "Humanity is nothing in itself but only as reflections of greater and more beautiful forms and forces, the active little bodies and the round bowls of fire, the brains, the bone skulls, the shells full brimming with vision" (CP 5:378). For Jeffers, at this point, we are not children of the fire but pans or barrows carrying it around. Such a view of consciousness puts him in a difficult position regarding language and the function of the poet, a position somewhere between the organicism of Emerson and Pound and the formalism of Poe or New Criticism. Consciousness is fire or wine, the Promethean or Bacchic force, and it requires form or shape to take part in natural process. Yet the forms— skulls, shells, bowls, vessels, vaults—are not shaped by the force themselves; they are only adequate structures created by natural process. The contemporary view is that mind and consciousness are not contained inside the skull with the world outside it; rather, they are so intimately involved in constituting the reality we perceive that inside and outside do not exist. Yet the image of the skull as the container of consciousness is hard to resist. As George Lakoff and Mark Johnson observe: "We conceptualize the mind metaphorically in terms of a container image schema defining a space that is inside the body and separate from it. Via metaphor, the mind is given an inside and an outside. Ideas and concepts are internal, existing somewhere in the inner space of our minds, while what they refer to are things in the external, physical world. This metaphor is so deeply ingrained that it is hard to think about mind in any other way."[3] Jeffers's quite understandable inability to think about mind any other way as he struggles with the consequences of his sacramental vision is at the core of his poetry in the 1920s. The container metaphor that will recur in his poetry is the "bone vault," which first appears in the short poem "Credo." Just as his fictional characters are vessels and idols invented to contain the wine or fire of divine force, the human skull is the container of consciousness.

This dualism is thus also a problem of language and poetic function. The pantheistic vision that Jeffers wants to communicate is beyond language but can be expressed only in language. One of the first expressions of it, also related to the "Alma Venus" materials (CP 5:348), is Orestes's concluding speech from "The Tower beyond Tragedy," Jeffers's version of Aeschylus's Oresteia. The speech is a passionate and eloquent expression of the oneness that mystics feel with God, but for Orestes it is a going beyond humanity to include a union with the universe-as-god, the synecdochal connection between part and whole:

> I was the stream
> Draining the mountain wood; and I the stag drinking; and I
>   was the stars
> Boiling with light, wandering alone, each one lord of his
>   own summit; and I was the darkness
> Outside the stars, I included them, they were part of me. I
>   was mankind also, a moving lichen
> On the cheek of the round stone . . . (CP 1:177)

Many years later, Jeffers read Orestes' speech as part of his presentation called "Themes in My Poems," commenting that it is an example of the "religious feeling" at the heart of his work and contrasting it with "Oriental pantheism" (CP 4:412).

Consciousness is intimately connected to the language centers of the brain, and it seems that the fall into consciousness is also the fall into language. Orestes describes his mystical knowledge as "a stranger language" (CP 1:175) but understands that "they have not made words for it" (CP 1:177). Orestes can at last give up the struggle to tell it—he "cast[s] humanity" and "enter[s] the earlier fountain" (CP 1:178)—but the poet cannot. In notes found among the "Roan Stallion" drafts, Jeffers writes: "The hardship and the power of poetry . . . to express, by means of the music-songs and cradle syllables of humanity, the wisdom of demons" (*CP* 5:358). Lacking an adequate theory of consciousness, Jeffers also lacks a biopoetic view of language that accounts for its capacity to express consciousness while at the same time to constitute consciousness. This dual aspect of language brings Jeffers to his most explicit theorizing about language and poetry. As we will see, Jeffers's experiments with inventing the language to tell it culminate in the poem "Prelude," which reveals the sacramental poet's ordeal in his attempt to discover the ontological basis of spirit in matter through the epistemological filter of language, and it is Jeffers's first approach to a "biopoetics." But first, we must look at the poems in which the fire of consciousness breaks out, "Tamar" and related lyrics, and the poem in which Jeffers reaches a temporary resolution in his struggle with consciousness, "Night."

From Noon to Night: "Tamar" and the Problem of Consciousness

In the early 1920s, Jeffers broke through to the regional impulse, found the sacrality of place, in the conception and composition of his narrative poem "Tamar," whose title character is a manifestation of the eroticism inherent in the biological connection to place. Along with some of his shorter poems written about the same time, "Tamar" reveals Jeffers's direct and indirect relations to romanticism and what Karl Kroeber calls romantic imagining. In the foreword to his *Selected Poetry*, Jeffers explicitly linked "Tamar" with Percy Shelley's *The Cenci* (*CP* 4:393), and in light of Kroeber's ecologically oriented reading of Shelley we can find deeper connections.[4] Kroeber examines *The Cenci* in relation to *Prometheus Unbound*, convincingly arguing that they are "counterdramas" presenting two opposing views on the value of human consciousness. He writes, "Prometheus embodies self-consciousness as a natural phenomenon manifesting the emergence of culture from material nature. . . . *The Cenci* is *Prometheus*'s mirror opposite in urging us to suspect these wonderful capacities."[5] Read alongside "Tamar," an early group of sonnets, "Consciousness," and the meditative lyric "Night" constitute a thematic cycle that shows Jeffers struggling with the Promethean implications of consciousness, confronting the destructive aspects of self-consciousness more thoroughly than Shelley, and, finally, reconciling what he's discovered about consciousness with his vision of a divine cosmos governed by the second law of thermodynamics.

Like two of his modernist contemporaries, William Carlos Williams and Gertrude Stein, Jeffers imbibed a "mechanistic anti-spiritual point of view from medical school"; however, neither Williams nor Stein fused it with "a mysticism that seems almost instinctive" (*CP* 4:552). In 1907, Jeffers was a medical student at the University of Southern California, and for two years he served as an assistant for Dr. Lyman Stookey, teaching physiology in the dental school. Before enrolling at USC, he had translated German medical papers and journals for a friend of the family.[6] Thus, as a young man, Jeffers was actively involved in the absorption and transmission of contemporary European biology and physiology. The story of nineteenth-century biology is largely the account of a narrowing focus on the cell as the basic form of life. In *Biology in the Nineteenth Century*, William Coleman details this process, emphasizing the progression from anatomy and organs, to the tissue doctrine, to early cell theory. As Coleman presents it, nineteenth-century biology progressed from simple observation of organ functions to the "tissue doctrine" by means of postmortem physical examination. Then, after microscopy advanced, the tissue doctrine gave way to "cell theory."[7] The cell was identified as the basis of life, and Coleman writes, "The 'cell' as recognized in 1875 was, in its broadest specifications, very much the same 'cell' so vigorously scrutinized by modern investigations."[8] Focused on reductive, positivistic, and material explanations of the vital forces essential to life, nineteenth-century biologists ignored issues of consciousness and mentation in order to prove that life sprang from the same energy that propelled the physical universe. Coleman discusses Max Rubner's "respiration apparatus" experiments, which proved that animal heat was derived from nutrients ingested and expelled by bodily process. He explains that Rubner showed that "the organism was a heat machine. Its forces were precisely comparable and most probably the same as those as the universe at large."[9] Coleman points out that William Bayliss, author of the 1913 textbook *Principles of General Physiology*, emphasized that Rubner's experiment determined that the only methods to study vital process were physical or chemical and that life was a product of energy produced and transferred by material means, not a metaphysical "life force." Coleman writes, "Bayliss was referring to the larger question of confining vitalistic explanation but he also exposes the conceptual power within biology of the doctrine of the conservation of energy. . . . The animal machine was still mysterious in its working parts but its general place in the universe—discounting the unresolved problems of psychic activity—seemed henceforth clear. The organism was no being apart, but an integral, interacting element in the physical universe."[10] Teaching physiology in the years just before Bayliss's textbook was published, Jeffers clearly adapted this biological position to his poetics and vision, but since physiology "discount[ed] the unresolved problems of psychic activity," the poet had to find his own way to resolving the problem of consciousness.

Sometime around 1920, Jeffers made his first attempt at this: a triptych of sonnets called "Consciousness" (*CP* 1:7–8), in which he invented a theory of dual creators in order to explain consciousness.[11] The first God is the inhuman one, creating everything material, including the human animal. The second is a Promethean fire-giver, endowing humankind with consciousness and putting it at odds with the rest of the material creation and itself. The poems follow this progression: the first poses the question "What is this unreasonable excess . . . this consciousness?"; the second posits a theory, the dual creators; the third explains that our allegiance between the two is divided because consciousness brings both joy and pain. The first sonnet concludes with this quatrain and couplet:

> Our nerves and brain have their own chemic changes,
> This springs of them yet surely it stands outside.
> It feeds in the same pasture and it ranges
> Up and down the same hills, but unallied,
> However symbiotic, with the cells
> That weave tissues and lives. It is something else.[12]

Jeffers cannot align the materiality of the organic brain processes and the apparent epiphenomenon of consciousness. Consciousness is "symbiotic" but also "unallied" with the cells from which it "springs." To be "allied" would mean that it was of a similar nature; *symbiotic* in a biological sense refers to a close association between two organisms, which may or may not be mutually beneficial. Consciousness here relies on the cellular basis of life for its existence, but the speaker cannot see that it is produced by the same process. Jeffers's expertise in physiology serves him well in these lines—they specifically describe the "animal machine's" biology. He understands cell theory and incorporates it into his poem, but like his scientific precursors he cannot account for the materiality of consciousness. The brain is a biologically determined organ, but the mind "is something else."

The second sonnet begins: "As if there were two Gods," and the bulk of the three quatrains describes the inhuman God who "made / All visible things":

The swift messenger nerves that sting the brain,
The brain itself and the answering strands that start
Explosion in the muscles, the indrinking eye
Of cunning crystal, the hands and feet, the heart
And feeding entrails, and the organs that tie
The generations into one wreath, one strand[.]

Here is the organism defined in Bayliss's *General Physiology*, the animal machine with a primary consciousness whose nerves and cells respond to external stimuli. Jeffers cannot see the evolution of a higher conscious-ness as an active process from the cell outward; to him, it simply must have been imposed from without—it isn't part of the animal. So "the other God comes suddenly and says / 'I crown or damn, I have different fire to add. / These forms shall feel, ache, love, grieve and be glad.'" The third sonnet comments on the paradoxical results of this gift:

There is the insolence, there is the sting, the rapture.
By what right did that fire-bringer come in?
The uncalled for God to conquer us all and capture,
Master of joy and misery, troubler of men.
Still we divide allegiance: suddenly
An August sundown on a mountain road
The marble pomps, the primal majesty
And senseless beauty of that austerer God
Come to us, so we love him as men love
A mountain, not their kind: love growing intense
Changes to joy that we grow conscious of:
There is the rapture, the sting, the insolence.
. . . . . Or mourn dead beauty a bird-bright-May-morning:
The insufferable insolence, the sting.[13]

Describing this intractable dilemma, neurologist Antonio R. Damasio underscores the difficulty of the task that Jeffers has set for himself: "No aspect of the human mind is easy to investigate, and for those who wish to understand the biological underpinnings of the mind, consciousness is generally regarded as the towering problem, in spite of the fact that the definition of the problem may vary considerably from investigator to investigator. If elucidating mind is the last frontier of the life sciences, consciousness often seems like the last mystery in the elucidation of the mind. Some regard it as insoluble."[14] In these sonnets, Jeffers approaches this problem poetically, but with a solid understanding of human physi-ology. Ultimately, he cannot comprehend "the biological underpinnings of the mind," but his diction and imagery represent the dilemma as accurately as possible. Damasio himself, writing for a general readership, speaks in the same terms as Jeffers's poem: "Consciousness is the critical biological function that allows us to know sorrow or know joy, to know suffering or know pleasure, to sense embarrassment or pride, to grieve for lost love or lost life. . . . Do not blame Eve for knowing; blame consciousness, and thank it too."[15] Jeffers, too, saw consciousness as the biological replacement for original sin, just as Emerson saw self-consciousness as the Fall. The poet concludes his sonnet triptych without the optimism of the neuroscientist, but with the same sense of the mixed blessing that is consciousness.

Two brief lyrics written in the same period as the sonnets on consciousness reconsider the idea of "this unreasonable excess," offering a slightly more sanguine view of the matter but not resolving it.[16] In "Divinely Superfluous Beauty" (CP 1:4), the speaker, because of the beauty of human passion, is himself in the "web" of natural process. In "The Excesses of God" (CP 1:4), the speaker steps out of the web, recognizing the "humaneness," "the extravagant kindness" that creates the superfluous beauty of nature. The implicit paradox of "Divinely Superfluous Beauty" is made explicit—writing a poem about process removes the poet from that process—and the role of consciousness in this paradox is expressed in the opening of "The Excesses of God": if consciousness is excess, then it is in fact by such superfluousness that we know our "God." Knowing and being, of course, are two different things, and the poem ends on a tension that strains the web of "Divinely Superfluous Beauty." Humans would be able to "flow" like the fountain of excess "if power and desire were perch-mates," but since our desires exceed our power (for fulfillment or restraint) we will continue to miss "the great humaneness at the heart of things."

These two lyrics are an advance over the sonnets because they posit a single force motivating both natural and divine process, rather than dual creators, but they still represent consciousness as an "unreasonable excess." Another key distinction between the sonnets and the two lyrics is the eroticism in the latter poems. The beauty of erotic desire is one of the excesses of God, but consciousness has the potential to corrupt and pervert it. Such perversion occurs when humanity turns consciousness in on itself, and Jeffers explores the consequences of this through the trope of incest in "Tamar." Tamar's action is in part determined by the sins of the father, and thus her immolation of the family and their farmhouse at the end is a ritual of purification. However, the incest also appears unmotivated to the narrator, who asks,

> Was it the wild rock coast
> Of her breeding, and the reckless wind
> In the beaten trees and the gaunt booming crashes
> Of breakers under the rocks, or rather the amplitude
> And wing-subduing immense earth-ending water
> That moves all the west taught her this freedom? (*CP* 1:25)

The excess of consciousness finds a parallel in Tamar's excessive transgression, which also breaks the bounds of human nature: "It was not good, not wise, not safe, not provident, / Not even, for custom creates nature, natural," the narrator says of her incestuous act (*CP* 1:25). The incest is committed in a cold and tranquil pool, an escape from the heat of "the mad white April sun" (*CP* 1:24), and after seducing her brother Tamar shivers with cold (*CP* 1:27). Thereafter in the poem, she is tortured by the excessive heat of summer, and fire imagery dominates in the foreshadowing of the holocaust of the ending. Images of the sun and daylight in "Tamar," and in a related lyric called "Noon," embody the power of consciousness and the pain its tensions produce.

The lyrical invocation of part V in "Tamar" calls on the "beauty of the fountains of the sun" to possess "the dark lamps" of poem's characters (*CP* 1:32), a conceit that echoes the dual creators of "Consciousness." The poet, imitating God, creates vessels to be filled by the divine force of consciousness. As the poem's plot unfolds against the seasonal progression, Tamar's pain increases as summer intensifies; she endures "the insufferable sun" (*CP* 1:40), and in a fever dream after her miscarriage she sees herself suspended between earth and sky "Burning with light" (*CP* 1:60). In the character of Tamar, consciousness turned in on itself burns with excessive clarity and intensity. "Noon" also presents the sun as the "pitiless God" of consciousness, and the heat and stasis of the noontide both compel and torment the speaker of the poem. Here, like one of his vessels, the poet and his pride are "thrown down," and he "lie[s] naked / In a hollow of the shadowless rocks, / Full of the God, having drunk fire" (*CP* 1:203). Consciousness, for characters and poet both, is the excessive force that "crowns" and "damns," and the tragic consequences of its containment in the barely adequate vessels of humanity are imaged in the burning of the farmhouse at the end of the poem.

Jeffers finds a momentary respite from the blaze of consciousness in his majestic meditation "Night," which celebrates the fading of daylight consciousness into the "night-intelligence."[17] Best read as a romantic ode in the mode of Wordsworth, Keats, and Whitman, it is, in fact, a crisis ode, but one in which the crisis has been omitted from the frame of the poem. Rather than a psychological crisis, it is the contradiction provoked by the harnessing of his scientific training and instinctive mysticism. In this sense, "Night," written during the "Roan Stallion" period (1924–25), completes the cycle begun in the "Consciousness" sonnets, written during the "Tamar" period (1920–23).[18] It provides a temporary resolution to the dilemma of consciousness, provoked by Jeffers's training in nineteenth-century biology, by counterbalancing that training with his understanding of nineteenth-century physics.

As William Everson has pointed out, "The cosmos of Jeffers is essentially a Newtonian one," and Max Oelschlaeger comments that "the two great nineteenth-century insights into the reality of becoming—the discovery of evolution and the second law of thermodynamics—provide a scientific backdrop against which the profile of the inhumanist can been seen most clearly."[19] The tension between physics and biology was the nineteenth-century legacy in Jeffers's early twentieth-century training. Drawing on the work of Sadi Carnot and Rudolf Clausius, William Thomson formulated the second law of thermodynamics in 1852, and in turn Clausius created the concept of entropy. Alfred Toffler writes, "The Second Law pointed toward an increasingly homogeneous—and from the human point of view, pessimistic—future." At the same time, Darwin was developing the theory of natural selection, which proposed that organisms become more complex over time. Toffler also observes, "It is interesting that the specific form in which time was introduced in physics, as a tendency toward homogeneity and death, reminds us more of ancient mythological and religious archetypes than of the progressive complexification and diversification described by biology and the social sciences."[20] Indeed, the second law and entropy comported perfectly with Jeffers's antiprogressive stance, historically as well as politically.[21] But as a poet who professed a sacramental materialism he had to confront the crisis that emerged from the collision of physics and biology.

It is my contention that Jeffers's thorough knowledge of nineteenth-century biology and physics was the precipitating factor of this crisis—that he was, in a sense, forced to choose between the second law of thermodynamics, which asserts that the energy in the universe inexorably tends toward disorganization, or entropy, and Darwinian evolution, which implies that organisms accumulate complexity and advantages over time, that life tends toward higher states of organization. Because at this point he could not find a material, biological basis for human consciousness, he turned to physics for his answers. As an embrace and celebration of the night-intelligence, "Night" (*CP* 1:114–16) resolves Jeffers's crisis by choosing the second law of thermodynamics over evolution.[22] It is an ode to entropy:

The ebb slips from the rock, the sunken
Tide-rocks lift streaming shoulders
Out of the slack, the slow west
Sombering its torch; a ship's light
Shows faintly, far out,
Over the weight of the prone ocean
On the low cloud.

Over the dark mountain, over the dark pinewood,
Down the long dark valley along the shrunken river,
Returns the splendor without rays, the shining of shadow,
Peace-bringer, the matrix of all shining and quieter of
    shining.
Where the shore widens on the bay she opens dark wings
And the ocean accepts her glory. O soul worshipful of her
You like the ocean have grave depths where she dwells
    always,
And the film of waves above that takes the sun takes also
Her, with more love. The sun-lovers have a blond favorite,
A father of lights and noises, wars, weeping and laughter,
Hot labor, lust and delight and the other blemishes.
    Quietness
Flows from her deeper fountain; and he will die; and she is
    immortal.

Far off from here the slender
Flocks of the mountain forest
Move among stems like towers
Of the old redwoods to the stream,
No twig crackling; dip shy
Wild muzzles into the mountain water
Among the dark ferns.

O passionately at peace you being secure will pardon
The blasphemies of glowworms, the lamp in my tower, the
    fretfulness
Of cities, the cressets of the planets, the pride of the stars.
This August night in a rift of cloud Antares reddens,
The great one, the ancient torch, a lord among lost children,
The earth's orbit doubled would not girdle his greatness, one
    fire
Globed, out of grasp of the mind enormous; but to you O

Night
What? Not a spark? What flicker of a spark in the faint far
    glimmer
Of a lost fire dying in the desert, dim coals of a sand-pit the
    Bedouins
Wandered from at dawn . . . Ah singing prayer to what gulfs
    tempted
Suddenly are you more lost? To us the near-hand mountain
Be a measure of height, the tide-worn cliff at the sea-gate a
    measure of continuance.

The tide, moving the night's
Vastness with lonely voices,
Turns, the deep dark-shining
Pacific leans on the land,
Feeling his cold strength
To the outmost margins: you Night will resume
The stars in your time.

O passionately at peace when will that tide draw shoreward?
Truly the spouting fountains of light, Antares, Arcturus,
Tire of their flow, they sing one song but they think silence.
The striding winter giant Orion shines, and dreams
    darkness.
And life, the flicker of men and moths and the wolf on the
    hill,
Though furious for continuance, passionately feeding,
    passionately
Remaking itself upon its mates, remembers deep inward
The calm mother, the quietness of the womb and the egg,
The primal and the latter silences: dear Night it is memory
Prophesies, prophecy that remembers, the charm of the
    dark.
And I and my people, we are willing to love the four-score
    years
Heartily; but as a sailor loves the sea, when the helm is for
    harbor.

Have men's minds changed,
Or the rock hidden in the deep of the waters of the soul
Broken the surface? A few centuries
Gone by, was none dared not to people

The darkness beyond the stars with harps and habitations.
But now, dear is the truth. Life is grown sweeter and lonelier,
And death is no evil.

Jeffers's poem begins where another early twentieth-century meditation on the consequences of materialism, "Sunday Morning," leaves off.
"Night," less familiar than Wallace Stevens's poem, of course, is more
than that poem an ode in the romantic tradition. It consists of seven
stanzas that alternate between groupings of seven lines with two to six
stresses and twelve lines with five to ten stresses. This structure emphasizes elements of the poem's content, rhetoric, and rhythm, and these
are significant distinctions from Stevens's classical, modernist arrangement. The seven-line stanzas, which frame the poem and separate the
three larger stanzas, are primarily imagistic, portraying the sea and
mountainside as night comes. The twelve-line stanzas are organized rhetorically by the apostrophe (a figure that appears in the third seven-line
stanza). The first twelve-line stanza apostrophizes the soul who worships
the night (the speaker's, but by extension any night-watcher's), and the
other stanzas apostrophize the night "herself." These stanzas present the
rhetorically framed thesis of the poem: that night is the ultimate reality,
the source from which light and life flow and to which they return. The
shorter stanzas provide the breaks between these idea-oriented sections,
lyrically imaging the nighttime scenes that surround the speaker, and
they create the rhythm of the poem—each is a pivot on which the longer
stanzas turn, and the alternating groups of lines create a regular, tidal
pulse.

The poem itself is about troping, or turning, and it takes the universe's major turning as its logic. Rhythmically and thematically, the
verse embodies the turning of the tide. The earth's diurnal turning
tropes the human life metaphorically; night becomes a metonym for
death, based on this trope; and the diurnal rotation of the earth becomes
a synecdoche for the universe's major turning—entropy. In contrast to
Wordsworth, Jeffers feels intimations of mortality; extending Keats, he
accepts not only autumn, the rich harvest of the seasonal turn, but the
nonreturning turn, the end of the universe's season; and like Whitman,
he embraces the message of the sea-mother—death. Thus the achievement of "Night" parallels "Sunday Morning" and inverts it. Both poems
seek a solution to the problem of an afterlife in a materialist universe,
but Stevens turns to an aesthetic naturalism whereas Jeffers embraces
physics. Stevens rejected the possibility of a new solar paganism when he
restored his ambivalent celebration of an unsponsored naturalism to the

final stanza after Harriet Monroe's preferred version had concluded with the nude men chanting in a circle to the sun.[23] But "Night" is literally an ode to entropy, an unambiguous celebration of the "hypothetical tendency for all matter and energy in the universe to evolve toward a state of inert uniformity."[24] There are no "ambiguous undulations" in "Night." Of course, entropy is the final turn, and the poem's ultimate trope; etymologically it means "in transformation," from the Greek *tropē*, a turning, change.

Embracing the second law of thermodynamics might appear to be the stance of a romantic fatalist. As Roger Penrose writes, "It might seem, perhaps, that the second law is like a counsel of despair, for it asserts that there is a relentless and universal physical principle, telling us that organization is necessarily continually breaking down,"[25] yet the laws of physics remained always a tonic for Jeffers, the reassurance that no matter how painful or pointless life was, it would always achieve the peace of night, death, entropy. Nonetheless, poetry is song, praise, noise; it, like life, is a self-organizing system that somehow, despite the second law of thermodynamics, manages to become more complex along the arrow of time. Consciousness, as we have seen, is one of the most complex biological phenomena, and without consciousness, no language, and without language, no poetry. Even with the grand resolution of "Night," the poet had to continue his investigation of consciousness.

Inventing the Language to Tell It: "Prelude" and "The Women at Point Sur"

The austere beauty of Jeffers's ode to entropy marks his acceptance of nineteenth-century physics, but, as we have seen, he was equally committed to the premises of nineteenth-century biology and its emerging interest in the cellular basis of life. Even though his medical training was inadequate to comprehend a biological theory of consciousness—to this day neuroscientists have yet to develop an adequate theory—it nonetheless drove him to inquire into the biology of mind. The answer propounded in the consciousness sonnets violates neuroscientist Gerald Edelman's requirements for an adequate theory—it "abandon[s] the materialism and hypothetical realism that the physical scientist applies to the world outside the observer" in favor of the epistemological dualism of the two creators.[26] Although "Night" provided him with a stabilizing position in line with the ineluctable laws of physics, the world outside and consciousness's relation to it still exerted their force on the poet. The major poems that follow "Tamar"—"Roan Stallion" and "The Tower beyond Tragedy"—return to the tensions produced by consciousness, and the strain and tension of the unreasonable excess come to a head again in the poem that Jeffers considered his greatest work and many of his readers considered his biggest failure, "The Women at Point Sur." The failure of "Point Sur" to hit its target is in fact the confirmation of Jeffers's project because the answers he sought at this time did not exist—to find his answer would be to falsify his materialism. The disastrous reception of "Point Sur" turned Jeffers's attention to more modest goals in the late 1920s and 1930s, and it would not be until after his consolidation of Inhumanism during World War II, discussed in chapter 4, that he would return to the question of the biology of mind.

My sense that "Point Sur" is primarily motivated by Jeffers's struggle with consciousness is supported by two shorter poems closely related to it, "Credo" and "Prelude." "Credo" (*CP* 1:239) was written about two years after "Night."[27] In this brief lyric, Jeffers compares two epistemologies, idealist and realist, using Eastern religious philosophy to represent the former and his Western sacramental materialism as the latter. However, this gambit is not mere curbstone-kicking. Both perspectives are presented as forms of mysticism, and the title signals that this is a statement of belief, not fact. Jeffers has considered this contrast in a comparativist mode before, notably in "Point Pinos and Point Lobos" (*CP* 1:92–98), so it is an honest inquiry into two ways of seeing reality. Nonetheless, his terms are loaded—his "harder mysticism" forces the Asian philosopher, although he has "powers and magic," into the subordinate position in a binary scheme. The Eastern perspective is soft, passive, feminized—in short, Jeffers's credo is in part based on orientalism. However, the poem still subtly engages issues at the center of the inquiry into the biology of mind. Any form of solipsism, Eastern or Western (and "Point Sur" itself takes on Western solipsism), is a mystical tradition's liability. Moreover, neuroscientists themselves argue about consciousness's role in constituting reality, and many are distrustful of any theory that claims unqualified access to the ocean's ocean "out there," as Jeffers puts it in "Credo." Edelman's "theory of neuronal group selection" (TNGS) also puts it in such terms. For Edelman, it is "naïve realism" to posit direct contact with material reality. TNGS, he claims, "lead[s] to the view that I have called qualified realism—realism admittedly affected by phenotypic limits on sensory qualities and perceptual categorizations."[28] Qualified realism requires a vigilant self-consciousness, but it can provide the grounds for investigation of the "out there." Jeffers may long for a "naïve realism," but he does not assert one. He acknowledges consciousness's constitutive

capacity. However, neither does he present a "qualified realism" here—
he asserts his "credo," his belief in such realism:

> My friend from Asia has powers and magic, he plucks a blue
> leaf from the young blue-gum
> And gazing upon it, gathering and quieting
> The God in his mind, creates an ocean more real than the
> ocean, the salt, the actual
> Appalling presence, the power of the waters.
> He believes that nothing is real except as we make it. I
> humbler have found in my blood
> Bred west of Caucasus a harder mysticism.
> Multitude stands in my mind but I think that the ocean in
> the bone vault is only
> The bone vault's ocean: out there is the ocean's;
> The water is water, the cliff is the rock, come shocks and
> flashes of reality. The mind
> Passes, the eye closes, the spirit is a passage;
> The beauty of things was born before eyes and sufficient to
> itself; the heart-breaking beauty
> Will remain when there is no heart to break for it.

"Credo" presents in miniature many of the issues and themes addressed
in "The Women at Point Sur," without the drama of coast-scouring storms
and exploding oil tanks that begin the action in the poem's "Prelude."

Both William Everson and Tim Hunt read "Prelude" as an essential
warm-up for an encounter with the narrative that follows it. Everson calls
it "one of the masterpieces of Jeffers' art, exhibiting to maximum degree
his complex technical skills," and asserts that it is "the threshold over
which we must pass in order to effect a shift in attitude from our normative consciousness, in order to leave the world of 'actuality' and enter the
world of 'myth.'"[29] Hunt observes, "It is important . . . for the reader of
the poem to understand how this first-person meditation controls the
narrative that follows, how Jeffers defines his own stake in his storytelling, and how the poet and story interact to form a poem that fuses lyric
and narrative elements."[30] Though "Prelude" involves minor characters
who will appear in "Point Sur," its primary purpose is to introduce the
main concern of the poem, not its main characters or story; the central figure of the narrative, Reverend Arthur Barclay, does not appear
in "Prelude." The theme is now a familiar one: the strain of divine force
against containment in natural form, and the necessary release of that
tension through violent action. The personal "stake" mentioned by Hunt

is the poet's need for the same release, which is made more problematic because the poet's action happens in language. Whereas the "multitude" outside the skull and the "multitude" inside were held in balance in "Credo," here an excess of multitude (in this case human presences) in the poet's imagination creates the strain in the skull that can be alleviated only through writing.

The first verse paragraph of "Prelude" recalls the tranquillity of "Credo" and its inevitable disruption:

> I drew solitude over me, on the lone shore,
> By the hawk-perch stones; the hawks and the gulls are never
>   breakers of solitude.
> When the animals Christ is rumored to have died for drew
>   in,
> The land thickening, drew in about me, I planted trees
>   eastward, and the ocean
> Secured the west with the quietness of thunder. I was quiet.
> Imagination, the traitor of the mind, has taken my solitude
>   and slain it.
> No peace but many companions; the hateful-eyed
> And human-bodied are all about me: you that love
>   multitude may have them. (CP 1:240)

Multitude is an ambivalent term for Jeffers. The imagination can contain the multitude of reality, the "out there," but turning in on itself, consciousness produces multitudes that strain the natural container of the bone vault. In "Birds" (CP 1:108), for example, the multitude of natural fact becomes the multitude of thought that produces the poem, and in "Bixby's Landing" (CP 1:388) the returning wilderness in the abandoned canyon is "a good multitude." But in "Point Sur," the multitude of imagined humanity is obsessively invoked, producing a strain in Barclay's mind (the word *multitude* occurs at least eleven times in the poem). In "Prelude," the forces of multitude are manifold—human, animal, atmospheric, molecular—and this multitude strains against all containment. The poet ritualistically calls a great storm down onto the coast, seeking release in its "kind violence" (CP 1:244). As more and more "actors" are added to the scene, the poet's stake in the drama is deemphasized. It is indeed a dazzling and overwhelming range of "characters": a woman whose adulterous desire strains against the bonds of marriage; a girl whose adolescent desire strains against parental morality and rural isolation; a visionary farmhand who messianically yearns to take the place of a crucified hawk; the ocean that strains against the shore; lightning that strains for release in its cloud; and, most explosively, oil that strains in its tanks for release.[31] Yet in all this tension and strain the poet reminds us that these external forces are also the excess of consciousness in the bone vault:

> O crucified
> Wings, orange eyes, open?
> Always the strain, the straining flesh, who feels what God
>   feels
> Knows the straining flesh, the aching desires,
> The enormous water straining its bounds, the electric
> Strain in the cloud, the strain of the oil in the oil-tanks
> At Monterey aching to burn, the strain of spinning
> Demons that make an atom, straining to fly asunder,
> Straining to rest at the center,
> The strain in the skull, blind strains, force and counterforce,
> Nothing prevails . . . (CP 1:244)

What "Prelude" reveals is an unforeseen image of Jeffers as an experimental poet, and it contains the lines that summarize the necessary conditions for a biopoetics that can accommodate the biology of mind. Here Jeffers is literally experimental—he puts his own experience to the test in language to discover God. In the second verse paragraph, he self-reflexively considers his role as poet:

> But why should I make fables again? There are many
> Tellers of tales to delight women and the people.
> I have no vocation. The old rock under the house, the hills
>   with their hard roots and the ocean hearted
> With sacred quietness from here to Asia
> Make me ashamed to speak of the active little bodies, the
>   coupling bodies, the misty brainfuls
> Of perplexed passion. Humanity is needless.
> I said "Humanity is the start of the race, the gate to break
>   away from, the coal to kindle,
> The blind mask crying to be slit with eye-holes."
> Well now it is done, the mask slit, the rag burnt, the starting-
>   post left behind: but not in a fable.
> Culture's outlived, art's root-cut, discovery's
> The way to walk in. Only remains to invent the language to
>   tell it. Match-ends of burnt experience
> Human enough to be understood,

Scraps and metaphors will serve. The wine was a little too
    strong for the new wine-skins . . .
(*CP* 1:240–41)

The language he invents to do this is his most effective combination of lyric and narrative technique, rhetorical and poetic effect, a seamless integration of the interior soliloquy and dramatic action (all the more powerful in that "Prelude" is a hybrid of two separate pieces that pre-dated "Point Sur" [*CP* 5:379]). However, this combination, because it turns on the contradiction between invention and discovery, increases the tension at the center of sacramental poetics rather than resolves it.

We are accustomed to seeing experimentation in modern poetry in terms of the materiality of language, the collage of fragments that Eliot and Pound invented, or the opacity of writing in Stein. The requirements of his sacramental materialism lead Jeffers to different conclusions, as we have seen, but the insistence on experience as the grounds for discovering truth places him in the company of Emerson, Thoreau, Dickinson, and Whitman as well as Eliot, Pound, and Stein. What is striking about Jeffers's experimentalism is that he rejects modernism's methods for making it new yet still follows a path of invention. If Jeffers initially fails to see that we are "children of the fire"—that our form coevolved with consciousness rather than merely providing a container for it—he advances on Emerson's organic theory of language that proposes that "words are signs of natural facts" and "language is fossil poetry."[32] Connecting word and thing by means of reference or analogy removes language from the realm of biology—it is no longer considered a functional part of an organism but an organism in and of itself, part of the world rather than part of one species' consciousness of the world. It is his investigation into the biology of mind that links him with the language experiment of American romanticism and modernism, but sacramental materialism demands a biopoetic rather than organic theory of language.

According to Brett Cooke and Frederick Turner, biopoetics is "the evolutionary study of art," combining Darwinian theory, evolutionary psychology, and sociobiology in order to understand the adaptive advantages of art and aesthetics.[33] It submits the "superfluous" activities of play and art making to the logic of natural selection, seeking evolutionary reasons for humans' artistic creativity. Another definition was proposed in the early 1970s, when the small press journal *Io* published a "Biopoesis" issue (number 20), edited by Harvey Bialy, who was "trained as a biochemist." Richard Grossinger, the publisher of *Io*, explains that biopoesis proposes "an exact correspondence between the genetic language (of the cells), which expresses us, and the poetic language (of the intelligence), by which we express our cellular and cosmic reality."[34] There is an Emersonian ring to Grossinger's definition, a sort of DNA-based doctrine of correspondence, but here the correspondence is at the level of code itself—language functions like genes, it organizes expression of mind in the same way that genes organize the expression (manifestation) of the body.[35] Unlike Emerson's romantic language theory, which became Pound's modernist language theory through the conduit of Ernest Fenollosa, biopoetics is based not on analogy between word and thing but on the similarity of the means by which word and thing engage in evolutionary process.[36]

Biologists and anthropologists discuss the coevolution of language and the brain, acknowledging that consciousness emerges in tandem with language, that in fact consciousness may not emerge without the language centers of the brain also in existence. Edelman proposes that we consider "language as *epigenetic* phenomenon," which makes its connection to biology structural rather than analogical.[37] Emerson's doctrine of correspondence and Pound's ideogram posit a referential or representational origin—words once referred directly to things or actually looked like them. Epigenesis proposes that individual organisms develop by successive differentiation rather than by a simple enlarging of a preformed entity. Language that develops this way comports more closely with structuralist linguistics—words function by difference rather than identity—and Grossinger's analogy describes process rather than appearance. In recognizing language's arbitrariness (it must be invented), Jeffers produces a language theory that is intimately involved with the processes of consciousness. Language, like consciousness, separates us from nature, but it is also the means by which we, the "symbolic species," in Terrence Deacon's phrase, realize our connection to and participation in nature. The materiality of language is its epigenetic form—the "natural fact" of language is that it coevolved with consciousness, not that it points to things or is itself a thing. Jeffers is as close to this discovery as he can be in "Prelude." He still has a way to go toward accepting the biology of mind, but his sacramental poetics, as opposed to Emerson's or Pound's organicism, does not rely on the "pictorial fallacy" of the ideogrammic method. Such organicism attempts to ground language in nature by negating its arbitrariness—an imposition rejected by structuralist and poststructuralist linguistics. However, language considered in a coevolutionary context can be seen as both natural and arbitrary. It is arbitrary because it is a conventional system of symbols created by humans; it is natural because it evolved by the same material processes that govern all living things. Thus, in a sacramental-materialist view, language is sacramental because it structures or expresses human consciousness, not because it symbolizes or refers to divinity in nature.[38] Language, and thus consciousness, is one of the means by which we participate in natural process as "natural aliens," in Neil Evernden's phrase.

Therefore, "Prelude" is at once language as experience (discovery) and language used to represent experience (invention). The telling is both the discovery and the invention—the experience happens outside language, but without language it is nothing at all. Seen this way, "Prelude" should supplement Jeffers's more doctrinal statements that emerge from the "Point Alma Venus" materials. In "Apology for Bad Dreams," part IV, he explains that his poetics is an imitation of divine poesis; in "Point Sur"'s part XII, as in the invocation to part V in "Tamar," he discusses his implication and investment in the narrative as the creator of idols or vessels; but in "Prelude" he tells the story of the storm because the storm is in his head. The invasion of his mind by the multitude of the imagination—the excessive force of consciousness—is the tension and strain that is also the characters' passion and lust; rather than explicitly telling us that he is aping God, he simply assumes divine power by poetic fiat when he invokes the storm: "I was calling one of the great dancers" (CP 1:241). The process that releases the invented characters from their straining limitations provides release for the speaker. All the straining forces are manifestations of divine force; "who feels what God feels" feels the strain—and the strain in the atom, the strain of desire, the straining of the tides, the strain of electricity in the clouds, the straining oil molecules are the blind forces mirrored by the strain in the skull.[39]

Just as Jeffers mutes his stake in the process in "Prelude," he privileges the doctrinal statements that permit him distance from his idols and vessels: he included "Point Sur"'s part XII in the 1938 Selected Poetry, not "Prelude." But it is the personal stake in "Prelude" that makes it so powerful, I think, and another indicator of this is its title. Of course, combining the first two verse paragraphs, which were originally published separately as "Preface" and "Storm as Galeotto," required a new title for the hybrid, but if the poem were intended solely as an introduction to "Point Sur," "Preface" would have indicated that relationship more clearly. Aside from the Wordsworthian allusion, "Prelude" is the more apt title. The musical analogy suggests a performance rather than merely prefatory remarks. The piece can be played prior to the more symphonic narrative it precedes, or it can be played on its own. It is also a microcosm of "Point Sur" itself, but with a crucial difference. The characters appear in various supporting roles in the "main" story, the storm is also invoked, but in "Prelude" there is no main character, no Barclay. The focus is on the tension of natural and divine process itself. To discover the divinity of the cosmos one must play the piece, invent the language, again and again. The strain and the tension matter, not the fable or the characters. And the person playing the piece is the poet, or the reader. Either one gets to experience both the strain of consciousness and its release through language, and this process expresses the biopoetic role of language in manifesting consciousness.[40]

In his struggle with the biology of consciousness, which is the divinely excessive force that is the tension and strain of the material world becoming aware of itself, Jeffers arrived at a comprehensive poetics not unlike Emerson's romanticism or Pound's modernism. "The Women at Point Sur" ends Jeffers's great period of experimentation in the 1920s.[41] He had extended his investigation into the nature of consciousness as far as it could go at that time, and the largely negative response to the poem most likely discouraged him from any further attempts in that direction. Although he joked that "Point Sur" was "perhaps unfit for human consumption" (CL 1:700), he nonetheless considered it his best work, the culmination of the concerns and issues that defined his mature poetry. Writing to Albert Bender in August 1927, he explained: "The book concludes a train of thought that began with Tamar; it was meant to complete the ideas but also to indicate the dangers and abuses of them, which it does pretty thoroughly. . . . It puzzles people; but will be understood eventually" (CL 1:693). In the same letter, he adds, "My next book will be chiefly shorter poems, I think." His next book turned out to be Cawdor and Other Poems, whose title poem, based on the story of Phaedrus and Hippolyta, is in fact one of Jeffers's longer poems, so he returned to the narrative form with success once the fallout from "Point Sur" cleared. Even though he continued to organize his collections around one or two long, narrative poems, he did begin to put more emphasis on shorter work, in both lyric and narrative modes, and the following ten-year period contains many of Jeffers's best poems in these forms. In fact, as we will see, he broke significant new ground in the poetry that turned away from the classical tragic plots that had defined his long poems in the 1920s.

3 /   The Whole Mind: Brains, Biology, and Bioregion in the Middle Period

That the reception of "The Women at Point Sur" did not damage Robinson Jeffers's reputation overall is indicated by the notice his 1932 collection, *Thurso's Landing and Other Poems*, received from the popular media. After the book was published in March, an Edward Weston photograph of Jeffers appeared on the cover of the April 4 issue of *Time* magazine, and later that same month a picture of the poet and his sons, also by Weston, was printed in *Vanity Fair*, which proclaimed: "In the eyes of many, Robinson Jeffers is America's greatest poet." The *Time* article included photos of the Jeffers family, Tor House and Hawk Tower, and the poet posing in the dining room addition that he was currently building. Certainly the media attention was also caused by the Jefferses' romantic and idyllic life in Carmel. If Jeffers's narratives were written to "magic horror away from the house," as he said in "Apology for Bad Dreams," in the late 1920s and early 1930s the magic would seem to have worked.[1]

In parallel with this circumstantial stability in his life and reputation, critics have noted a shift in Jeffers's attitude and work in this period. According to Arthur Coffin, along with the lyric sequence *Descent to the Dead*, also published in 1932, "*Thurso's Landing* marks the beginning of Jeffers' second phase of development in which he tries to apply his theories to a broader segment of society." Terry Beers sees this change in part as a shift toward an "epic," or historical, mode as Jeffers left behind the tragic and mythical themes of twenties-era work such as "Cawdor." According to Beers, *Thurso's Landing* "marked a new creative dimension in Jeffers's verse, one noticed at the time by many reviewers. Granville Hicks, writing for [the] *Nation*, found it 'Perhaps the most human poem he had written.'"[2] Moreover, as Robert Zaller points out, characters in the middle-period narratives such as Reave Thurso embody human values in a way that archetypal characters such as Tamar Cauldwell do not. They are, Zaller writes, "deliberately antiheroic, men of tough fiber but of limited ambition and imaginative capacity. Their moral gravity derives from their capacity to endure an unsought (though not necessarily an unmerited) suffering; they are not men who have rashly dared fate but whose very humanity has enmeshed them in it."[3]

I believe these distinctions are valid, and I would like to add more types to this schema of the Jeffersian character. Although this shift is made definitively by the early 1930s, as Beers and Zaller note, it starts becoming apparent immediately after "The Women at Point Sur." Even though "Cawdor" is still a long, tragic narrative in his myth-ritual mode, its titular hero, a rancher referred to only by his last name, is more in the mold of the historical or antiheroic character Thurso than a Tamar or Barclay.[4] Cawdor is not tormented by consciousness but rather motivated by more basic concerns such as the follies of desire, filial betrayal, and the diminishments of aging. This is not to say he is necessarily a more realistic character—critics of Jeffers's narratives often complain about the lack of depth or individuality of his characters. It is a valid complaint because Jeffers was not concerned with rendering fine-grained human emotions or intimacies—his narrative characters are acting out dramas of consciousness in large-scale productions. However, we can, I think, distinguish character types based on the level of consciousness that is being experienced.

Many neuroscientists distinguish between two levels of consciousness: primary consciousness, which all animal life possesses to certain degrees, and higher-order consciousness, which only humans possess to a significant degree (though it may be present in some primates). As Gerald Edelman describes it: "Higher-order consciousness confers the ability to imagine the future, explicitly recall the past, and to be conscious of being conscious."[5] In a loose sense, the people in Jeffers's narratives can be divided into characters entrapped in a higher-order consciousness and characters encountering the demands of life at a "primary" consciousness level. This is not to say that they lack all self-consciousness or are animalistic characters, but their problems and failures result from an engagement with the world and its forces rather than from a struggle with self-consciousness itself. Furthermore, I think that with the shift from myth-ritual plots and themes to the historical-antiheroic, we can separate Jeffersian characters into a rough, fourfold schema based on the mode of the poem. In this chapter, I will make a case for Jeffers's "comic mode"—not comedies per se but nontragic narratives.[6] Jeffers's vision is predominantly tragic, so the tragic are the types of characters we are most familiar with. On this side of the schema, there are "high tragic" characters who are manifestations of higher-order consciousness turned in on itself (Tamar, Barclay, and Margrave) and "low tragic" characters who escape the trap of self-consciousness and are a sort of primary consciousness turned out to the world but still in conflict with it (Cawdor, Thurso, and Ferguson).

On the other side of the schema, there are "high comic" characters whose higher-order consciousness is successfully turned outward. It might be more appropriate to say that of this type there is only one, the old caretaker from "The Inhumanist," because he is the only character who survives the breakthrough to the inhumanist perspective (we might include Orestes, but he is involved in a predominantly tragic plot). The "low comic" characters appear in the shorter narratives, which I will define as bioregional later in this chapter, and they are examples of a more basic, primary consciousness, engaged in the processes of nature but not in conflict with them. These figures range from minor characters in the longer narratives, ranchers and coastal inhabitants portrayed in brief, episodic narratives, and nameless interlocutors Jeffers meets in his excursions. Again, these people are not devoid of an actual higher-order consciousness, but they live in such a way as to avoid its dilemmas and experience nature in a seemingly direct, or primary way. In a late, untitled poem, Jeffers imagined such a consciousness this way:

> What's the best life for a man? To ride in the wind. To ride
>   horses and herd cattle
> In solitary places above the ocean on the beautiful
>   mountain, and come home hungry in the evening
> And eat and sleep. He will live in the wild wind and quick
>   rain, he will not ruin his eyes with reading,
> Nor think too much. (CP 3:424)

As I will argue, these characters deserve to be acknowledged in Jeffers's work because they constitute a model of consciousness that doesn't estrange the human from the world. What's more, the shorter, episodic narratives in the comic mode set the groundwork for Jeffers's environmental narrative, "The Inhumanist," which will be discussed in the next chapter. Before turning to the bioregional narratives, let's look at this middle period's approach to the biology of consciousness in the tragic mode—Jeffers's fascination with consciousness in the dying brain.

Jeffers's Brains: Death and the Biology of Consciousness

Jeffers does not abandon consciousness as a subject in the 1930s, though it does not have the central place in his work that it had in the 1920s. One indicator that Jeffers sought a biological understanding of consciousness is his attempt to render portraits of the human mind nearly postmortem, upon the moment of death. The first critic to examine science in Jeffers's poetry, Hyatt Howe Waggoner, observed: "The general term *biology* may be used to include the various specialized sciences of physiology, bacteriology, neurology, physiological chemistry, and the like, from which since the publication of *Roan Stallion* Jeffers has borrowed so heavily. When old Martial dies, and once again, when young Hood Cawdor's life is splattered out at the bottom of the cliff, and finally when the caged eagle is shot, we have images of brain decomposition . . . and we have imaginative speculation as to the mental accompaniment of the chemical changes."[7] Waggoner refers to the set piece "death dreams" of "Cawdor," the long narrative poem that followed "The Women at Point Sur." Although it is not an explicit motivating force in "Cawdor" as in the previous poem, Jeffers uses these passages to put forward a theory of consciousness that locates human mind in the cells and distinguishes between higher-order consciousness, which is unstable and easily dissolved, and the primary consciousness of animals, which, represented by the bird of prey, is more direct and enduring. Of course, the biology of the theory is based in Jeffers's medical training, even though it is entirely speculative; the distinction between higher-order and primary consciousness comports with Edelman's distinction discussed above, following it more closely in the human-animal distinction but going far beyond science in representing what the eagle's consciousness looks like.[8]

In "Cawdor," old Martial is a failed rancher who, having fled a wildfire with his daughter, takes refuge at Cawdor's farmhouse as an invalid. The tragic plot of the story is based on Phaedra and Hippolytus: Cawdor agrees to give Martial shelter because he wants to marry his daughter, Fera, who falls in love with Cawdor's estranged son, Hood. When Hood rejects Fera, she tricks Cawdor into killing him. In Martial's death dream, the loss of consciousness is connected to the dying brain:

> Gently with delicate mindless fingers
> Decomposition began to pick and caress the unstable

chemistry
Of the cells of the brain; Oh very gently, as the first weak
    breath of wind in a wood: the storm is still far,
The leaves are stirred faintly to a gentle whispering: the
    nerve-cells, by what would soon destroy them, were
    stirred
To a gentle whispering. Or one might say the brain began to
    glow, with its own light, in the starless
Darkness under the dead bone sky; like bits of rotting wood
    on the floor of the night forest
Warm rains have soaked, you see them beside the path shine
    like vague eyes. So gently the dead man's brain
Glowing by itself made and enjoyed its dream. (CP 1:449–50)

In such a description, consciousness is biologically based, dependent
upon living cells, and the dream that the decomposing cells produce,
imagined here as a kind of bioluminescence, is a vision of an eternal
pleasure, a wish fulfillment that "Resembled the eternal heaven of the
Christian myth" (CP 1:451). However, before its demise, consciousness is
rendered as a complex set of integrated cells and neural processes: "the
interconnections between the groups of the brain / Failing, the dreamer
and the dream split into multitude. Soon the altered cells became unfit
to express / Any human or at all describable form of consciousness" (CP
1:450–51). As I noted in the previous chapter, *multitude* is a crucial word
in Jeffers's vocabulary, and here it evokes the disunification of human
consciousness, which is a key insight into the biology of consciousness.
Edelman writes, "What is particularly striking about the operations of
the conscious human brain is the necessity for integration, for a unitary picture, for construction, and for closure. . . . The conscious brain
in health or disease will integrate what can be integrated and resists a
fractured or shattered view of 'reality.'"[9] In imagining the decomposition
of consciousness, Jeffers appears to get it right—the integrated connections in the brain create a unified consciousness that breaks down when
the interconnections are destroyed.

The description of Hood's dying consciousness also emphasizes the
human mind's need for unity:

The vivid consciousness
That waking or dreaming, its twenty years, infallibly
Felt itself unitary, was now divided:
Like the dispersion of a broken hive: the brain-cells
And rent fragments of cells finding

After their communal festival of life particular deaths.
In their deaths they dreamed a moment, the unspent
    chemistry
Of life resolving its powers; some in the cold star-gleam,
Some in the cooling darkness in the crushed skull.
But shine and shade were indifferent to them, their dreams
Determined by temperatures, access of air,
Wetness or drying, as the work of autolytic
Enzymes of the last hunger hasted or failed. (*CP* 1:479–80)

Just as Old Martial's dying brain dreams heaven, Hood's decomposing consciousness passes through cycles of recalled pleasures punctuated by "a wave of infinitesimal pains."

These waves both lessened
In power and slowed in time; the fragments of consciousness
Beginning to lapse out of the frailties of life
And enter another condition. The strained peace
Of the rock has no repose, it is wild and shuddering, it
    travels
In the teeth of locked strains unimaginable paths;
It is full of desire; but the brittle iniquities of pleasure
And pain are not there. These fragments now approached
What they would enter in a moment, the peace of the earth.
    (*CP* 1:480)

Completing the consideration of consciousness in "Cawdor" is another set piece, the "Eagle's Death Dream," as Jeffers titled it for his *Selected Poetry*. The narrator begins by comparing humanity's higher-order consciousness to the eagle's primary consciousness:

The nerves of men after they die dream dimly
And dwindle into their peace; they are not very passionate,
And what they had was mostly spent while they lived.
They are sieves for leaking desire; they have many pleasures
And conversations; their dreams too are like that.
The unsocial birds are a greater race;
Cold-eyed, and their blood burns. What leaped up to death,
The extension of one storm-dark wing filling its world,
Was more than the soft garment that fell. Something had
    flown away. (*CP* 1:510)

Expanding on his description of the mercy killing of an injured hawk presented in "Hurt Hawks," Jeffers here imagines the primary consciousness of the eagle as both concentrated and released. In reconnecting with the life of the universe, primary consciousness rises to its power, as opposed to the leaking, exhausted consciousness of the dying human brain. The following lines are an apostrophe to the bird's consciousness that emphasizes its continuity with natural process: "Oh cage-hoarded desire, / Like the blade of a breaking wave reaped by the wind, or flame rising from fire, or cloud-coiled lightning / Suddenly unfurled in the cave of heaven" (*CP* 1:510–11). The description of the eagle's death dream goes on for many lines—the desire, which can be referred to only as "it" or "this," rises above the canyon and the coast, finally seeing all living beings from a God's-eye view. It is described as "the archetype / Body of life" that takes the form of a bird of prey. Finally,

> Pouring itself on fulfillment the eagle's passion
> Left life behind and flew at the sun its father.
> The great unreal talons took peace for prey
> Exultantly, their death beyond death; stooped upward, and
>   struck
> Peace like a white fawn in a dell of fire. (*CP* 1:513)

The bird's predatory behavior is archetypically and paradoxically inverted—instead of stooping to strike it rises—and peace is figured as its natural prey. Along with the well-known "Hurt Hawks," I think other lyrics inform Jeffers's view of aquiline consciousness as it appears in "Cawdor."[10] In "Rock and Hawk," written half a decade later in the mid-1930s, the falcon possesses the "bright power" of a "fierce consciousness"—its emblematic value is its capacity to connect with reality through action. Another 1930s lyric, "Fire on the Hills," describes a wildfire that calls down predatory birds to hunt the small game that flees the fire, a scene that is the ecological equivalent of the "dell of fire" here. A more tenuous, but revealing, connection can be made with a very early lyric, "The Excesses of God." This poem does not feature a hawk or eagle, but it deploys avian imagery in explaining human consciousness's inability to connect directly to nature. Although consciousness, like beauty and desire, is an excess, a superfluity that signals divinity in natural process, humanity's higher-order consciousness, which allows it reflexively to know itself and thereby know the God of the world, is nonetheless corrupted by its higher-order status:

> There is the great humaneness at the heart of things,
> The extravagant kindness, the fountain
> Humanity can understand, and would flow likewise

If power and desire were perch-mates. (*CP* 1:4)

The eagle's consciousness in "Cawdor" can "flow likewise" because its power and its desire are "perch-mates." Its total consciousness is to see and to strike its prey, and it wants nothing beyond that. Human consciousness, in projecting a future, in remembering a past, can never be equal to its desire—the past is gone and the future does not exist; there is nothing to stoop to and strike.

These portraits of dying brains inform Jeffers's major statement about consciousness in the 1930s, the midlength narrative "Margrave." The narrator opens the poem with a meditation on consciousness and its place in the universe, condemning it as an infection that the rest of the galaxies are fleeing in their apparent movement away from the earth's solar system. The conceit does not quite work—Robert Brophy points out that it is a forced and sentimental instance of the pathetic fallacy[11]—but if we keep in mind Jeffers's investigation of primary and higher-order consciousness it is perhaps less objectionable (though he still attributes consciousness to inanimate objects). In the middle of the poem, the narrator interrupts the story to confess his complicity in the "contagion" of consciousness:

I also am not innocent
Of contagion, but have spread my spirit on the deep world.
I have gotten sons and sent the fire wider.
I have planted trees, they also feel while they live.
I have humanized the ancient sea-sculptured cliff
And the ocean's wreckage of rock
Into a house and a tower,
Hastening the sure decay of granite with my hammer,
Its hard dust will make soft flesh;
And I have widened in my idleness
The disastrous personality of life with poems,
That are pleasant enough in the breeding but go bitterly at
    last
To envy oblivion and the early deaths of nobler
Verse, and much nobler flesh;
And I have projected my spirit
Behind the superb sufficient forehead of nature
To gift the inhuman God with this rankling consciousness.
(*CP* 2:166–67)

Earlier, the protagonist of the poem, Walter Margrave, a medical student convicted of the abduction and murder of a young girl, was offered as an example of "the fruits of consciousness" (CP 2:161), so the narrator's confession here aligns him with the criminality of his character. The story concludes with Margrave's hanging, which entails a description of the end of his consciousness:

> At last the jerked hemp snapped the neck sideways
> And bruised the cable of nerves that threads the bone rings;
>   the intolerably strained consciousness in a moment
>   changed.
> It was strangely cut in two parts at the noose, the head's
> Consciousness from the body's; both were set free and
>   flamed; the head's with flashing paradisal light
> Like the wild birth of a star, but crying in bewilderment and
>   suddenly extinguished; the body's with a sharp emotion
> Of satisfied love, a wave of hard warmth and joy, that ebbed
>   cold on darkness. After a time of darkness
> The dreams that follow upon death came and subsided, like
>   fibrillar twitchings
> Of the nerves unorganizing themselves; and some of the
>   small dreams were delightful and some slight miseries,
> But nothing intense; then consciousness wandered home
>   from the cell to the molecule, was utterly dissolved and
>   changed;
> Peace was the end of the play, so far as concerns humanity.
>   (CP 2:170–71)

The elements of his investigation of consciousness in the 1920s are present here—the strain, the unnecessary excess of consciousness, and the entropic dissolving of it back into matter, night, and death.[12] Brophy, echoing other critics who object to Jeffers's biological view of consciousness, observes, "The glandular-anatomic reduction of consciousness to a labyrinth of nerve-cables seems excessively mechanical while explaining nothing; Jeffers would later gift the very stones with consciousness."[13] However, it is this reductive tendency that gets Jeffers closer to a biological understanding of consciousness. Higher-order consciousness is centered in the skull—throughout life it is connected to the body's proprioceptive apparatus, but in the literal severing of the connection in Margrave's snapped neck, embodied consciousness returns to its primary components. The body experiences what appears to be an orgasmic spasm ("a sharp emotion of satisfied love, a wave of hard warmth and joy"), and the brain loses its unity in the same way that old Martial's and Hood's minds did. To describe it as "the nerves unorganizing themselves" is, once again, apt. Though Jeffers here focuses on the cell and the molecule, the patterns of organization are what constitute consciousness. The cells and molecules are the material substrate for consciousness. Terrence Deacon identifies three general problems in considering the connection between brain process and consciousness, the first of which is "the binding problem": How does brain structure, which involves millions of separate "parts" and activities, "produce a unified subjective experience of self?"[14] In his imagining of higher-order consciousness in dying brains, Jeffers emphasizes the "unbinding" of these parts and activities.

Furthermore, Edelman observes: "Consciousness is a process occurring separately in each individual; it is historical, changing, partial, and linked to the perception of objects. It is therefore not a property of particles of matter or even of most biological arrangements of matter. Matter exists prior to mind, and on death individual minds are doomed to extinction in the sense that the conscious processes and thoughts possessed by those individuals are no longer possible."[15] Jeffers does emphasize particles of matter in Margrave's dying consciousness, but I think this is his way of expressing an incipient sense of consciousness's evolutionary status. In the early sonnets, it was "unallied, / However symbiotic, with the cells / That weave tissues and lives" (CP 1:7). In "Margrave," consciousness is allied with cells, which, in the biological usage of the term allied, means it is related by similarity or structure or common descent. Its explanation no longer requires a second creator, outside natural process.

For Brophy, "Margrave" is less a transitional poem in Jeffers's view of consciousness than a retrenching of his earlier position: "He seems not yet ready fully to concede . . . that this ambivalent function, human consciousness, is a necessary evolutionary process, a step in the cosmos's own becoming conscious of itself."[16] However, I believe that it does represent something of an advance in his thinking about consciousness in that it extends the meditations of the 1920s into his middle-period work and expands his imagining of the biology of consciousness. Responding to a query about themes in his poems of the 1920s, Jeffers himself connected "Margrave" with the earlier work. He writes that in "The Women at Point Sur," "I was thinking of human and non-human as one substance—or energy!—different (not very different) manifestations of the same thing. (I am afraid the poem called 'Margrave' in my latest book exaggerates the difference. From that point of view it is just a poem. I was irritated into extravagance by the excessive value that people seem to attribute to human consciousness)" (CL 2:81).[17] Or, we might say, he was irritated by the excessive value people attribute to higher-order, tragic consciousness. As he sought other ways of thinking about the "fire" of consciousness, he found ways of imaging it outside the brain vault that led him to a realization of the "whole mind" not just in human biology but in a bioregional sense of place.

Idylls of the Coast: The Bioregional Narratives of the 1930s

Fire is the primary trope for consciousness in the major work of the 1920s, and even in "Margrave" Jeffers still expresses his guilt that he "sent the fire wider" in having sons, planting trees, building Hawk Tower, and writing poems. But fire is not just figurative in his poetry—it is also an integral part of the ecology of his region. One particular aspect of place that constitutes Jeffers's bioregional experience is California's fire ecology. Each of California's nine bioregions has a distinct fire regime that affects its ecosystem at all levels, but fire plays a key role in Jeffers's bioregion. As the authors of *Fire in California's Ecosystems* point out, "Nowhere in California . . . is fire more dramatic than in the chaparral-covered mountains of the South and Central Coasts."[18] Jeffers describes natural wildfires, human-caused wildfires, and the use of fire in ranching and other human activities. His awareness and understanding of fire's role in ecological process offer a primary example of the material basis on which his religious holism is founded.

Bioregionalism did not emerge as a concept until the 1970s, more than a decade after Jeffers's death, but the detailed representations of California flora and fauna, climate, geology, and geography in his lyric and narrative poems add up to an incipient bioregional awareness of the Central Coast. Recognizing the bioregional aspect of Jeffers's poetry further grounds his moral and religious vision in natural process. The Californian poet most directly linked with bioregionalism, Gary Snyder, writes, "Bioregional awareness teaches us in *specific* ways. It is not enough just to 'love nature' or want to 'be in harmony with Gaia.' Our relation to the natural world takes place in a *place*, and it must be grounded in information and experience."[19] Snyder's 1974 *Turtle Island* was the first collection of poetry that defined itself bioregionally—he explained the book's title as the "old/new name" of North America, a term he introduces so "that we may see ourselves more accurately on this continent of watersheds and life-communities—plant zones, physiographic provinces, culture areas; following natural boundaries."[20]

Turtle Island also includes a section of didactic and political essays. One of them, "What's Meant by 'Here,'" is a rambling description that includes impressions of the landscape based in daily activities and sensory perception, detailing flora and fauna, federal and local land use, and various community activities, and presents a bioregional definition: "Watershed: west slope of the northern Sierra Nevada, south slope of the east-west running ridge above the south fork, at the level of Black oak mixed with Ponderosa pine."[21] Compare the first two paragraphs of Jeffers's "A Note about Places" from *Californians* (1915):

> The Monterey Peninsula takes [its] name from the town of Monterey, capital of California in Spanish and Mexican times, situated some ninety miles south of San Francisco. The peninsula is a little one, about four miles wide and as many long. The Carmel River empties just south of it. . . . The peninsula is heavily forested; its westward rocks, and those of Point Lobos, a little to the south, are fringed with Monterey cypresses, trees of tempestuous grandeur, and of a sort peculiar to the place. Pines compose the bulk of the forest.
>
> The Santa Lucian hills overlook the Carmel River and extend southward along the coast. Their northernmost slopes are pine-crested; the valleys beyond are forested with redwoods (sequoias) and oaks and Santa Lucian firs. This region, and the peninsula, are made aerially beautiful by cloud-play and the frequent ocean mists.
> (*CP* 4:176)

Snyder has a distinct political agenda to present to his readers, and he deliberately sets out to invent a bioregional poetics. Jeffers, of course, aware of his early twentieth-century audience's lack of familiarity with California, helpfully offers a description of his place as they will find it in his poetry, but "A Note about Places" also constitutes an incipient bioregional definition that anticipates Snyder's sense of the watershed. One of bioregionalism's foremost theorists, Kirkpatrick Sale, proposes that to "relearn the laws of Gaea," as he puts it, is "to understand *place*, the immediate specific place where we live. The kinds of soils and rocks under our feet; the source of the waters we drink; the meaning of the different kinds of winds; the common insects, birds, mammals, plants, and trees; the particular cycles of the seasons; the times to plant and harvest and forage." These things, along with the cultures native to the place, are the essence of bioregionalism. For Sale, a bioregion is "a life-territory, a place defined by its life forms, its topography and its biota, rather than by human dictates."[22]

Obviously, "Jeffers Country" is a small portion of the "separate country" of Northern California that bioregionalist Peter Berg defined in the mid-1970s.[23] As with Snyder's more precise definition of what *here* means, we can get a more precise sense of Jeffers's place if we think about it as a subsection of the Central Coast bioregion. Tor House is located in the North Coastal Santa Lucia Range subsection of the Central Coast bioregion. "The Southern Coastal, North Coastal, and Interior Santa Lucia Ranges form a distinctive subregion characterized by extreme ruggedness, moderate rainfall and continentality, extensive shrublands, montane hardwood forests and mixed hardwood-conifer forests, and a high occurrence of wildfire."[24] Wildfire appears quite often in Jeffers's poetry. In narrative poems such as "Cawdor," "The Women at Point Sur," and "The Double Axe," wildfires occur as important plot elements, and in some of his lyrics he demonstrates a sophisticated understanding of fire ecology in California. For example, his training in forestry informs his description of the coastal redwood ecosystem in "The Summit Redwood." The tree has been struck by lightning, "the fire from heaven," and, he writes,

> it has felt earth's too
> Roaring up hill in autumn, thorned oak-leaves tossing their
>   bright ruin to the bitter laurel-leaves, and all
> Its under-forest has died and died, and lives to be burnt; the
>   redwood has lived. (CP 1:389)

"Fire on the Hills" (CP 2:173), published in 1932, describes animals fleeing a wildfire and an eagle that comes to hunt the small game. The poem's speaker painfully realizes that "the whole mind" that encompasses the destruction is better than the individual mind that just sees the suffering and the need for mercy:

> The deer were bounding like blown leaves
> Under the smoke in front of the roaring wave of the
>   brushfire;
> I thought of the smaller lives that were caught.
> Beauty is not always lovely; the fire was beautiful, the terror
> Of the deer was beautiful; and when I returned
> Down the black slopes after the fire had gone by, an eagle
> Was perched on the jag of a burnt pine,
> Insolent and gorged, cloaked in the folded storms of his
>   shoulders.
> He had come from far off for the good hunting
> With fire for his beater to drive the game; the sky was
>   merciless
> Blue, and the hills merciless black,

The sombre-feathered great bird sleepily merciless between
   them.
I thought, painfully, but the whole mind,
The destruction that brings an eagle from heaven is better
   than mercy.

It is "the whole mind" of natural process that can see the beauty of the wildfire's destruction, and this kind of fire, rather than the Promethean fire of consciousness, indicates a bioregional awareness that informs Jeffers's holistic view of the natural world, an awareness that leads to a new narrative mode in the 1930s.

After "The Women at Point Sur," Jeffers developed a short narrative form that departed from the tragic structures of his major long poems and incorporated the ecological and bioregional sense of place found in his lyric poems. These shorter narratives provide a middle ground on which Jeffers can explore the implications of human survival within the community of nature that can rightly be considered a "comic" counterpart to his more famous tragic narrative poems.[25] The earliest of these poems, grouped together in the *Collected Poetry*, first appeared in *Cawdor and Other Poems* in 1928: "The Humanist's Tragedy" (*CP* 1:379–83), based on the Bacchae; "The Dead Men's Child" (*CP* 1:384–86), a "folk" legend invented from a combination of sources; and "An Artist" (*CP* 1:390–92), a self-referential parable that most likely responds to Jeffers's fame after "Tamar" reached its wider audience.[26] Beginning with a brief narrative in a myth-ritual mode, with the word *tragedy* in its title, this cluster of poems ranges across dramatic story, anecdote, and parable, exhibiting the diversity of narrative techniques that will develop in the 1930s.

As Robert Brophy demonstrates in *Robinson Jeffers: Myth, Ritual, and Symbol in His Narrative Poems*, Jeffers's long poems are dominantly tragic in structure and purpose, and the choice of this mode is intended to expose human self-involvement and reveal a way out of it. Discussing the famous passage on tragedy in "Roan Stallion," Brophy, writes, "Tragedy 'breaks man's face'; tragedy slits eye-holes in the previously blind mask man wears in his role of tragic actor." The tragic mode of the major narratives is, as Brophy asserts, Jeffers's main statement against a human-centered vision of God and the universe: "Since the time of Copernicus, astronomy has attempted to correct the Ptolemaic bias that put earth and man in the center. On the contrary, man is a speck on Earth which is but a minor satellite to a sun which is millions of light-years off center in a galaxy which is light-centuries off center in the universe—if there actually is a center to be contemplated. Once reoriented within such a realm, man cannot be comfortable in his solipsistic, presumptuous complacency."[27] Brophy convincingly argues that to understand Jeffers's pantheistic vision of a divine cosmos, the tragic element in his narrative poems must be experienced and the basis of their plots in myth-ritual structure must be understood.

It is here that a split between myth-ritual and psychoanalytical readings of Jeffers's longer poems and ecocritical readings of his shorter poems becomes apparent. Even though his tragedies are intended to slit eyes in the mask of homocentrism and show us the beauty of the divine universe, ecocritical interest in Jeffers focuses mainly on the lyrics, which present that beauty directly through description and offer moral statements on humanity's obligations toward it.[28] In one sense, Jeffers's great contribution to the post-Darwinian attack on homocentrism may also be his great flaw to a readership that has already accepted the necessity of leaving behind "the arrogance of humanism," in David Ehrenfeld's phrase. In fact, a year after Brophy's book was published, Joseph Meeker advanced a theory of "literary ecology" that proposed that comic modes such as the picaresque and dramatic comedy are better suited to an ecological view of humans as members of an ecosystem rather than lords of creation. In *The Comedy of Survival*, Meeker writes, "Tragedy is ultimately metaphysical, and it is always evident that biological problems of survival and welfare are of small concern."[29] Tragedy's basis in myth-ritual orients Jeffers's narrative structures toward action that emphasizes humanity's disconnection and away from the biological processes that integrate it into nature; with a singular attention to the tragic in Jeffers's narratives, we lose the opportunity to see how his narrative reinventions of place can reveal characters' biological connection to the community of nature in which they exist. If we look past the simple binary division between narrative and lyric, we can find a variety of poetic forms in Jeffers's work, especially shorter narratives and discursive lyrics in the 1930s that operate in a comic mode that supplements the tragic nature of Jeffers's major work as well as the ecological witness of the short lyric poems.

In ecological terms, one might suppose that if we stripped away myth or narrative, and focused intently on objective description of place, we would get closer to the actual environmental particulars, but such scientific objectivity would deny Jeffers the power of his ability with narrative. Environmental philosopher Jim Cheney proposes another way to think about myth and story: "A Western scientific description of the specifics of the ecosystem within which one lives is not adequate. It provides the wrong kind of myth. It can and ought to *inform* our construction of appropriate mythical images, but it cannot function as the centerpiece of a viable environmental ethic, much less a mythos for our times." What Cheney proposes instead is what I think becomes apparent in many of Jeffers's shorter narrative works, poems in which he drops the myth-ritual structure and the tragic imperatives and deploys a comic mode. Cheney writes, "The task then is to tell the best stories we can. The tales we tell of our . . . 'storied residence' in place are tales not of universal truth, but of local truth, bioregional truth."[30] If Brophy's version of myth connects Jeffers's narratives with their deep sources in ritual, Greek and Nordic myth, and tragic drama, Cheney's environmental mythos connects story with ecosystem, or bioregion, and reading Jeffers's "non-archetypal," shorter narratives in light of this concept adds another layer to our understanding of his narrative practice.

One clue for discovering Jeffers's comic mode is in fact exposed by the thoroughness with which Brophy explores tragedy in the longer narratives. The appendix of *Myth, Ritual, and Symbol* presents a "Schema for Jeffers' Myth-Ritual Patterns," derived in part from Northrop Frye's *Anatomy of Criticism*. Brophy adapts Frye's "theory of myths," which is meant to encompass the narrative patterns of Western literature, to the work of a single author. The schema puts into graphic form the myth-ritual patterns that Brophy discusses in detail throughout his study, thereby offering a concise summation of his argument about the meaning and structure of Jeffers's major narrative poems of the 1920s. By schematizing the seasonal pattern to which Frye's *mythoi* correspond, Brophy confirms the importance of myth and ritual in Jeffers's work, and he establishes the context in which the narratives offer their richest meanings. Frye's theory of myths posits that there are "four narrative pregeneric elements of literature . . . *mythoi* or generic plots," and he connects each of the four *mythoi* with one of the four seasons, emphasizing the cyclical patterns of action in natural process that correspond to "divine activity."[31] Brophy's schema puts Frye's model into action, imaging the seasonal cycle as the driver of the circle of *mythoi*, and the circular graph shows "*the seasonal context of tragedy*," indicating that "Jeffers' poetry accents the tragic autumn phase of the cycle."[32]

Whereas placing Jeffers's narratives in this context reveals the tragic nature of his storytelling, it also raises the question of these other *mythoi* in his work as a whole. If Jeffers's poetry is dominantly autumnal and tragic, is it exclusively (some might say relentlessly) so? Where might we look in his work for examples of the solstice modes of romance and satire, or the other equinoctial mode of comedy? Brophy does not deny other *mythoi* in Jeffers's work, and he points us to the most likely of the other modes, comedy, as the essential counterpart of tragedy. He writes, "Though his poetry touches all four seasonal phases (see, for instance, 'The Maid's Thought' for the motif of spring resurgence), his vision characteristically is tragic."[33] "Spring resurgence" does indeed find expression in Jeffers's poetry, and Brophy's example is apt, as would be the two poems that follow it in the *Collected Poetry* ("Divinely Super-fluous Beauty" and "The Excesses of God"). However, as lyrics, these examples fall outside Brophy's concern in his study, and in Frye's system they would have to wait until the "theory of genres" to be accounted for because the *mythoi* are "pregeneric." The power of Brophy's applica-tion of Frye's theory lies in its focus on narrative, Jeffers's major poetic strategy for expressing his cosmic vision.[34] Identifying and assessing Jeffers's comic mode supplements Brophy's account by adding an "eco-logical" dimension, in Meeker's sense, to his narrative practice. Rather than demonstrating humanity's disconnection from the divine cosmos through tragic, incestuous self-involvement, the comic mode indicates humanity's biological integration into the natural cycles of particular ecosystems and the possibility of its continued survival and satisfaction (if not happiness) there.

After "The Humanist's Tragedy," these shorter narratives also are a sign of Jeffers's exhaustion of, and with, tragic themes. As Tim Hunt explains, by the mid-1930s Jeffers started thinking in terms of group-ings of brief narratives rather than a single, longer, tragic poem. Most significantly, he considered the shorter works "idyls." Hunt observes that in spring 1936, "Una Jeffers wrote Albert Bender that 'Robin is working on a new book, a group of idyls,'" and he proposes that "the timing of her comment suggests this was about the time Jeffers recognized that he might have to focus for a time on narratives that were briefer (and less tragically intense and violent) and that this move—allowing nature's tragic violence to be more an implicit frame for the narrative than its dramatic center—was successful enough that he was able to imagine organizing a collection around such pieces rather than around one or two long narratives" (*CP* 5:99). The irregular and unrestricted formal qualities of the idyll make the term perhaps a better descriptor for these poems of the mid-1930s than *comedy*, but *idyllic mode* carries a much too quaint association for the characters and action of the various stories. An idyll "describes a picturesque rural scene of gentle beauty and inno-cent tranquillity and narrates a story of some simple sort of happiness."[35] Obviously, the setting itself, and the types of local characters that Jeffers encountered, call for adjustments to this formula.

The comic aspects of the shorter narratives in this period also in part derive from the local and personal context of their composition. The stories came to the poet as part of his own "idyllic" life on the coast rooted in his marriage; they were often collected by Una or by the couple together on their excursions through the canyons and coastal mountains near their home. Mabel Bennett points out that Una's "part in the making of" Jeffers's mature work "was important, for it was she who brought home incidents about the coast people which stirred Jeffers to weave his stories around them," and Brophy also emphasizes the link between the grander tragic narratives and local anecdote and legend: "The tragedies are discovery, self-education, and daily insight. At the core of Jeffers' 'imagined' tales were actual incidents which were part of the lore in the Carmel-Sur area."[36] When integrated into his major work, such lore grounds the excess of the plots and the wildness of the characters in reality; on their own, they provide instances of the local culture and bioregion detached from the mythic structures and can then generate a meaning different from that produced by tragedy. This comic mode is most evident in the brief, anecdotal narratives that Jeffers categorized as idylls: "The Stone Axe," "The Wind-Struck Music," "All the Little Hoof-Prints," "Going to Horse Flats," and "Steelhead, Wild Pig, The Fungus."[37] In such poems, Jeffers blends his skill in narrative technique with the ecological witness of his lyric mode and produces what might be considered a bioregional narrative poetry. Without denying his primarily tragic view of human existence, the comic mode allows him to consider the possibilities of human survival and integration.

"The Stone Axe" (*CP* 2:306–8) may be the most identifiably comic narrative that Jeffers wrote: it ends with a happy couple and an impending birth, and it presents an ironic yet sympathetic view of humanity's ignorance of the larger natural cycles that both decenter its importance and give it its meaning. The poem tells the story of a stone hand-axe that finds its way to America from the coast of Scotland. Through a series of misidentifications and mishaps, the axe arrives in California and finds itself behind glass at a local museum. Civilization goes through "strange growths and changes and ghastly fallings" while the axe waits. Then, in some Edenic future, the axe is found by a pregnant young woman dressed in deerskin, and she brings it to her mate, believing it is the tool he lost the day before. The poem concludes with this exchange:

> He took it and said, "That's a good thing.
> I was greatly afraid I'd lost it, but here it is." She said, "How
> lovely the world beginning again.

Look, dear, there comes the sun. *My* baby be born as quietly
    as that."

Most likely, Jeffers saw such a stone-age relic in Scotland, noticed its
similarities to one in California, and invented the story in order to demonstrate a basic human nature and intelligence that runs through history
while also meditating on his theme of culture cycles (and also on another
favorite theme, the endurance of stone). Whatever its genesis, the anecdotal presentation achieves the comic effect with efficiency and grace.[38]

"All the Little Hoof-Prints" (*CP* 2:538–40) narrates an encounter from
a daylong hike taken by the poet and his wife, blending bioregional detail
and anecdotal incident. The hikers pass an old man, who has nodded off
while sharpening a cross-cut saw, on their way up the canyon. Richard
Kohlman Hughey and Boon Hughey have identified the location as Palo
Colorado Road. They write, "One of the best places to get a good look
at the Ventana backcountry is at Bottchers Gap . . . . [The] road leads
through a magnificent stand of coastal redwoods in the gorge of the canyon and then begins an ascent that takes one to Bottchers Gap. . . . [Jef-
fers] also called it 'Pigeon Gap' in the poem 'All the Little Hoof-Prints,'
which is more solidly based on the fact that the area was a Mecca at one
time for pigeon hunters."[39] After taking in this view, the speaker says that
on their return down the canyon the couple

> had the picture in our minds of magnificent regions of
>   space and mountain not seen before. (This was
> The first time that we visited Pigeon Gap, whence you look
>   down behind the great shouldering pyramid-
> Edges of Pico Blanco through eagle-gulfs of air to a forest
>   basin
> Where two-hundred-foot redwoods look like the pile on a
>   Turkish carpet.) With such extensions of the idol-
> Worshipping mind we came down the streamside.

As in other poems of this idyllic period, most notably "Oh Lovely Rock,"
the narrative provides a frame for the environmentally oriented vision.
Rather than the lone witnessing eye of the poet-speaker, there is a com-
plementary human presence (here his wife, in "Oh Lovely Rock" the boys
whom he accompanies on their camping trip) that links him to both
human and nonhuman. In this case, the inhumanist point of view develops out the couple's shared experience of the place in the ludic context of
their recreation, and, in turn, their receptive states of mind provide a foil
for the old man's passionate attachment to his canyon home.

When he sees them on their way down, the old man confronts them because he fears they have camped out and might have left a fire. "I'll kill anybody that starts a fire here," he tells them. His concern about wildfire combines with the story he tells them of falling off his horse and cracking his skull. His fever of "a hundred and two every afternoon" echoes the imagined heat of fire, and both are contrasted in the darkness and coolness of the canyon. The poet says,

> "Darkness comes early here." He answered with pride and
>   joy, "Two hundred and eighty-
> Five days in the year the sun never gets in here.
> Like living under the sea, green all summer, beautiful."

Despite Una's concern that he is at risk alone with such a wound, the old man refuses to leave for treatment until the fire season has passed:

> "The doctor. He said the bone
> Presses my brain, he's got to cut out a piece. I said All right
>   you've got to wait till it rains,
> I've got to guard my place through the fire-season. By God,"
>   he said joyously,
> "The quail on my roof wake me up every morning, then I
>   look out the window and a dozen deer
> Drift up the canyon with the mist on their shoulders. Look
>   in the dust at your feet, all the little hoof-prints."

The old man's sensitivity for and intimacy with the canyon allows him to point out the small beauties that the daytrippers may have overlooked in their "extensions of the idol- / Worshipping mind." The poet lets his insight stand without comment or addition.

In "Hoof-Prints" the encounter with the old man reaffirms that the harshness of life on the coast is compensated by the daily presence of beauty. In "Going to Horse Flats" (*CP* 2:541–43), the poet, hiking alone this time, encounters another old local, but this one is distracted by concerns with the outside world rather than guarding and defending his home. As they pass a campsite left by hunters, the old man finds a recent newspaper among the litter. Farsighted from old age, he asks the speaker to read him the news. In response to the rising antagonisms in the news—the Spanish Civil War, Stalinist aggression—the old man pessimistically says "there is no way out" of such "crimes and cruelties" and he argues with the speaker who replies, "There are ways out." The poet eggs the old man on, just "to try him," making the outrageous suggestion that the winning side should just exterminate the losers and "the feud will then be / Finished forever," to which he responds, "*You're* the fool" and stomps off. Alone in the now quiet canyon, the speaker observes the natural beauty and turns to his reflections on the story he has just related.

This episode allows Jeffers both to indulge in a little self-parody, revealing to readers that his more extreme statements are perhaps meant to be more provocative than literal, and to represent himself as much more sympathetic to human suffering than his reputation would indicate. He wonders why the old man would seek news of the world when he has the advantage of living in a wilderness, when he should know that "He could do nothing / To help nor hinder. Nor you nor I can . . . for the world." The speaker continues,

> Man's world is a tragic music and is not played for
>   man's happiness,
> Its discords are not resolved but by other discords.
>
>   But for each man
> There is real solution, let him turn from himself and man to
>   love God. He is out of the trap then. He will remain
> Part of the music, but will hear it as the player hears it.
> He will be superior to death and fortune, unmoved by
>   success or failure. Pity can make him weep still,
> Or pain convulse him, but not to the center, and he can
>   conquer them . . . . But how could I impart this knowledge
> To that old man?

Rather than merely restating the inhumanist perspective as it is expressed in "Shine, Perishing Republic" ("the trap" and how to avoid it [*CP* 1:15]) or in "The Answer" (love the whole, "not man / Apart from that" [*CP* 2:536]), the narrative frame here allows Jeffers to present his solution in a comic mode, with restrained humor and compassion. The musical metaphor is one of Jeffers's more appealing figures for inhumanist detachment. The music may be tragic, but it is possible to participate in it and stand outside it at the same time. What is more, the inhumanist perspective, rather than being made the product of a tragic rending in the blind human mask, emerges out of a localized narrative, as part of Jeffers's "storied sense of place."

The most important benefit of realizing Jeffers's comic mode, implicit in "The Stone Axe," is that it provides a balanced view of sexuality and survival in Jeffers's narrative voice. His inclination to deploy sex as an element of his tragic vision through the trope of incest, especially in his narratives of the 1920s, creates a negative view of sex and sexuality by necessity. As Brophy explains, "'Tragedy,' etymologically the 'goat-song' from the rites of Dionysus (god of fertility and father of Priapus), necessarily involves overtones of dark sexuality." Zaller also remarks on this dominant characterization of sex in the poet's work: "Jeffers was preoccupied with the destructive and apocalyptic side of human sexuality. For Jeffers, as for Lawrence, sexuality was a fundamentally anarchic force, capable of overturning all convention and law." Calvin Bedient also compares Jeffers's and Lawrence's "ultra-modernist" leap "over the ethical (as too humanistic) into the sacred" by "straining and contorting and hurting the beautiful into something inhumanely sublime."[40] Overall, sex in Jeffers's narratives is a negative force, but a comic mode, in Meeker's sense of it, provides opportunities for humanity's biological participation in natural process through sexuality.

Bedient provides an extended analysis of the negative power of sex in Jeffers and Lawrence as it is manifest in "the erotic sublime." His reading of the major narrative poems connects Jeffers's tragic view of sexuality with Julia Kristeva's notion of the abject. He writes, "On the relation between art and incest, Julia Kristeva is . . . absolute: simply, poetic language 'utters incest.' It traffics in abjection, the field of attraction and repulsion regarding fleshly things. . . . Not even T. S. Eliot's lines are so loaded as Jeffers's are with expressions of revulsion at female flesh, appetite, and filth." In terms of Jeffers's tragic heroes and heroines, in their stories in which a break into the apocalyptic occurs, tragedy and the abject combine to create a revulsion at the reintegration into natural process: "An abject apocalypse occurs, in other words, where the 'I' collapses back toward the matrix from which it once extricated itself reluctantly, angrily, perhaps inevitably."[41] For Bedient, the only character who escapes the abjection of the erotic sublime is Clare Walker of "The Loving Shepherdess." He writes,

> Simply by inventing a heroine as reluctant as he himself is to face the meaninglessness of an existence not already and invariably a fusional bliss, Jeffers here bypasses abjection, the vortex of summons and repulsion, that gives "The Roan Stallion" and "Cawdor" and "The Women at Point Sur" their rending fury and frightening exaltations. For all the cruelty of Clare's story, the sacred and hence the sublime do not break into it, because in it the maternal is not a forgotten bliss but tenderly preserved in a memory that seems to belong to the very cells of Clare's body. As a protagonist of peace and love, not of power, Clare is the exception in Jeffers's work.[42]

Most interesting, Bedient finds a tension in "The Loving Shepherdess" that expresses Jeffers's contradictory views of the tragic pain of sexuality and the comic acceptance of biology's imperatives. He notes the moment at the poem's conclusion in which Clare unknowingly recognizes her fate reflected in the salmon swimming up the Carmel River to spawn and die. "So it is," Bedient observes, "in one poem, Jeffers tenderly promotes (if not promulgates) a suicidal regret of birth and praises the life-adventure of 'dear flesh' and a dedication to the continuation of the species (albeit not the human species)."[43] If Clare Walker is the exception in Jeffers's longer tragedies, then her appearance signals other exceptions in Jeffers's 1930s narrative works. As Brophy implies in his comment on "The Maid's Thought," Jeffers's celebrations of a rejuvenating sexuality characteristic of spring are more likely found in his lyrics. In the 1930s, Jeffers used the shorter narrative form to present characters whose sexuality, like Clare's, even in violent and sometimes cruel contexts, is grounded in the seasonal cycles through biology rather than myth-ritual. In a group of three related short narratives from *Such Counsels You Gave to Me*, he also uses the violence and fecundity of nature to mirror human sexuality and passion without a break into the sacred or the sublime.

"Steelhead, Wild Pig, The Fungus" (*CP* 2:549–57) presents three stories of infidelity, passion, and sexuality as correlatives to natural process. The characters, rancher Hugh Flodden, his father and brothers, his young wife June, her friend Florrie, and Vina, his mistress, act out scenes of desire and passion that, rather than alienating them from natural process, reveal them as human correlatives of its fecundity. The narrative is divided into three sections, each one represented by the natural object in the title. These stories, like other shorter narratives of this period, are probably material that Jeffers intended to include in the major narratives but for whatever reason left out. Tim Hunt supposes that "'Wild Pig' . . . either evolved from a partially drafted discarded scene for *Such Counsels You Gave to Me* or it and *Such Counsels* both evolved from something else, in which the Floddens (*Steelhead, Wild Pig, The Fungus* [*sic*], and 'Memoir'), the Howrens (*Such Counsels*), and Tom Birnam ('The Wind-Struck Music') would all have been characters" (*CP* 5:597).[44]

By grouping these three narratives together, Jeffers emphasizes the seasonal cycles that organize Brophy's myth-ritual account, but rather than functioning by archetypal patterns of tragedy that rise dialectically into the apocalyptic, these stories achieve integration as bioregional narratives. As in Meeker's comedy of survival, sexuality functions to locate the characters within their environment—not by synecdoche, as parts that metaphorically stand for the whole, but by metonymy, as signifiers that take on meaning by their contiguity with other signifiers in the system. The structure and arrangement of the poems indicate this allegorical rather than symbolic patterning. The natural objects that contribute their names as titles function less as totems than as metonyms, names that transfer their meaning onto the sexuality and conflict that the human actors participate in. Each one—the steelhead salmon, the invasive wild boar, and the mushroom—is a signifier of phallic power. Nonetheless, each one is placed in the context of its environment, an integrated part of the seasonal round that all the characters are enacting.

The three poems span the central coast's fertile period, winter through spring, and the poet's attentiveness to environmental particulars discloses one liability of following Frye's seasonal *mythoi* too rigidly. As the dramatic action of "Tamar" shows, summer's stasis of intense heat and light inverts Frye's winter stasis. In winter, on the coast, verdure reappears out of late summer's and autumn's desiccated landscape. The first poem is set in December, when, with the rivers running full, the steelhead return to spawn. Hugh Flodden catches Vina poaching salmon from the creek on his ranch and makes her "pay" the fine with sexual favors. Vina's poaching is completely part of the natural process—it comes from instinctive impulses in response to the overwhelming fecundity of the fish, and the description of her as she spears the salmon is sexually charged and naturalizing: her actions are like a heron's, she "pant[s] hard" as "she lean[s] on the shaft, looking down passionately"; as she lifts her prey, "her slender body / Rock[s] with its writhing." When Hugh "catches" her, she tells him, "Take half o' them, honey. I loved the fun." As an analogue to a predatory bird, Vina exercises her natural power over the fish. To get what he wants, Hugh invokes patriarchal law—she has to pay the "fine" levied on her instinctive passion. Her only scruple is her sense of self-preservation: "Your wife would kill me." Nevertheless, she allows herself to be carried off "to [an] island in the willows."

Jeffers wryly implies the excess of her sexual appetite—she pays two "fines" for poaching and exceeding the legal limit, "and would willingly / Have paid a third for trespassing," but Hugh declines, lamely masking his sexual exhaustion with an excuse about being discovered. The concluding scenes emphasize the parallels between the state of natural struggle for survival and reproduction and the reflexive consciousness of humanity. Leaving their trysting spot, they see gulls gorging on the steelhead running up the creeks. Vina sees her own behavior reflected in the gulls and is repulsed by it: "That's a horrible thing. . . . They're worse than I am." Her moral assessment of the gulls indicates that she, momentarily, is self-reflexively outside the flow of natural process, while at the same time it connects her to the birds as predator and scavenger, and it recalls Jeffers's characterization of herring gulls from the lyric "Birds": "ungainly / Gray hungers fledged with desire of transgression" (*CP* 1:108). Although Vina's observation is projected outward onto the gulls, it is an external manifestation of her recognition that she has poached more than salmon. On the other hand, Hugh Flodden identifies with the salmon, not as a victim but as an inverted mirror-image of his momentary good fortune. Returning along the beach alone, seeing that they have caught one of the fish in shallow water, he scatters the gulls:

> Young Flodden rode into them and drove them
> up; he found the torn steelhead
> Still slowly and ceremoniously striking the sand with his tail
> and a bloody eye-socket, under the
> Pavilion of wings. They cast a cold shadow on the air, a
> fleeting sense of fortune's iniquities: why should
> Hugh Flodden be young and happy, mounted on a good
> horse,
> And have had another girl besides his dear wife, while others
> have to endure blindess and death,
> Pain and disease, misery, old age, God knows what worse?

The second poem begins with an explanation of the presence of exotic, Eurasian boars in the coastal mountains: "a wealthy amateur up the Carmel Valley brought in wild pigs / From the Urals to stock his hunting-park: they overswarmed it and broke his borders and roam the coast-range, beautiful / Monsters, full of fecundity." In this story, Hugh's father traps a boar in a thicket and prepares to enter it and kill the boar, which has killed one of his dogs, with a knife. Hugh and the old man quarrel over this, but the old man tells his son that he's bothered by the young couple's nightly lovemaking, which constantly reminds him of his lack of sexual satisfaction—such pointless and risky hunting is now his only pleasure. However, old Flodden finds only "the two living dogs, meek and subdued, and the dead one / Trampled in a jelly of its own entrails, . . . the tall boar had vanished, like a piece of sea-fog / That blows up-canyon into warmer air and instantly vanishes." A rockslide, marking this poem's place in the seasonal cycle at the end of winter, abruptly brings this section to a close:

> It was now broad daylight, and old Flodden
> Returned out of the thicket, jeering at the cowardly dogs:
> that moment a heavy

Noise like distant cannon-fire roared at the mountain-top,
    the horses pasturing in the valley below
Raced up the opposite slope; then some great stones and a
    storm of fragments came bounding
Down the rock-face, felled an oak-tree or two, and cut
    several straight paths through the brush and chaparral.
The winter had been very rainy, a high blade of rock
Had settled and split away and rolled down; but it seemed as
    if the mountain had said something, some big word
That meant something, but no one could understand what it
    meant. Or the other mountains did.

Such a conclusion is enigmatic, just as the poem's narrative episode is unresolved, the vanishing boar leaving the old man with no outlet for his sexual frustration. The rockslide gives the impression of significance, that nature has purpose and intent, but its meaning is unknowable except perhaps to nature itself. Without a tragic plot at the center, this shorter narrative can leave its characters to continue their daily lives; the only meaning necessary, or possible, is the "local truth" of what has happened in place.

The final story involves June Flodden and her friend Florrie Crawford. It takes place in March, at the early beginning of spring, and it focuses on female sexuality exclusively. The two women are gathering mushrooms:

Florrie found a thick-stemmed toad-stool with a close
    purplish cap,
She plucked it and giggled at it, showing it to June, who
    couldn't think what she meant; then Florrie formed
An oval doorway between the finger and thumb of her left
    hand, she forced the odd-looking fungus
Into the slot and made it play back and forth. When its head
    broke off
She screamed with pleasure, threw it on the ground and
    trampled it, her little white teeth grinning maliciously,
    "I'd love to
Do that to all of them."

Florrie's sexual explicitness and anger cause June to break into tears, and she confesses her knowledge of Hugh's dalliance. Florrie forces June to reveal all the details, and June describes spying on Hugh and Vina from a distance and then fleeing to the beach, where she saw a dying pelican, its wings coated in oil. She identifies with the pelican: "I guess

that bird and I were the very wretchedest / Lives in the world." Florrie
advises a "tit-for-tat" solution to June's marital problems: when Florrie's
husband cheats on her, she cheats on him. They are happy, she says, and
"You'll find revenge / Is sweeter than love or honey." June won't accept
her friend's advice, saying she would rather die like the pelican than take
a lover. The poem concludes with Florrie comforting her:

> "Ah, Ah, never say die,"
> Florrie answered quickly, "it's wicked for a married woman
>   to talk like that, we must not be abject. Look, darling:
> There's the first yellow violet, yellow outside and brown
>   underneath, just like your hair."

The end of "The Fungus," like that of "Wild Pig," is inconclusive in
that no resolution is apparent in June Flodden's situation. However, in
giving Florrie Crawford the last word, Jeffers allows a comic, natural
attitude toward sexuality to prevail. Florrie's observation aligns June's
beauty with nature's resurgence, and her willed optimism, her marital
advice notwithstanding, corresponds to her ability to see the beautiful
in nature, which is also confirmed in her name.

Multiple elements of these poems from the 1930s indicate a comic
mode in Jeffers's narrative work: the fanciful lightness of "The Stone-
Axe" and its positive view of human survival; the humor and humanity
of "All the Little Hoof-Prints" and "Going to Horse Flats"; the ambiguity
and suspension of tragic sexuality in "Steelhead, Wild Pig, The Fungus."
Such narrative techniques supplement both the overwhelmingly tragic
character of Jeffers's major poems and the dominantly lyric qualities of
his ecologically oriented short poems. With some adjustments, Brophy's
schema for his myth-ritual readings of the 1920s work indicates where
we might look to find elements of the other *mythoi* in Jeffers's poems in
the 1930s and beyond. Shorter narratives based in anecdotal plots and
incidents continue to appear in his later work: "Come Little Birds" (*CP*
3:5–9), written in the late 1930s, and "The Inquisitors" (*CP* 3:209–10), written in the mid-1940s, are two tales of the uncanny that add another style
to Jeffers's narrative practice, the latter being an environmental fantasy
of the earth's judgment of humanity.

In fact, the shorter narratives of the 1930s might be the groundwork
for Jeffers's most important environmental long poem, "The Inhumanist." It makes a pair with "The Love and the Hate," the two narratives
that constitute his major poem of the World War II period, "The Double
Axe" (*CP* 3:214–312). William Everson, sensing the presence of the comic
element in "The Inhumanist," describes the two parts of the title poem:

"If 'The Love and the Hate' is the darkest narrative Jeffers ever penned, then 'The Inhumanist' is, by far, the lightest."[45] The lightness of the poem derives from the title character, the nameless old caretaker of the abandoned ranch. The old man is an imaginative projection for Jeffers, and as such he can go further than the poet himself in practicing an inhumanist detachment. In this character the poem finds its comic aspect. Not only does the old man possess the aloofness required to make wry comments on the other characters' and his own actions throughout the poem, but he himself survives the process of breaking through to the inhumanist vision, a process that no other Jeffers character, with the exception of Orestes in "Tower beyond Tragedy," has survived. "The Inhumanist" is a narrative hybrid, mixing together tragedy, comedy, fantasy; history, myth, and current events, even, a rarity in Jeffers, poetry and prose. Yet what marks it as most distinctive is the survival of the protagonist, which in effect makes it Jeffers's major contribution to the "comedy of survival." The shorter narratives of the 1930s provide the context for this most surprising of narrative developments in Jeffers's work, but the later 1930s were a time of trial and crisis, as Jeffers anticipated the coming of the Second World War. He had to endure a crisis of holism before he could invent the character of the Inhumanist.

4 / To Keep One's Own Integrity: "The Inhumanist" and the Crisis of Holism

In the relative calm of the "idyllic" years of the early and mid-1930s, Jeffers resolved the tensions of his struggle with the biology of consciousness into a philosophical holism. He expressed it succinctly in a 1934 letter: "I believe that the universe is one being, all its parts are different expressions of the same energy, and that they are all in communication with each other, influencing each other, therefore parts of one organic whole. (This is physics, I believe, as well as religion)" (*CL* 2:365). Although the drift of ecological and biological science in the twentieth century was toward increasing reductionism and away from holism, Jeffers affirmed his belief that his sacramental vision was confirmed by science.[1] The mysticism and materialism that Jeffers acknowledged as central to his worldview were now harnessed together by an explicit organic holism, and as another war in Europe began to emerge throughout the decade the efficacy of this position was tested by a crisis that returned the poet to the conflicts and tensions that marked his work in the 1920s and resulted in his most ecological narrative poem, "The Inhumanist." Indeed, considering its concluding image of a nuclear holocaust, we might designate "The Inhumanist" as the inaugural poem of Donald Worster's "Age of Ecology," which began with the first atomic bomb tests in New Mexico in 1945. "For the first time in some two million years of human history," Worster writes, "there existed a force capable of destroying the entire fabric of life on the planet." Arthur Koestler proposed a "new calendar" for the new age, with the year zero beginning on that specific day in August. "The reason is simple," he writes. "From the dawn of consciousness until

6 August 1945, man had to live with the prospect of his death as an *individual*; since the day when the first atomic bomb outshone the sun over Hiroshima, mankind as a whole has had to live with the prospect of its extinction as a *species*."[2] The sad irony of the Age of Ecology is that it took science's ability to reduce the physical world to its smallest parts—to split the atom—to bring about a new consciousness of the whole.

Other major poets of Jeffers's modernist cohort responded to the bomb, but because of the organic holism he had developed during the thirties only Jeffers was prepared to fit it into his worldview. Wallace Stevens's apocalyptic vision was parallel to Jeffers's in many respects, and Charles Berger reads his "Auroras of Autumn" (1947) as a figure for the bomb: "What triggered the finding of the auroras by Stevens was not so much a text as an event: the dropping of the atomic bomb, the epitome of all great explosions. . . . The auroras merged old and current versions of apocalypse in a dense textual weave." Berger points to the phrase "gusts of great enkindlings" in canto II as an example of imagery based on the atomic blasts, though any explicit mention of the war is absent in the poem.[3] The bomb, it seems, becomes just one version of the apocalypse for Stevens, who later wrote, "I cannot say that there is any way to adapt myself to the idea that I am living in the Atomic Age and I think it a lot of nonsense to try to adapt oneself to such a thing."[4] In "Reflection on the Atomic Bomb," written in 1946, Gertrude Stein simply proclaimed the bomb to be uninteresting.[5] Perhaps Robert Frost comes closest to Jeffers's holism in his dual response in two poems from *Steeple Bush* (1947). "One Step Backward Taken" is his comic response, judging, not unlike Stein, the bomb to be much ado about nothing: feeling his "standpoint shaken / In the universal crisis," all he has to do is take a step backward from the precipice and watch the world go by him. His more serious response was "Directive," which, not unlike Jeffers, points his readers in the direction of healing: "Here are your waters and your watering place. / Drink and be whole again beyond confusion."[6] However, rather than an allegorical journey back in time leading to a source and a grail, Jeffers offers his readers the more rigorous and paradoxical remedy of his organic holism, now formally introduced after the war as "Inhumanism."[7]

World War II and Holism

Even as he was writing and publishing the shorter narratives that I have identified as being in a comic mode, stories that emphasize characters' integration into the coastal environment, Jeffers began composing lyric poems on the worsening turn in current events in Europe. The first round of these poems was collected in *Such Counsels You Gave to Me and Other Poems*, published on September 27, 1937 (*CP* 5:574). It contained "Air-Raid Rehearsals," an antiwar poem that anticipates the coming conflict in Europe, as well as other poems that comment on the news, including "Blind Horses" (which remarks on Stalin's consolidation of power), "Memoir" (which mentions "Russian labor-camps" and "German prison-camps" [*CP* 2:525]), and "Thebaid" (with a passing reference to Hitler).

"Air-Raid Rehearsals" and its twin, "Rearmament," which was published in *Solstice and Other Poems* (1935), reveal the tension between detachment and involvement, a crisis of integrity precipitated by the collision of Jeffers's organic holism and his concern with the emerging war. "Rearmament" (*CP* 2:515) comments on Germany's weapons buildup in the midthirties:

> These grand and fatal movements toward death: the
>   grandeur of the mass
> Makes pity a fool, the tearing pity
> For the atoms of the mass, the persons, the victims, makes it
>   seem monstrous
> To admire the tragic beauty they build.
> It is beautiful as a river flowing or a slowly gathering
> Glacier on a high mountain rock-face,
> Bound to plow down a forest, or as frost in November,
> The gold and flaming death-dance for leaves,
> Or a girl in the night of her spent maidenhood, bleeding and
>   kissing.
> I would burn my right hand in a slow fire
> To change the future . . . I should do foolishly. The beauty of
>   modern
> Man is not in the persons but in the
> Disastrous rhythm, the heavy and mobile masses, the dance
>   of the
> Dream-led masses down the dark mountain.

"Air-Raid Rehearsals" (*CP* 2:516) addresses the same situation in Europe but might also be considered the poet's "rehearsal" of his response to the war that he knows is coming:

> Unhappy time why have you built up your house
> So high that it cannot stand? I see that it has to fall:
> When I look closer I can see nothing clearly, my eyes are
>   blinded with rain.

I see far fires and dim degradation
Under the war-planes and neither Christ nor Lenin will save
    you.
I see the March rain walk on the mountain, sombre and
    lovely on the green mountain.

I wish you could find the secure value,
The all-heal I found when a former time hurt me to the
    heart,
The splendor of inhuman things: you would not be looking
    at each others' throats with your knives.

These two poems are genetically linked—evidence presented by Tim
Hunt in volume 5 of *The Collected Poetry* shows they probably began as
the same poem; at one point, each was subtitled "March 1935." In both,
the speaker laments the oncoming conflict, seeing its inevitability yet
still wanting to present an alternative. The poems also share images of
tears and weeping, indicating the speaker's emotional involvement taking its color from the equinoctal rains, and both make direct reference to
current events in Europe. Although "Rearmament" resolves on a note of
fatalism, the gesture toward personal sacrifice is telling. Hunt points out
that the image of burning his hand in a fire appeared in a draft of "Air-
Raid," then was included in "Rearmament" (*CP* 5:577).[8] The third stanza
of "Air-Raid" offers healing rather than sacrifice. The publication history
supports a speculation that Jeffers truly believed he had a viable solution
to offer: "Rearmament" was a late addition to *Solstice and Other Poems*,
sent to Random House after the table of contents had been determined.
"Air-Raid Rehearsals" was first published in the *Saturday Review*, Janu-
ary 4, 1936, the only short poem from *Such Counsels You Gave to Me and
Other Poems* to appear in a magazine prior to being collected for the
book. Jeffers went to the trouble of getting these two poems into print as
soon as he could, yet by 1938 he seems to have decided that fatalism was
better than healing: he didn't include "Air-Raid" in the Random House
Selected Poetry. Perhaps the teary sympathy of "Air-Raid" just didn't
hold up for him; the stoic sacrifice of "Rearmament" and its equally stoic
rejection were emphasized.

    Another of the topical lyrics in *Such Counsels You Gave to Me and
Other Poems*, "The Answer" (*CP* 2:536), echoes the organism of his 1934
letter quoted above, and it is, in effect, Jeffers's "answer" to the questions
implied by the other poems on current events. It is the clearest poetic
expression of his theory of holism:

Then what is the answer?—Not to be deluded by dreams.
To know that great civilizations have broken down into
    violence, and their tyrants come, many times before.
When open violence appears, to avoid it with honor or
    choose the least ugly faction; these evils are essential.
To keep one's own integrity, be merciful and uncorrupted
    and not wish for evil; and not be duped
By dreams of universal justice or happiness. These dreams
    will not be fulfilled.
To know this, and know that however ugly the parts appear
    the whole remains beautiful. A severed hand
Is an ugly thing, and man disseevered from the earth and
    stars and his history . . . for contemplation or in fact . . .
Often appears atrociously ugly. Integrity is wholeness, the
    greatest beauty is
Organic wholeness, the wholeness of life and things, the
    divine beauty of the universe. Love that, not man
Apart from that, or else you will share man's pitiful
    confusions, or drown in despair when his days darken.

This poem is one of Jeffers's best-known statements of a holistic ecological ethics; it is often quoted by environmentalists, and the Sierra Club used the phrase "not man apart" for the title of its coffee-table book of photos and selections from Jeffers's poetry. What is significant is that the poem proposes organic holism as the "answer" to the social and political confusions of the time, and the complexity of his answer turns on the key term of the poem, *integrity*.[9]

Of course, Jeffers is well aware of the pun in his definition of *integrity*. His first use of the term applies one of the dictionary definitions, "steadfast adherence to a strict moral or ethical code." His second evokes the word's derivation from the Latin *integer*, whole, complete, which is traced to the Indo-European root *tag-*, "to touch, handle." Jeffers makes the pun on *integrity* explicit in his second use of the term, "Integrity is wholeness." Wholeness is etymologically connected to health—the Indo-European root *kailo-*, from which derive *whole, wholesome, health, heal, holy,* and *hallow.* So Jeffers's answer is associated with health and wholeness, and integrity implies being able to stay in *touch* with these values.[10]

In a poem written not long after "The Answer," "Theory of Truth" (*CP* 2:608–10), Jeffers says that Arthur Barclay (the main character of "The Women at Point Sur") "touched his answers," and the poet ponders the truths touched by other seekers (Lao-tze, Christ, Buddha), each of whom "stained" the truths he found with his own "private impurit[ies]." "The greatest have achieved answers, but always / With aching strands of insanity in them," he writes. The speaker poses another question: "Then search for truth is foredoomed and frustrate? / Only stained fragments? // Until the mind has turned its love from itself and man, from parts to the whole." Wholeness is a thing that can be touched; insanity is being "touched" in the head. The hand both confirms the answer—that which is whole, an integer, is that which can be handled—and creates the disease. There is a hand in "The Answer," of course—it just happens to be cut off. Surely, Jeffers chose this image for its instinctive repugnance, but, as I am arguing here, the severed hand in "The Answer" belies a deeper contradiction indicative of the dilemma inherent in the inhumanist perspective.

These manual images offer a key to understanding how Jeffers's inhumanism is entangled in the classic deconstructive double bind between synecdoche and metonymy, and they reveal the difficulty of maintaining an integrity based in a holistic view of the universe. Throughout his career, Jeffers offered "signs manual" as figures for synecdochal wholeness or metonymical detachment, and his back-and-forth between these two mutually exclusive tropes suggests the difficulty of escaping the structure that produces the binary opposition. To sever oneself from humanity is to cut off one's hand because the hand makes us human through its relation to language. Jacques Derrida, paraphrasing Heidegger, proposes "that the animal has no hand, that a hand can never upsurge out of a paw or claws, but only from speech."[11] And in another iteration of the deconstructive double bind, the hand is connected to speech through writing, but that connection is metonymical—the hand is associated only with writing.[12] The hand as a synecdoche for humanity is based in its connection to the body.

In "Hands" (*CP* 2:4), written in the late 1920s, Jeffers himself saw this connection between our hands and our humanity:

Inside a cave in a narrow canyon near Tassajara
The vault of rock is painted with hands,
A multitude of hands in the twilight, a cloud of men's palms,
    no more,
No other picture. There's no one to say
Whether the brown shy quiet people who are dead intended
Religion or magic, or made their tracings
In the idleness of art; but over the division of years these
    careful

Signs-manual are now like a sealed message
Saying: "Look: we also were human; we had hands, not
    paws. All hail
You people with the cleverer hands, our supplanters
In the beautiful country; enjoy her a season, her beauty, and
    come down
And be supplanted; for you also are human."

The hand as a sign of humanity is metonymical—the connection is contingent rather than necessary. Furthermore, the hand's association with language is through writing, not speech. Structuralist linguistics underwrites this tension: Roman Jakobson's bipolar structure of language based in metaphor and metonymy, and, more specifically, Paul de Man's deconstructive versions of synecdoche and metonymy. De Man rejected the romantic symbol as mystification and valorized allegory as the trope based in the reality of a contingent and arbitrary semiological system. Two types of metaphor are parallel to these terms, synecdoche and metonymy. In synecdoche a part represents the whole, and in metonymy the name or image of one thing stands for another. For de Man, the synecdochal symbol evokes the illusion of unity, identity, wholeness, and eternity; the metonymical allegory represents the reality of separation, difference, fragmentation, and temporality.

If we take the hands of Tassajara and the hands from the World War II period poems, we have the terms of the crisis brought on by the nonanthropocentric perspective. It is a deconstructive crisis between synecdoche and metonymy. An artificial detachment has to happen metonymically, while at the same time an organic wholeness, the proper relation between part and whole, has to be maintained synecdochically. The hand as sign of the human is detachable because it is a metonym; the hand as symbol for wholeness is integral because it is a synecdoche. Inhumanism asks us to subordinate our metonymical associations to our synecdochal connections. We have to sacrifice our metonymical privilege, singular existence, for synecdochal healing, holistic being. Yet the means by which this endeavor gets expressed, writing, requires our detachment from the whole; it severs us from the world so that we may comprehend, grasp, it. How can one write poetry that imagines our integration in nature when writing requires that we sever ourselves from nature?

Integrity is wholeness, then, and wholeness is health, yet to recognize and value this wholeness, indeed to participate in it, we must sever ourselves from our own humanity. In the various prefaces to *The Double Axe and Other Poems*, Jeffers speaks in terms of sanity, which is mental wholeness, derived from the Latin *sānus*, healthy. In the 1947 preface, he evokes its inversion in his example of the "insane man" who represents humanist anthropocentrism (*CP* 4:418–19). In a paragraph drafted as an alternate introduction, he explicitly equates his inhumanism with sanity: "The attitude they [the poems] suggest—the devaluation of human-centered illusions, the turning outward from man to what is boundlessly greater—is a next step in human development; and an essential condition of freedom, and of spiritual (i.e. moral and vital) sanity" (*CP* 5:998).[13] As we can see, the "organic wholeness" presented in "The Answer" connects with Jeffers's most ecological narrative—"The Inhumanist," which is the second half of "The Double Axe"—the long poem that most clearly presents his sacramental solution to the dilemma of consciousness.

"The Inhumanist" and Holism

The Double Axe and Other Poems follows a period of intense political awareness for Jeffers; in a note to *Be Angry at the Sun and Other Poems* (1941), he writes, "I wish also to lament the obsession with contemporary history that pins many of these pieces to the calendar, like butterflies to cardboard" (*CP* 4:417). The goal of *The Double Axe and Other Poems* is to reinstate the integrity of inhumanist detachment. However, the book contains many explicitly political poems—some so critical of U.S. involvement in the war that its publisher, Random House, printed a disclaimer on the dust jacket and as a prefatory note to the poems. Nonetheless, the position Jeffers takes in "The Double Axe," especially the poem's second half, "The Inhumanist," rejects the world of contemporary politics in favor of the possibility of individual transformation. Jeffers experienced a crisis of integrity in the mid- to late 1930s, precipitated by his compulsion to write poems that commented on the historical events leading toward war. Although in "The Answer" he had reminded himself not to love "man apart" from the whole, by the time the United States entered the war, and even after the war, he had yet fully to overcome the compulsion to write about politics, about the parts rather than the whole.

While this account of a sacramental nature poet's turn away from politics may seem to be an iteration of Jerome McGann's "romantic ideology," it is only from the perspective of a historicist ideology that politics can be posited as a source of value. Phenomenologist Erazim Kohák describes the philosophical position that accommodates the goals of Jeffers's sacramentalism: "A far more basic reason for questioning the utilitarian justification of the historicist vision is its effect on the only lives that humans actually live, those of the perennial present. The power of the historicist vision is that it seems to endow that present with a time-relative meaning. It does so, however, only at the frightful cost of draining the present of all absolute, perennial present meaning."[14] "The Double Axe" responds to this condition. It rejects the "historicist vision" that denies individuals the reality of their lived experience and seeks to discover a new system of value that connects the individual with an absolute reality. On the surface, Jeffers's "answer"—inhumanism—might appear opposed to a revaluation of historicism, since it denies the individual as the source of value. However, the poem presents a process in which the individual sheds the anthropocentric perspective in order to recognize the absolute reality of the perennial present, the intersection of time and being, in Kohák's phenomenological terms, or the chiastic crossing of matter and spirit in the figurative terms of the poem.

The attempt to negotiate the reintegration of the individual by means of figurative thinking locks sacramental poetics in the deconstructive double bind of synecdoche and metonymy. A synecdochal relationship is the classic trope for this reintegration—value is produced by being a part of the whole—yet writing always undermines that connection in its metonymical operations. In one sense, this is a productive tension—the poet is forced, as Emerson would have it, into a double consciousness, ably leaping back and forth between the synecdochal and metonymical.[15] However, a sacramental poet is driven to attempt, at least, to break out of language, to find a connection that moves through dualism to the whole. To do this, Jeffers writes a long poem that rejects the modernist strategy of resolving fragmentation through the materiality of language, charting instead a route out of the double consciousness by locating an absolute value. In this way, sacramental poetics is able to achieve a momentary reconciliation of the one and the many, to envision a healing and wholeness, because the long poem can encompass dualism and unity. Once Jeffers steps back from the achievement of his poem, he has to make compromises with the historicist vision that rejects absolute value. Nonetheless, the ambitions of "The Double Axe" mark a signal achievement in his sacramental poetics.

In the preface to *The Double Axe*, Jeffers writes that the title poem's "burden . . . is to present a certain philosophical attitude, which might be called Inhumanism, a shifting of emphasis from man to not-man; the rejection of human solipsism and recognition of the transhuman magnificence. It seems time that our race began to think as an adult does, rather than like an egocentric baby or insane person" (*CP* 4:428). "The Double Axe" is Jeffers's reworking of the issues that arose in the prewar poems of the 1930s—it is the "answer" again, this time in the form of a two-part narrative poem. If the lyrics and shorter narratives of the 1930s reveal Jeffers developing an environmental ethics based in his theocentric vision, then "The Double Axe" is the testing of this system on a larger scale.[16] In this sense, "The Double Axe" is a return to an experimental approach to storytelling that he abandoned after the disastrous reception of "The Women at Point Sur." Not since that poem, which was discussed in chapter 2, had Jeffers invested such personal stakes in a narrative. William Everson suggests that the two poems of "The Double Axe," linked internally only by their setting, actually are joined by the psychological purpose of expressing Jeffers's rage at U.S. involvement in the war and of purging that emotional overinvolvement with politics, which violated his own principle of detachment.[17] The two narratives taken together, then, embody the opposing forces that complicate inhumanism's nonanthropocentricism, what Arthur Koestler calls the "dichotomy of wholeness and partness."[18] The sacramental logic of the poem requires a transformation of the atomistic partness of the metonymical into the synecdochal partness that creates wholeness.

The first half of the title poem, "The Love and the Hate," is split psychically between the emotions that, for Jeffers, were the cause of the greatest problems because they demand a solipsistic involvement of humanity. It is the gruesome story of a soldier, aptly named Hoult Gore, who returns from the dead (quite literally, as a reanimated corpse) to act out an Oedipal drama in which he purges himself of both love and hate by avenging himself on his parents. These are typical themes for Jeffers's long poems, incest and parricide being his master metaphors for the human race's introversion, but in the context of the war they also take on political significance: the young taking revenge on the corrupt patriarchs who sent them to their deaths. The main character of the second half, "The Inhumanist," is a nameless old man who has become the caretaker of the abandoned Gore ranch. The passions of the previous narrative's characters haunt the subplot of "The Inhumanist," in which the old man witnesses another tale of betrayal and vengeance involving his illegitimate daughter, her lover, and his wife.

However, the main action of "The Inhumanist" centers on the old man's daily activities, in the course of which he meets various refugees from the crumbling postwar civilization outside his sanctuary. Aside from his daughter and his half-feral pet dog, Snapper, the characters he meets are either archetypal or allegorical figures: a doppelgänger ("the man of many terrors" [CP 3:298]), a nuclear physicist with a German accent, an aspiring disciple, a fugitive with radiation sickness.

All appear so that the old man may comment on the world events that brought about the disasters or so that he may be taught a lesson that brings him closer to achieving the inhumanist vision. Considering the dichotomies and contradictions that mark the World War II period for Jeffers—roughly 1938 to 1948, a span of years that begins with the publication of his *Selected Poetry*, which stayed in print for nearly fifty years, and ends with the Broadway success of his adaptation of *Medea* but that also includes political poems that garnered some of his worst reviews and censure from his own publisher—it is not surprising to find that his major narrative poem of this time splits in two, one part of which focuses on the twin manifestations of human solipsism ("the love and the hate") and the other part of which involves a solitary figure constantly beset by reflections of himself (daughter, dog, doppelgänger). The poem itself is a double axe, a tool (or weapon) the poet uses to sever the androcentric from the nonanthropocentric, thereby restoring his own sense of integrity or wholeness. As in "The Answer," it is only through the paradoxical idea of a severed part that we can reconnect with the whole.

As a detailed articulation of the nonanthropocentric perspective, "The Inhumanist" should be considered a key text in literary environmentalism's canon. One of the main goals of environmental classics such as Mary Austin's *The Land of Little Rain*, Aldo Leopold's *A Sand County Almanac*, and Edward Abbey's *Desert Solitaire* is to present models of environmentally ethical behavior, which often looks unethical from the humanist perspective. In the old man, Jeffers invented such a model, specifically an example of the stoic, detached life, worshipful of the divine universe. Even though he struggles, the old man falls in love outward, doting lovingly on the beauty of place; he pays homage to patron saints of the nonanthropocentric worldview, Copernicus and Darwin; he cares for his dog and his daughter, yet with proper detachment so that he is glad to see them leave him to pursue their own destinies. What's more, had Jeffers included some plot elements found in his notes for the poem, the old man would have been a proto-monkeywrencher or ELF (Earth Liberation Front) activist. At one point, he considered having the Inhumanist kill another character for torturing a fox in a trap (*CP* 5:787), and another note reads: "Surveyers: 'We are plotting a road.' He shot from ambush and killed them" (*CP* 5:789). However, the old man is ultimately a model for, as one draft of the preface puts it, "[a] new philosophy, which is both practical and religious" (*CP* 5:998). Even from an inhumanist perspective, one hopes, killing for such reasons is neither practical nor religious. The murder that the old man does commit in the poem—the killing of his doppelgänger human half—is both practical, because it is the only way to achieve the inhumanist perspective, and religious, because it is done ritualistically, not by bullet but by axe.

"The Inhumanist" is also Jeffers's full-scale return to the problem of the biology of consciousness, beginning from the position of the organic holism of the 1930s. A brief verse paragraph introduces the old man and the setting—"the infamous house" that no one ever comes to. The narrator says, "Old men and gray hawks need solitude, / Here it is deep and wide" (CP 3:256). In his solitude, as the caretaker of an abandoned ranch with nothing on it that requires much caretaking, the old man thinks his way through a series of propositions that set the groundwork for inhumanism's theocentric position, elaborating on the holism of the 1930s and resolving some of the tensions of the 1920s. His questions and proposed answers also lead to the crux of the poem, Jeffers's notion of the beauty of things, that will be resolved only after the old man's solitude is disrupted by multiple intrusions.

In the first section, pondering the cycles of natural and historical process—the turning of the seasons, the alternations between war and peace—the old man sees them as iterations of divine process and asks, "Why does God hunt in circles? Has he lost something? Is it possible— himself?" In section II, the questioning continues:

"Does God exist?—No doubt of that," the old man says. "The
   cells of my old camel of a body,
Because they feel each other and are fitted together,—
   through nerves and blood feel each other,—all the little
   animals
Are the one man: there is not an atom in all the universes
But feels every other atom; gravitation, electromagnetism,
   light, heat, and the other
Flamings, the nerves in the night's black flesh, flow them
   together; the stars, the winds and the people: one energy,
One existence, one music, one organism, one life, one God:
   star-fire and rock-strength, the sea's cold flow
And man's dark soul." (CP 3:256–57)

Section III, just a single sentence, dismisses the notion of "an anthropoid God," and section IV extends on the old man's theology to consciousness: "A conscious God?—The question has no importance. But I am conscious: where else / Did this consciousness come from? Nobody that I know of ever poured grain from an empty sack" (CP 3:257). Thus, at the start of the poem, the old man expresses the core principles of the inhumanist perspective, principles that are the foundation of a nonanthropocentric, ecological ethics and that can be found in similar terms in the poetry of the 1930s.

After these initial propositions, the various secondary characters appear and subplots begin to unfold—the old man's solitary mediations are interrupted, and he is gradually pulled back into social concerns as he acquires a pet dog, reunites with his illegitimate daughter, and encounters numerous refugees from the collapsing postwar society. In this way, Jeffers invents an allegorical narrative to illustrate the difficulty of maintaining the inhumanist perspective. For the old man, the climactic event is the ritualized slaying of his doppelgänger, "the man of many terrors," who represents his human half. It is only after he makes this final break with humanity that the Inhumanist can see the whole rather than the parts.

The conclusions reached by the Inhumanist result in a reconsideration of one of Jeffers's most important poetic *topoi*, the beauty of things. The radical proposal of Jeffers's inhumanism is to make beauty an ontological rather than epistemological category. The old man's most extreme statement comes after he breaks from the anthropocentric perspective by killing the doppelgänger. Early in the poem, the Inhumanist proclaimed, "The beauty of things— / Is in the beholder's brain—the human mind's translation of their transhuman / Intrinsic value. It is their color in our eyes: as we say blood is red and blood is the life: / It is the life. Which is *like* beauty. It is *like* nobility" (CP 3:260). After his sacramental murder of his human half, he amends his statement: "The beauty of things is not harnessed to human / Eyes and the little active minds: it is absolute" (CP 3:311).

Although he speaks of its beauty, Jeffers is not moralizing or even aestheticizing nature—he is sacramentalizing it. Without this distinction, the old man would appear to be suffering from what Timothy Morton has diagnosed as "beautiful soul syndrome"—the romantic condition that Hegel described as the unhappy consciousness that separates humanity from nature. From Morton's Marxist perspective, "The beautiful soul fuses the aesthetic and the moral. The aestheticization has a moral dimension, the result of an achieved distance. The beautiful soul maintains a split between self and world, an irresolvable chasm created by the call of conscience. . . . Yet the beautiful soul also yearns to close the gap."[19] Thus, with the perceiver separated from the perceived, the concept of "beautiful Nature" becomes the object on the other side of the chasm from the subject. Without the "beautiful soul" there can be no "beautiful Nature." Absolute beauty, the old man's ultimate value, is an impossibility from an aesthetic-historicist perspective; therefore, as we have seen, the goal of "The Double Axe" was to escape from this perspective. Albert Gelpi's assessment of Jeffers's achievement is right—"Jeffers's poetry . . . constitutes the effort . . . to stand apart from yet be a part of sublime Nature"[20]—but the conceptual frame of sublimity locks the perceiver into the syndrome critiqued by Morton just as surely as the concept of beauty does. The sublime, as relevant as it is to Jeffers's idea of nature, nonetheless requires an anthropocentric subject standing apart from an aestheticized object. Thus the importance of Jeffers's reiterated phrase: the beauty of things. Gelpi writes, "Jeffers speaks of 'the beauty of things' often, but he really means the sublimity of things."[21] In terms of his rugged coastal environment, and in terms of the ego-negating response he had to that landscape, sublimity is an important concept, as Gelpi and Robert Zaller, in *Robinson Jeffers and the American Sublime*, have shown. However, sublimity is not an inherent quality in a thing any more than beauty is. Jeffers's inhumanist gamble is to objectify—indeed, to reify—the concept of beauty. In fact, to make it no concept at all. This is the import of his recurring phrase, "the beauty of things." He embraces the Cartesian term for nature, *res extensa*, and proposes to eliminate the subject, the *cogito*, from the equation. The inhumanist challenge—impossible to be sure—is to see the beauty of things without the aesthetic concept of beauty. It is the falling in love outward that the old man experiences, and it is a condition closer to Morton's idea of "dark ecology" than to his "beautiful soul syndrome." In dark ecology, he writes, one attempts "to love the thingness, not in a Heideggerian sense, but actually the mute, objectified quality of the object, its radical nonidentity. Nature is *not* a mirror of our mind."[22] If we can look at nature and not see our mind reflected in it, we are seeing through inhumanist eyes.

Of course, the inhumanist position is not one we can dwell in for long. In fact, it is not a position—it is, as the old man says, a remedy (*CP* 3:312). It is a curative to bring one back to health, which is wholeness. Jeffers created a character to present it to his readers because he could not kill his human half and still write. He himself had discovered "the beauty of things" twenty or more years prior, but he still lapsed into "the love and the hate" when the Second World War came along. After writing "The Inhumanist," he too came back to the relativist, aesthetic perception of beauty. In "De Rerum Virtute," even as he strains for the inhumanist perspective ("Look," he directs us, "without imagination, desire nor dream"), he admits the role of human perception in the conception of beauty:

The beauty of things means virtue and value in them.
It is in the beholder's eye, not in the world? Certainly.

It is the human mind's translation of the transhuman
Intrinsic glory. It means that the world is sound,
Whatever the sick microbe does. But he too is part of it.
(*CP* 3:403)

He hedges—there is another language, inherent in the things themselves, and we merely translate that language—and he leaves it at that.[23] From the human (metonymical) perspective, required for rational discourse and writing poetry, he must accept the relative value of beauty. Yet he provides his readers with a double axe, a rhetorical and figurative tool, the sign of doubleness that paradoxically and sacramentally can help readers cut through the anthropocentric screen that keeps them from seeing the thingness, the oneness, of nature and their part in it.

The caretaker of the Gore ranch is the final iteration of one of Jeffers's favorite themes, the meditation on saviors, final in that he at last imagines an alternative to the salvific model. The old man is a figure of sacramental value, but that value is based in a materialist conception of the universe-as-god, not a god who exists apart from the universe and therefore would have to intervene in its processes in the form of a savior. This distinction is crucial. William Everson, Jeffers's best reader in many respects, assesses the old man as a savior, thereby missing the ecological advantage he represents. Everson claims that Jeffers "created, despite himself, something suspiciously like a savior figure . . . a savior figure, that is, who constitutes some kind of model for human conduct, an intellectual and moral attitude appropriate to mankind in the dilemma of existence which now confronts it." He, too, hedges here somewhat, allowing the old man to be a model for behavior rather than a divine intervention in human history. However, he immediately turns to the archetype: the old man is "the only viable savior figure in his writing. The surfacing of the redeemer archetype here is revealing, given Jeffers' efforts to deny it."[24] Jeffers may be an archetypal thinker in many ways, but this assertion is more about Everson than Jeffers. What is revealing, to me, is Everson's insistence on reading for the archetype. The conclusion of "The Inhumanist" presents the old man not as a savior or redeemer but as a healer. When an atomic holocaust has destroyed the cities, refugees arrive at the ranch. At the advent of Worster's Age of Ecology, Jeffers's caretaker has already seen its consequences and solutions. For humanity to endure, he says, it must abandon its "human God" and also its "human godlessness" (*CP* 3:311). The personal god of salvific religions will not redeem it, nor will the secular savior of humanism. After the last refugee dies of radiation exposure, the poem concludes:

>   "There is," he said, "no remedy. —There are *two*
> remedies.
> This man has got his remedy, and I have one. There is no
>   third."
> About midnight he slept, and arose refreshed
> In the red dawn. (*CP* 3:312)

Of course, a remedy is a medicine or therapy—it relieves pain and cures disease. The old man's remedy is the "answer" of the lyrics from the midthirties; it is "the splendor of inhuman things," the "all-heal" that Jeffers offered to readers in "Air-Raid Rehearsals" (*CP* 2:516). Even though he continued to imagine human consciousness as "original sin," he offered remedy rather than salvation, the choice to return to health rather than the possibility of being saved. It wasn't until the 1970s that another sacramental nature poet, Gary Snyder, stated it as plainly: "heal-ing, / not saving."[25]

In "The Inhumanist," for once in all of Jeffers's narrative poems, the reader sees the rebirth of the individual after the inhumanist break-through. The old man, because he is a comic figure, survives and is able to articulate what Jeffers can only imagine: a view of the universe beyond humanity. The major portion of Jeffers's narratives is based on themes from classical tragedy—archetypal plots taken from Euripides and Sophocles—and his intention in such redactions is to reveal the tragedy of humanity violently and fatally centered on itself. As we saw in the pre-vious chapter, in his study of "literary ecology," *The Comedy of Survival*, Joseph Meeker argues that tragedy is an inherently "unecological" form, and he proposes comedy, in the Shakespearean mode, and the picaresque as the literary forms most capable of expressing the ability of human consciousness to find harmony with and comfort in its natural habitat. Jeffers's violent narratives are thus cautionary tales at best, not models of how to live but dramatized metaphors of what we have done and what we are when separated from nature, and for this reason they are a necessary counterweight to Meeker's comic mode. As a species, we have excelled at survival, gaining such mastery as to threaten the survival of many other species and our own as well. The old man's "comedy of survival" is surprising, almost out of the blue, and "The Inhumanist" is Jeffers's most "ecological" narrative in Meeker's sense. Yet the dramatic masks always come as a pair, so the dual structure of "The Double Axe" in its totality is the best indicator of Jeffers's sacramental poetics.

The double axe itself is in fact the most surprising aspect of "The Inhu-manist." The old man's axe is not just a prop and a symbol—it is also a character. The caretaker talks to it and it responds with screams, squeals, and giggles; it makes oracular comments, and even more bizarrely, it takes action on its own, at one point killing some intruders while the old man sleeps. It also flies and swims.[26] Early in the poem, the old man reveals his—and Jeffers's—knowledge of the religio-mythic history of the symbol: "He considered the double-bladed axe: 'In Crete it was a god, and they named the labyrinth for it. . . . It was a symbol of generation: the two lobes and the stiff helve: so was the Cross before they christened it. But this one can clip heads too. Grimly, grimly. A blade for the flesh, a blade for the spirit: and truth from lies'" (*CP* 3:258).[27] Thus the poem's titular figure is elaborated as divine, linked with the cross as a religious symbol, and encoded as a signifier of dualism. The axe also retains a closer connection to sacrificial violence than the cross, and its ability to "clip heads" is demonstrated in the poem when the old man beheads his doppelgänger, thereby killing the fearful and human-centered "half of himself" (*CP* 3:301). Although the axe's status as a fertility symbol is read as phallic here, it is interesting that the old man and his axe may be "priest" and "attribute" of a pre-Hellenic Earth Mother. In this sense, the old man's role as caretaker takes on the valence of a sacred duty, yet another model of ethical environmentalist behavior.

Regardless of how one chooses to read this uncanny figure, it is clear that Jeffers has tapped into a deep source of myth and symbol that embodies the dilemma of part and whole at the center of a sacramental poetics. Contemporary poet Clayton Eshleman has also adopted the figure of the double axe and the labyrinth to examine the evolutionary wound in the human mind known as consciousness. In an essay called "Placements II," he writes,

> It is possible to formulate a perspective that offers a life continu-
> ity, from lower life forms, through human biology and sexuality, to
> the earliest imaginings of our situation, which now seems to be bio-
> tragically connected with our having separated ourselves out of the
> animal-hominid world in order to pursue that catastrophic miracle
> called consciousness. If the labyrinth is a Double Axe, one might see
> it as humanity's anguished attempt to center an unending double-
> ness that is conjured by the fact that each step "forward" seems to be,
> at the same moment, a step "backward." And the haft? Phallocentric-
> ity which fuses the menstrual/ovulatory cycles in to an instrument of
> inner and outer ceremony that injures but does not restore.[28]

Seen in these terms, Jeffers's double axe participates fully in the circuit of healing and wholeness that is at the core of a sacramental poetics.

The weapon/tool that splits and divides, makes things into parts and fragments, becomes a symbol of the physical journey and psychological process that leads to the whole.

"The Inhumanist" is one of many sacramental long poems written by West Coast poets that William Everson, as we will see in the Conclusion, intuited as a regional response to the destruction of the war and its atomic aftermath, including his own "Chronicle of Division" and Kenneth Rexroth's "The Phoenix and the Tortoise." This impulse extends into the postwar generation with Gary Snyder's "Myths and Texts" and *Mountains and Rivers without End*. In fact, response to the "nuclear sublime" brings Jeffers and Snyder together in a chiastic crossing of beginnings and endings.[29] At the conclusion of Jeffers's last great experimental narrative poem, the Inhumanist meets the refugee who describes the nuclear apocalypse: "The fire, the blast and the rays. The whiffs of poisoned smoke that were cities" (*CP* 3:310). However, the old man has found his remedy and sees the larger whole beyond the destruction. He awakes "refreshed / In the red dawn" (*CP* 3:312). In a group of poems on Mount St. Helens in his first collection of new poetry (*Danger on Peaks*) after completing his long poem *Mountains and Rivers without End*, Snyder returns in his memory to the nuclear advent of the Age of Ecology. The prose poem "Atomic Dawn" begins, "The day I first climbed Mt. St. Helens was August 13, 1945," and continues:

> Spirit Lake was far from the cities of the valley and news came slow. Though the first atomic bomb was dropped on Hiroshima August 6 and the second dropped on Nagasaki August 9, photographs didn't appear in the *Portland Oregonian* until August 12. Those papers must have been driven in to Spirit Lake on the 13th. Early the morning of the 14th I walked over to the lodge to check the bulletin board. There were whole pages of the paper pinned up: photos of a blasted city from the air, the estimate of 150,000 dead in Hiroshima alone, the American scientist quoted saying "nothing will grow there again for seventy years." The morning sun on my shoulders, the fir forest smell and the big tree shadows; feet in thin moccasins feeling the ground, and my heart still one with the snowpeak mountain at my back. Horrified, blaming scientists and politicians and the governments of the world, I swore a vow to myself, something like, "By the purity and beauty and permanence of Mt. St. Helens, I will fight against this cruel destructive power and those who would seek to use it, for all my life."[30]

For both poets, the mountains are symbols of permanence, even within the dynamic flux of geological process and catastrophic change (the Mount St. Helens sequence is in part motivated by Snyder's revisiting of the mountain after the eruption). Snyder, even before the beginning of his career as a poet, and Jeffers, nearing the end of his, both witness the atomic dawning of the Age of Ecology and look to the sacramental wholeness of nature to heal the wounds that created it.

5 / The Wound in the Brain: The Discoveries of the Later Poetry

As we saw in chapter 3, Jeffers explores the "comic" potential for human integration in nature in other poems of the 1930s, and in chapter 4 we examined the crisis of holism brought on by the Second World War and resolved in "The Inhumanist." In his later poems, Jeffers returns to the biology of consciousness and confronts many of the questions left unanswered in the 1920s. One of the most important advances is a more developed understanding of cells and their role in the evolution of consciousness. In late poems and fragments he revises his earlier opinion that consciousness is only contained in the human mind, that there is "no thought apparent" outside the brain vault, as he once supposed in "Apology for Bad Dreams." He comes a long way toward resolving the tension of the two-creators dualism in the early poems on consciousness, modifying it by seeking an evolutionary cause of and justification for consciousness, yet a strain still remains between the two horses in his harness. If the power of Jeffers's poetry of the 1920s emerged from the tension produced by the strain in the skull, the shift in his views on consciousness lowered the personal stake he had in writing poetry about consciousness. Without the release of the tension as the motivation to write, he had to seek other sources of power to drive his verse, though the goal of his writing was the same: discovery. The power of the poetry of the 1920s is the paradox that art and culture are ended, that the poet's discoveries will be beyond them, and yet the poet must invent a language to tell of his discoveries. Jeffers's discovery in the 1920s was the divinity of the universe and the individual's relation to it. In the 1950s, of course, his discoveries were of a different order. After the death of his wife, and looking toward his own demise, Jeffers's own consciousness turned toward entropy—if "Night" was an abstract consolation in 1924, it became a consoling prospect to him in the last decade of his life. The strain in the skull was diminished, and therefore the sacramental poetics that it produced is less pronounced. In fact, the sacramentality of the later work is an inversion of the earlier poems. Rather than struggling to place consciousness in an evolutionary frame, the poet turns his attention to the more personal concerns of accommodating consciousness to the losses and changes of aging and death.

The last major poem that Jeffers completed, "Hungerfield," which first appeared in the May 1952 issue of *Poetry*, bears the last traces of his use of the narrative form to release the tensions of consciousness. The poem includes a lyric elegy for his wife that frames the story of a man, Hawl Hungerfield, who wrestles with Death for the life of his cancer-stricken mother. In this way, the poem addresses consciousness, though its story is not directly concerned with it. The opening verse paragraph presents a moving meditation on memory and loss, in which the poet tries to convince himself that his wife is not actually gone. He writes, "If time is only another dimension, then all that dies / Remains alive; not annulled, but removed / Out of sight. Una is still alive" (*CP* 3:375). The rest of the paragraph is a series of vivid memories of Una, and the next paragraph begins: "It is possible that all these conditions of us / Are fixed points on the returning orbit of time and exist eternally . . . / It is no good. Una has died, and I / Am left waiting for death, like a leafless tree / Waiting for the roots to rot and the trunk to fall" (*CP* 3:375–76, ellipses in original).

After directly addressing Una, the poet goes on to say that it is not loneliness or old age that bothers him but rather "my torment is memory" (*CP* 3:376). As he observed thirty years before, consciousness is the "insufferable insolence, the sting" that makes us "mourn dead beauty a bird-bright-May-morning" (*CP* 1:8), an image that probably referred to a daughter who died the day after she was born but now can be appropriately applied to his wife. The desperate and heroic Hungerfield is then a wish fulfillment of sorts, as well as a warning against such wishes: his mother curses him for prolonging her life, and the story ends with multiple deaths in the family, after which Hungerfield immolates himself inside the farmhouse. Only his mother survives. The story may serve to remind the poet that the hubris of interfering with natural process leads only to tragedy, but more significantly he sees it as an escape from rather than exploration of consciousness. After recalling his feelings of guilt and helplessness as he cared for Una in her illness, he writes, "For these reasons / I wish to make verses again, to drug memory, / To make it sleep for a moment" (*CP* 3:378). "Hungerfield" is, then, a late-period engagement with the dilemma of consciousness, but one in which the poet turns to narrative to distract himself from it rather than attempt to solve it.

Skulls, Cells, and the Song Called Language

Nonetheless, the biology of consciousness retains a central place in Jeffers's late work, and after writing "Hungerfield" he developed a more integrated view of human consciousness in the context of evolution. A poem from *Hungerfield and Other Poems* (1954), "De Rerum Virtute" (*CP* 3:401–3), is the major late-period statement of his new view of consciousness. It is a five-part poem, and the composition history recounted in volume 5 of *The Collected Poetry* indicates that Jeffers assembled the parts from various drafts and false starts. It begins with a familiar image from the 1920s work—the container of consciousness, the bone vault—and provides an index of the shift in Jeffers's stance toward the question of consciousness once he no longer has a personal stake in that question. It variously extends certain figures and rhetorical techniques from the "Point Sur" period—such as the bone vault and the statement of belief ("Credo")—and revises other ideas—such as the self-torturing God and the poet's imitation of him ("Apology for Bad Dreams"). The first verse paragraph of "De Rerum Virtute" reads:

> Here is the skull of a man: a man's thoughts and emotions
> Have moved under the thin bone vault like clouds
> Under the blue one: love and desire and pain,
> Thunderclouds of wrath and white gales of fear
> Have hung inside here: and sometimes the curious desire of
>   knowing
> Values and purpose and the causes of things
> Has coasted like a little observer air-plane over the images
> That filled this mind: it never discovered much,
> And now all's empty, a bone bubble, a blown-out eggshell.

Here Jeffers inverts the classical trope of the memento mori, the contemplation of a skull. Normally, the memento mori should provoke thoughts of the poet's mortality, the vanity of human desires and ambitions, the themes of time and loss, yet this skull turns the speaker to a meditation on consciousness and the beginning of life.[1] The first line of the next section picks up the image of the eggshell: "That's what it's like: for the egg too has a mind." Rather than using the container metaphors from the earlier period—vessels, wineskins, bowls—the poem analogizes the skull to a form that partakes of natural process. Bringing him closer to an image of embodied consciousness, the contemplation of the skull allows Jeffers a way to imagine consciousness as thoroughly integrated into the universe.

It is unlikely that Jeffers had an actual skull at hand, but skulls do in fact bear the literal traces of consciousness.[2] Anatomist Philip V. Tobias explains how endocasts of skulls reveal the brain contained within: "Pulsating, as the brain does with the beating of the heart, the outer surface of the brain imprints itself upon the interior of the brain case." The trace left by the pulsating brain is not just a marker of physiological process, a beating heart and pulsing brain; it can also be the trace of consciousness. On the basis of his study of endocasts of *Homo habilis* skulls from Olduvai and Koobi Fora, Tobias revised his earlier view that language would not have emerged at so early a stage in human evolution. Now he proposes that "the endocast markings, especially those representing Broca's area and Wernicke's area, coupled with the cultural evidence, point to the likelihood that articulated language, albeit rudimentary, was within the capacity of *H. habilis*."[3] Thus, in contemplating skulls and cells, Jeffers arrives at a statement of belief in which he revises his earlier theory of consciousness and biology—that mind and brain are unallied, though symbiotic—and proposes that eggshells, like skulls, contain a mind, and that consciousness does in fact inhere in cells. This "credo" is formulated late in his career, possibly after the discoveries of microbiology. Perhaps Jeffers was aware of them. Such discoveries revealed the cell to be an active, open system as opposed to just a container, as the very word *cell* implies.[4]

The notes and drafts described in volume 5 of *The Collected Poetry* reveal that "De Rerum Virtute" emerged from a composition history of self-interrogation and revision. Originally it seems that this section bore the title "No Thought Apparent," an allusion to a statement from "Apology for Bad Dreams" (CP 5:842). In the earlier poem, an *ars poetica* that is also related to the "Point Alma Venus" materials, Jeffers proposes a theory of poetry that links the poet with the divine force manifest in natural process. The poet "ape[s]" the creative force of the universe, the "God" who tortures himself in the continual cycles of death and rebirth. Nuclear fission becomes the symbol of human imitation of divine process: splitting the atom releases the same force that powers the stars. The poet says,

I have seen these ways of God: I know of no reason
For fire and change and torture and the old returnings.

He being sufficient might be still. I think they admit no
    reason; they are the ways of my love.
Unmeasured power, incredible passion, enormous craft: no
    thought apparent but burns darkly
Smothered with its own smoke in the human brain-vault: no
    thought outside: a certain measure in phenomena:
The fountains of the boiling stars, the flowers on the
    foreland, the ever-returning roses of dawn. (*CP* 1:211)

Jeffers's idiosyncratic syntax and punctuation make these last lines frustratingly ambiguous.[5] The "ways of God" have no motive, and so, in one sense, neither does the poet have any motivation for what he does. Nonetheless, they are the ways of his "love" as well. As Robert Brophy explains it, this love is the "expression of the poet's desire to participate in beauty and discovery."[6] Georges Bataille's meditations on, or theories of, excess provide a gloss for these lines:

> There is in nature and there subsists in man a movement which
> always exceeds the bounds, that can never be anything but partially
> reduced to order. We are generally unable to grasp it. Indeed it is by
> definition that which can never be grasped, but we are conscious of
> being in its power: the universe that bears us along answers no pur-
> pose that reason defines, and if we try to make it answer to God,
> all we are doing is associating irrationally the infinite excess in
> the presence of which our reason exists with our reason itself. But
> through the excess in him, that God whom we should like to shape
> into an intelligible concept never ceases, exceeding this concept, to
> exceed the limits of reason.[7]

Jeffers's God exceeds reason—the thought inside the brain vault cannot comprehend the ways of God; no matter how we conceptualize God, his unmeasured power will escape those concepts. It is only humans who are "conscious of being in its power," and therefore we must rely on something other than thought or reason to make sense of it. There is "a certain measure in phenomena"—they are not an excessive aspect of God and can be comprehended by our reason, and they do not require thought to take part in the life of the universal God. The poet can only imitate God; "the ways of [his] love" must also be the ways of God: "unmeasured power, incredible passion, enormous craft." The poet aping God is the human species falling into consciousness, torturing itself for no reason other than to discover itself. Brophy writes, "Reason is not essential to the universal process, though consciousness, in order fully to apprehend beauty, may be an exquisite attainment and a prerequisite for a formal participation in the god-life."[8] Jeffers is trapped in the contradiction of the Derridean supplement: consciousness, as a function of mind (and at least the substrate for reason), is not essential to natural process, but it is a prerequisite, a requirement, for our participation in the ways of God, who is imminent in natural process. The unacceptable split is here—consciousness, which the poet cannot at this point account for by natural process, is the awareness of the "infinite excess" that self-reflexively detaches us from it.

Nearly thirty years later, interrogating (and misquoting) himself in the draft of "De Rerum Virtute," Jeffers writes,

No mind except in man? I said that once—
I was ridiculous.
"No thought apparent but glows darkly
Muffled in its own smoke in the human brain-vault, no
    mind outside—"
I was a fool.

    certain measure in phenomena"—
I said wrote when I was young and a fool. (CP 5:843)

None of this self-interrogation was retained in the published version of the poem, but it reveals that the second section of "De Rerum Virtute" began as a retraction of the earlier claim that no thought exists outside the brain vault. However, even this more generous view of natural intelligence, which may be based on the discoveries of microbiology in the early 1950s, does not resolve the dilemma of consciousness.[9] Even if cellular development controlled by DNA coding can be seen as a form of mind, Jeffers says it is "a limited but superhuman intelligence." Natural process still happens within limits; it is not excessive, even if it is beyond our intelligence to replicate such processes (at least for the time being). The conclusions that Jeffers draws from this metaphor—that natural process has intention, direction, and purpose—might be warranted if the egg's "mind" were not limited, but he cannot make that leap logically, and therefore he turns to the credo formula:[10]

    I believe the first living cell
Had echoes of the future in it, and felt
Direction and the great animals, the deep green forest
And whale's-track sea; I believe this globed earth
Not all by chance and fortune brings forth her broods,
But feels and chooses. And the Galaxy, the firewheel

On which we are pinned, the whirlwind of stars in which
    our sun is one dust-grain, one electron, this giant atom of
    the universe
Is not blind force, but fulfills its life and intends its courses.
(*CP* 3:401–2)

Jeffers considered "I Believe" as a possible title before settling on the Latin one, a selection that, in its allusion to Lucretius, garners him the authority of the Roman poet-philosopher as a counterweight to the religious phrasing. Nonetheless, unlike Lucretius, who made claims about the nature of things and how they work, here the emphasis is on the "virtue" of things, their aesthetic and moral qualities (and, paradoxically, this emphasis relates them to human concerns by means of a buried pathetic fallacy— *virtue* derives from the Latin *vir*, man). Darwinian theory, the best explanation that we have for how evolution works as a material process, does not account for intentionality. As John Maynard Smith states, "Evolution does not happen because of its future consequences."[11] A credo is the best Jeffers can offer for such a view of "mind" in nature.

In a late fragment, "The unformed volcanic earth," Jeffers sketched out his final attempt at understanding the biology of mind. Hunt describes what seem to be Jeffers's intentions for a major narrative poem: "The various sketches for the projected sequence show that Jeffers wanted it to have the scope of a narrative and intended to explore the nature and implications of consciousness" (*CP* 5:130). The first part of the poem describes the formation of the earth and the creation of its atmosphere. The second part treats the emergence of life, "biogenesis," as Jeffers calls it in his notes. He also sketched out a plan in which the second section of a narrative poem would be called "Consciousness whence? —one life, one God" (*CP* 5:880). Of the three sections, this middle section is the most tentative in its claims for science's discoveries, indicating a lack of certainty in his experience. The first section can confidently join science and myth together in its account of geogenesis, but as the story transitions to biogenesis, the credo formulations creep back in: "What is this thing called life?—But I believe . . ." and "I think . . ." (*CP* 3:431–32).[12] In the notes, Jeffers returns to his dual-creator theory, struggling to answer the question he has posed to himself—"It seems indeed / That a second creative God must have come in" (*CP* 5:881)—before settling on his creed: "I believe the universe / Is all one God" (*CP* 5:882). Also, in a characteristic gesture, he notes: "I am near to death, / And all this fantasy springs from a dying man's brain. / I should love silence" (*CP* 5:881). The typed version that constitutes the middle section reads:

> I think the rocks
> And the earth and the other planets, and the stars and
>   galaxies
> Have their various consciousness, all things are conscious;
> But the nerves of an animal, the nerves and brain
> Bring it to focus; the nerves and the brain are like a burning-
>   glass
> To concentrate the heat and make it catch fire:
> It seems to us martyrs hotter than the blazing hearth
> From which it came. So we scream and laugh, clamorous
>   animals
> Born howling to die groaning: the old stones in the dooryard
> Prefer silence: but those and all things have their own
>   awareness,
> As the cells of a man have; they feel and feed and influence
>   each other, each unto all,
> Like the cells of a man's body making one being,
> They make one being, one consciousness, one life, one God.
>   (CP 3:432)

This credo bypasses the need for a dual-creator theory, but it certainly does not account for the biology of consciousness. Neuroscience accepts the cellular basis of consciousness, but it cannot accept an answer that proposes that there is a continuum of consciousness from rocks to humans. Only a poet can say that, so here the poet speaks as a matter of belief, adjusting his diction to the only slightly stronger "I think." However, regardless of where the knowledge comes from and how it is phrased, from poetry or from neuroscience, the fact remains that human consciousness is different. If Jeffers is satisfied with his answer, then he need not worry about the origins of consciousness any longer, but its effects are another matter. Here, as in the earlier poems, fire is the metaphor for consciousness, and humans' experience of it makes them martyrs—even though he "knows" whence it came, the passions it provokes and the tensions it creates still make it seem excessive.

The third section of the poem is the account of human evolution. Here the poet says he will make a "guess," but his diction is more certain in this section, the repetition of "therefore" and "it is" indicating his confidence in his anthropological knowledge and revealing that he is even more certain in his judgments about human nature. Jeffers writes,

> But whence came the race of man? I will make a guess.
> A change of climate killed the great northern forests,

Forcing the manlike apes down from their trees,
They starved up there. They had been secure up there,
But famine is no security: among the withered branches blue
    famine:
They had to go down to the earth, where green still grew
And small meats might be gleaned. But there the great flesh-
    eaters,
Tiger and panther and the horrible fumbling bear and
    endless wolf-packs made life
A dream of death. Therefore man has those dreams,
And kills out of pure terror. Therefore man walks erect,
Forever alerted: as the bear rises to fight
So man does always. Therefore he invented fire and flint
    weapons
In his desperate need. Therefore he is cruel and bloody-
    handed and quick-witted, having survived
Against all odds. Never blame the man: his hard-pressed
Ancestors formed him: the other anthropoid apes were safe
In the great southern rain-forest and hardly changed
In a million years: but the race of man was made
By shock and agony. Therefore they invented the song called
    language
To celebrate their survival and record their deeds. And
    therefore the deeds they celebrate—
Achilles raging in the flame of the south, Baltic Beowulf like
    a fog-blinded sea-bear
Prowling the blasted fenland in the bleak twilight to the
    black water—
Are cruel and bloody. Epic, drama and history,
Jesus and Judas, Jenghiz, Julius Caesar, no great poem
Without the blood-splash. They are a little lower than the
    angels, as someone said.—Blood-snuffing rats:
But never blame them: a wound was made in the brain
When life became too hard, and has never healed.
It is there that they learned trembling religion and blood-
    sacrifice,
It is there that they learned to butcher beasts and to
    slaughter men,
And hate the world: the great religions of love and kindness
May conceal that, not change it. They are not primary but
    reactions

Against the hate: as the eye after feeding on a red sunfall
Will see green suns.
(CP 3:432–33)

Jeffers's story of human evolution is highly condensed and simplified, but it is essentially accurate. He links bipedalism to climate change and locates the basis of culture in the adaptations required by the violence of meat eating and survival in a terrestrial rather than an arboreal environment. He posits a much more linear path to human evolution than allowed for by current anthropology, which emphasizes the "radiation" of many species of bipedal hominids and early humans prior to the reduction to the single species of *Homo sapiens*. Also, it is unclear where Jeffers thinks the first humans emerged: he supposes that early humans descended from the "northern forests" and says that "the other anthropoid apes were safe / In the great southern rain forest." The current consensus is that the earliest humans were restricted to the African continent until at least sixty thousand years ago.[13] Regardless of such simplifications or inaccuracies, what is significant about these lines is that Jeffers treats the evolution of human consciousness in a strictly Darwinian context. The crux in this account is the appearance of language.

He proposes two theories of language in "The unformed volcanic earth," the one quoted above that treats language as a tool that results from human evolution, and another that offers a biopoetic role for language and poetry in human evolution. One essentially separates language and discovery, the other combines them. Theories of the coevolution of mind and language discount the first story about language that Jeffers tells here. According to Terrence Deacon, language is not merely a device that humans invented to record experience. Language, in a very material sense, invented us. Deacon argues that we are a "symbolic species"—that humans are defined by their ability to create symbolic representations and share them with others of their species. His is an evolutionary account of Kenneth Burke's definition of humans as symbol-using animals.[14] Our ability to use symbols evolved along with our brains, and this process of coevolution means that this tool that we invented to help us shape and manipulate reality in turn became a reality that shaped and manipulated us. Deacon writes, "The origin of 'humanness' can be defined as that point in our evolution where [stone and symbolic] tools became the principal source of selection on our bodies and brains."[15] Jeffers's first account of language is not coevolutionary because it is linear and instrumental. Burke explicitly argues against such a view of language: "Those who begin with stress upon *tools* proceed to define language itself as a species of tool. But though instrumentality is an important aspect of language we could not properly treat it as the *essence* of language. . . . Language is a species of action, symbolic action—and its nature is such that it can be used as a tool."[16]

Even though he accepts consciousness at large in the universe now, there still is the human difference to be accounted for, and even without the coevolutionary advantage Jeffers's evolution story comports with Deacon's in a significance sense. After "life became a dream of death," according to Jeffers's story, language recorded the fight for survival, and religion was invented to mask humanity's hatred for the world that rejected it. It is the knowledge of death that distinguishes the human mind and turns it in on itself, as well as outward against the world. For Deacon, as for Jeffers (and Emerson as well), the discovery of the mortal, finite self, the awareness that we exist and the knowledge that we will cease to exist, is the fall into consciousness. And it is a fall into symbols. The self that will die is the symbolic self, a real but virtual self that did not exist prior to the "invention" of language because it is a self that exists only in the symbolic realm shared with other symbol users. Deacon writes,

> Knowledge of death, of the inconceivable possibility that the experiences of life will end, is a datum that only symbolic representation can impart. Other species may experience loss, and the pain of separation, and the difficulty of abandoning a dead companion; yet without the ability to represent this abstract counterfactual (at least for the moment) relationship, there can be no emotional connection to one's own future death. But this news, which all children eventually discover as they develop their symbolic abilities, provides an unbidden opportunity to turn the naturally evolved social instinct of loss and separation in on itself to create a foreboding sense of fear, sorrow, and impending loss with respect to our own lives, as if looking back from an impossible future. No feature of the limbic system has evolved to handle this ubiquitous virtual sense of loss. Indeed, I wonder if this isn't one of the most maladaptive of the serendipitous consequences of the evolution of symbolic abilities.[17]

Deacon and Jeffers agree on the consequences of this knowledge, both positing religion as a strategy for dealing with this painful knowledge, and the characterization of it as a maladaptive trait in evolution sounds a lot like Jeffers's sense that self-consciousness is one of evolution's botched experiments. But Deacon's argument points to another of Jeffers's insights, one that he struggled with as he drafted these lines. The brain structures that we share with most other mammals, the limbic system, have not evolved to help us with this suffering. Jeffers says this is a wound in the brain—his diction invoking the perplexing connection between brain and mind, one that he purposely elided in "De Rerum Virtute." The wound in the brain is a figure for this painful and tragic knowledge in physical terms; it is a symbolic cause of a physical hurt. The wound in the brain is mind. The conclusion of the "Unformed" fragment allows for the possibility that humans might overcome this hurt and do something great with their "imagination and mind," and Deacon himself says that the symbolic response to this wound "is the source both of what is most noble and most pathological in human behaviors."[18]

The second theory of language that Jeffers presents in "The unformed volcanic earth" is a biopoetics. This version of biopoetics is particularly sacramental—it accommodates both the symbolic and the material (instrumental) effects of language:

> The human race is one of God's sense-organs,
>
> . . . .
>
> As Titan-mooded Lear or Prometheus reveal to their
>   audience
> Extremes of pain and passion they will never find
> In their own lives but through the poems as sense-organs
> They feel and know them. (CP 3:434)

"Poems as sense-organs" is another way of conceiving a biopoetic function for language, an aesthetics for Jeffers's experimental poetry: invent to suffer to discover. In this scenario, he does not include the poet-as-ape-of-God element. The readers are invoked as an audience of a drama, an externalization that emphasizes its basis in action and directly connects it to Aristotelian poetics. The daring of "Prelude" or "The Women at Point Sur" is absent, the risk of his own involvement in the process, the strain in his skull, but the effect is the same. The symbolic action executed in language provides physical release.

Most intriguing in this late fragment are the various strategies Jeffers attempted to use to bring the material together. Without narrative, he was at a loss as to how to create the epic poem that he wanted. In another fragment he comments that Darwin, along "with Roman Lucretius and several others," "formed" the largest poem up to this time (CP 4:536). "The unformed volcanic earth" is his attempt to add to that tradition, intended to take its place in a line running from De Rerum Natura to

Origin of Species. The problem is that the poem simply tries to the tell the story of geo- and biogenesis—that is, to tell the story of science's discoveries, not the poet's—and therefore lacks force to make the poet invent the language to tell it. Part of this, of course, is a factor of age. In another late poem that invokes "Apology for Bad Dreams," Jeffers explains that his narratives were devices to "magic horror away from the house" and that his motivation for writing them was self-protection. The implication of the poem is that despite having "been warned," he no longer follows this imperative because "time sucks out the juice, / A man grows old and indolent" (*CP* 3:447). The narratives of the 1920s were strategies for dispelling the excess of consciousness—"life's passions" that were flung over the poet, who then created characters on which to displace them, the "strain in the skull" that pulled the poet into the creative process of God and the violent upheavals of natural process. The "juice" being sucked out is desire, the "sexual compulsions" (*CP* 3:475) that unbalance and disturb the human self-consciousness.

Old Age and New Discoveries

If Jeffers was too "indolent" to write narratives after "Hungerfield," he nonetheless remained committed to another of the imperatives from the 1920s. In "Prelude," he determined that "discovery's the way to walk in" and in the 1950s the discoveries he made tell us about the confrontation of consciousness with its individual demise. These are poetry's discoveries more than the discoveries of science that he intended to narrate in "The unformed volcanic earth."

In "The Deer Lay Down Their Bones" (*CP* 3:407–8), published in *Hungerfield and Other Poems*, Jeffers describes a discovery made while rambling the coastal hills alone after his wife's death.[19] This poem sets the terms for the poet's resolution to endure old age for the sake of discovery. It begins, "I followed the narrow cliffside trail half way up the mountain / Above the deep river-canyon," and the first verse paragraph describes the speaker finding a streamside clearing filled with bones and antlers of wounded deer that have gone there to die. He declares, "I wish my bones were with theirs," but quickly chastises himself for such sentimentality in the second verse paragraph:

> But that's a foolish thing to confess, and a little cowardly. We
>   know that life
> Is on the whole quite equally good and bad, mostly gray
>   neutral, and can be endured

To the dim end, no matter what magic of grass, water and
    precipice, and pain of wounds,
Makes death look dear. We have been given life and have
    used it—not a great gift perhaps—but in honesty
Should use it all. Mine's empty since my love died—Empty?
    The flame-haired grandchild with great blue eyes
That look like hers?—What can I do for the child? I gaze at
    her and wonder what sort of man
In the fall of the world . . . I am growing old, that is the
    trouble. My children and little grandchildren
Will find their way, and why should I wait ten years yet,
    having lived sixty-seven, ten years more or less,
Before I crawl out on a ledge of rock and die snapping, like a
    wolf
Who has lost his mate?—I am bound by my own thirty-year-
    old decision: who drinks the wine
Should take the dregs; even in the bitter lees and sediment
New discovery may lie. The deer in that beautiful place lay
    down their bones: I must wear mine.

Drafting the poem, Jeffers had considered the lines: "We are produced
as experiments, / We are brought into the world for experience, mouse,
lion and man. God, who pervades all natures, / Wants something new:
old age is an old story but man's mind is not" (*CP* 5:851). Although many
of Jeffers's last poems do tell the old story of old age—such as possibly
the last poem he attempted to write, which reports that growing old "is
very unpleasant and humiliating" (*CP* 3:485)—many of them also find in
the experience of old age new justifications for his sacramental poetics.

In "Not Solid Earth" (*CP* 4:539–40), written sometime around the *Hungerfield* poems but never published (*CP* 5:1039), Jeffers draws together the
various components of his sacramental materialism—discovery, beauty,
and consciousness:

      There is one way of peace: to know all
That men know or discover, and make it vital in the mind,
    the enormous and terrible beauty of things.
—Never fear that: it will be beautiful: whatever we know or
    discover
Is as beautiful as fire.

The terms here show that only through a sacramental poetics can "peace"
be achieved—to understand what is discovered we need to recognize it as

beautiful, which requires the "fire" of consciousness. Science can analyze and test the discovery, but only poetry, or the aesthetic sense, can make it "vital" or alive.

This discovery may be the central one that Jeffers makes in the late work—the confirmation that no matter how important science is to our understanding the divine cosmos, poetry is a different way of achieving that knowledge. In another late poem, Jeffers poses the question, "What's the best life for a man?" (*CP* 3:424–25), and answers:

> To ride in the wind. To ride horses and herd cattle
> In solitary places above the ocean on the beautiful
> mountain, and come home hungry in the evening
> And eat and sleep. He will live in the wild wind and quick
> rain, he will not ruin his eyes with reading,
> Nor think too much.

The speaker realizes the too easy simplicity of this answer and admits that civilization requires division of labor and specialized professions, but he offers a series of substitutions—shepherds for philosophers, lunatics for poets, and "old women gathering herbs on the mountain" instead of doctors. He continues,

> That would be a good world, free and out-doors.
> But the vast hungry spirit of the time
> Cries to his chosen that there is nothing good
> Except discovery, experiment and experience and discovery:
> to look truth in the eyes,
> To strip truth naked, let our dogs do our living for us
> But man discover.

> It is a fine ambition,
> But the wrong tools. Science and mathematics
> Run parallel to reality, they symbolize it, they squint at it,
> They never touch it: consider what an explosion
> Would rack the bones of men into little white fragments and
> unsky the world
> If any mind should for a moment touch truth.

These lines recall "Theory of Truth" (*CP* 2:608–10), a meditation that begins with a comment on Arthur Barclay, the main character of "The Women at Point Sur," "who touched his answers . . . But presently lost them again in the glimmer of insanity."[20] Once again, Jeffers uses the word *touch* to evoke a range of meanings associated with the search for truth: to be in contact with it, to grasp or understand it, but also to affect and be affected by it. Approached solely from a materialist perspective, contact with truth is destructive—the mind grasping reality through science alone "unsk[ies]" it: in one sense, it removes that which covers it, it reveals, but "unsky" also suggests undoing it, removing it from its place in the universe.

A later companion poem to "The Deer Lay Down Their Bones," "Vulture" (CP 3:462), demonstrates how Jeffers's sacramental materialism operates contrariwise to the discoveries of science:[21]

> I had walked since dawn and lay down to rest on a bare
>   hillside
> Above the ocean. I saw through half-shut eyelids a vulture
>   wheeling high up in heaven,
> And presently it passed again, but lower and nearer, its orbit
>   narrowing, I understood then
> That I was under inspection. I lay death-still and heard the
>   flight-feathers
> Whistle above me and make their circle and come nearer. I
>   could see the naked red head between the great wings
> Beak downward staring. I said "My dear bird we are wasting
>   time here.
> These old bones will still work; they are not for you." But
>   how beautiful he'd looked, gliding down
> On those great sails; how beautiful he looked, veering away
>   in the sea-light over the precipice. I tell you solemnly
> That I was sorry to have disappointed him. To be eaten by
>   that beak and become part of him, to share those wings
>   and those eyes—
> What a sublime end of one's body, what an enskyment; what
>   a life after death.

Albert Gelpi's description of "Vulture" is succinct: it "is about dying back into nature, about death and transfiguration deferred yet anticipated, anticipated yet deferred. The extinction of the conflicted human consciousness and the assimilation of the body into organic process are, for the pantheist, the sublime consummation." As Gelpi observes, for this consummation to be expressed in language it must be deferred—"At this penultimate point the enskyment is and can only be an enwordment"[22]—but it is Jeffers's coinage that reveals the difference between science's running parallel to reality and contact with it through sacramental poetics. Imagining the enskyment and bringing it into language puts us in touch with it. To "ensky" puts human consciousness back into the world's consciousness, purging it of the conflicted rationality that can only be "unskied" when it touches the truth.

Jeffers's sacramental poetics requires the materialism of science, the bedrock knowledge of the reality "out there." However, what makes the relationship to that material reality sacramental is its transmutation into symbol through poetry. The poet makes his discoveries through "symbolic action," and he in turn tells us the story so that we may realize his discovery. In one of his few explicit statements of poetics, which I quoted in the Introduction, Jeffers distinguishes poetry's synthesizing mode of discovery from science's analytic mode and observes that "something new is found out, something that the author himself did not know before he wrote it" (CP 4:416). Paraphrasing Frost, we might say, "No discovery in the poet, no discovery in the reader." Again, the idea of touching the truth, coming into contact with it, is the crux of a sacramental poetics. Science is parallel to the truth, whereas poetry's discoveries are tangential: it comes at truth indirectly, at an angle, and touches it but does not bisect it. It is a point of contact, not cutting through reality but stopping at it, seeing it for the first time. Science is not sacramental because it has only one horse in its harness—it operates only by reason, which is its liability. Poetry's liability is that it is truly tangential to reality: it is irrelevant, it really doesn't matter. Poetry's discoveries are irrelevant to the workings of the cosmos, and rightly so—the universe just does what it does. Only science can make the claim of relevance because it can show, by experiment, how the universe works; it can refer directly to the world out there even though it never touches it. Poetry, by its necessary indirection, its figurative language, cannot make the same claims.

Finally, poetry is tangent in the etymological sense—it touches its answers, a dangerous endeavor that science sidesteps. Poetry risks, as Jacques Derrida says of interpretation generally, getting its hand caught in the process: "There is always a surprise in store for the anatomy or physiology of any criticism that might think it had mastered the game, surveyed all the threads at once, deluding itself, too, in wanting to look at the text without touching it, without laying a hand on the 'object,' without risking—which is the only chance of entering into the game, by getting a few fingers caught—the addition of some new thread."[23] A new thread in the text is added, or, as Jeffers says, something new is made. Poetry invents to discover. A credo can proclaim belief in one God, one consciousness; it can offer a description of the discoveries of science, but compelling sacramental poetry demonstrates its own discovery, invents the language to tell it. Science discovers the complexity, diversity, and vastness of the universe; poetry discovers (and dangerously invents) its beauty and divinity, and thereby sacramentalizes it. For Jeffers, poetry is better than religion for doing so because it does not harden into a system of belief and does not require followers, disciples, or converts. It requires only readers: solitary individuals, who, if they are moved by the poem, experience something of the tangential discovery too. If not, no harm done.

The test for sacramental poetry's discovery of the biology of consciousness is not the accuracy with which a poet recounts the scientific evidence but rather the force with which he shows us what it means. If we believe in the divinity of the cosmos, what does it mean that we now understand more about the "biological underpinnings of mind"?[24] If we believe that it is the divine universe's intention to discover itself through the suffering of being aware of the violent processes of cosmological and biological creation, then the evolution of the human mind's ability to experience that self-awareness is also a part of that process. That the divine universe discovers its wholeness and oneness through the experience of its parts suggests the synecdochal relationship that we also experience in discovering that we are microcosms of the macrocosm. The paradox, of course, is that poetry, despite its liability to metonymical partness and deconstruction, is the best way to express the discovery of this condition. Science can provide theories of emergent wholes and can offer proof of them based in empiricism and mechanical reductionism, but it is the feeling of oneness or wholeness that is the ultimate proof, and that is what poetry is best at: inventing the language that allows us, or at least encourages us, to know what that experience feels like. That it happens when we break through the invented metaphors and images, or feel their inadequacies, is the happy contradiction of Robinson Jeffers's sacramental nature poetry, and it is the feeling of the biology of consciousness.

Conclusion: The Jeffers Influence and the Middle Generation

The introduction to this study outlined Robinson Jeffers's reputation as it relates to modernist poetry and environmental history. As I pointed out there, Jeffers is often omitted from the literary history of American poetry even as he finds a prominent place in the evolution of environmental literature and ethics. The significance of Jeffers in both areas can be found in what Michael Davidson calls the "sacramental impulse" of West Coast poetry in the mid-twentieth century. Jeffers's sacramental poetics is the Ur-expression of that impulse, yet, as I observed earlier, he finds no place as a precursor in Davidson's account of the San Francisco Renaissance or in Charles Altieri's discussion of Gary Snyder's and Robert Duncan's postmodern nature poetry in *Enlarging the Temple*. The exception to these studies is David Wyatt's *The Fall into Eden: Landscape and Imagination in California*. Although his historical survey of California literature is not limited to any one genre, Wyatt devotes a chapter to Jeffers and Snyder as the "two poets who have had the most to say about California landscape" because "both ground their vision in the building of a house" in distinctive regions of the state. Along the way, he also glances at Kenneth Rexroth, William Everson, and Yvor Winters in between his discussions of Jeffers and Snyder. Of Jeffers, Wyatt writes, "His stance overshadows all subsequent projects, yet few poets from his region display any outright signs of influence."[1] The question of the "Jeffers influence," especially with regard to middle-generation figures such as Duncan, Rexroth, and Everson, is the concern of this conclusion. If Jeffers is the dominant West Coast poet of the modernist generation, and if his poetics is the key expression of the sacramental impulse that characterizes his region, why is his influence so difficult to detect?[2]

I believe the answer, in part, can be found in an examination of the middle generation's response to Jeffers as a precursor. As in Wyatt's *Fall into Eden*, Jeffers is often paired with Snyder, but it is usually in order to study poetic representations of the West, or to investigate poetry's role in the environmental movement, as in Max Oelschlaeger's *The Idea of Wilderness*. Examining the connections between Jeffers and Snyder in these ways effectively suppresses the role of poets in the generation between the modernists and postwar poets. In a conversation with Snyder, Eliot Weinberger sought to make the middle-generation link: "It's interesting that the American West is essentially invented in literary American poetry by two of your immediate predecessors, Robinson Jeffers and Kenneth Rexroth. Did you feel that they opened it up for you somehow, made it acceptable to write about?" Snyder responded, "Definitely. Jeffers and Rexroth both, as you say, were the only two poets of any strength who had written about the landscapes of the American West, and it certainly helped give me the courage to start doing the same myself."[3] As we saw in chapter 1, Rexroth certainly is the direct link between Jeffers and Snyder in many respects, but he so adamantly denied the influence of Jeffers that he succeeded in breaking that link and obscuring his own place in the tradition of sacramental nature poetry. In displacing Jeffers, Rexroth effectively removed himself and his cohort of California poets from the ranks of the middle generation, those writers born in the first ten or fifteen years of the twentieth century such as Robert Lowell, Elizabeth Bishop, and John Berryman. Because of the East Coast bias of American literary history, which Rexroth and Everson were painfully aware of, as well as the New Critical consensus that dominated academic and mainstream publishing in the midcentury, there was no impetus to look for a West Coast group of poets carving out their place in the aftermath of modernism.

World War II and the Californian Middle Generation

The concerns of the Californian middle generation can be seen in a letter drafted by William Everson in December of 1947, when he was working as a janitor at the University of California Press.[4] Addressed to his fellow Californian poets Kenneth Rexroth, Robert Duncan, Thomas Parkinson, and Harry T. Moore, the letter proposes that they publish an anthology of their recent long poems, written during or just after World War II. In making his pitch for the project, Everson presciently describes the conditions that would obscure the achievements of these middle-generation poets of the West:

> And it is precisely because of a genuine and passionately felt *need* of motivation, rather than any mutual interest in mode, that brings these poems into alignment, just so much deeper becomes their mutual interest. The identity is in no wise literary. It is rather that each man, in his own way, borne upon by the very forces of place time and situation, had need to stand up and say his say. . . . Beyond these aspects of course the more obvious parralleisms [*sic*]—the western landscape, the ranginess of line, the impact of nature discription [*sic*], the sense [illegible] of a mutual landscape and sense of a mutual culture. I think that applies even though my own poem was actually written in Oregon. It is the West, the Pacific, the rim of a continent, ~~three thousand miles from a publisher~~ that underlying sense of apartness psychology of the western poet, written three thousand miles from a regular publisher and the established coteries.[5]

Lack of interest from East Coast publishers is, of course, a long-standing problem for poets in the West, and Everson's awareness of the importance of coteries is also telling. For example, discussions of midcentury poets, such as Eric Haralson's *Reading the Middle Generation Anew: Culture, Community, and Form in Twentieth-Century American Poetry*, still gravitate primarily around the East Coast centers and "established coteries," especially Lowell, Bishop, Berryman, and Jarrell. As Haralson notes, these poets are "the usual suspects" in discussions of the middle generation, but he emphasizes that his collection supplements this group with essays on a few lesser-known or studied figures. Midwesterners Lorine Niedecker and Robert Hayden are included, but both are connected to East Coast coteries—Niedecker is closely associated with the objectivists, especially Louis Zukofsky, and Hayden studied with W. H. Auden early in his career. Theodore Roethke, also included in *Reading the Middle Generation Anew*, lived many years in the West, teaching at the University of Washington in Seattle, but his work was also closely associated with the midwestern settings of his boyhood in Michigan rather than a West Coast ethos. Roethke was also championed by Auden early in his career, an imprimatur from an establishment forebear that confirms his status a middle-generation poet poised to shape the postwar generation.

Trenton Hickman's essay on Roethke in *Reading the Middle Generation Anew* demonstrates the importance of middle-generation figures that link the modernist and postwar cohorts; it also reveals how the absence of a West Coast, modernist-generation figure such as Jeffers further obscures the presence of the Californian middle generation. In "Theodore Roethke and the Poetics of Place," Hickman observes that in the 1950s Roethke offered Gary Snyder "a stylistic exemplar . . . as well as a precedent for paying close attention to nature and physical place as poetic subjects in their own right." He also associates other postwar poets—Richard Hugo, Robert Bly, James Wright, and James Dickey— with Roethke's influence and asserts that "Roethke taught these later poets an ethical commitment to the earth itself, eschewing an easy anthropocentrism in favor of a more complicated communion with the natural world."[6] Certainly, Jeffers, and then Rexroth, Everson, and Duncan, among others, provide a more direct, and proximate, line for this sacramental impulse than Roethke. I make this point not to disparage Roethke's achievement or influence, both of which are formidable, but only to demonstrate the distortion of literary history that ignoring Jeffers can produce. Until a modernist-generation figure is recognized in the West, the middle-generation poets themselves will continue to be overlooked. As we will see, there was a conversation about Jeffers among Rexroth, Everson, and Duncan, but because of these regional and critical biases, and Rexroth's animus toward the elder poet, that discussion was effectively silenced and with it Jeffers's influence on the middle generation.

Middle-generation poets not only serve as models for absorbing and adapting modernist poetics but also demonstrate how modern poetry can respond to the historical events and cultural shifts of the mid-twentieth century. In his attempt to organize his fellow Californian poets in a united publishing endeavor, Everson acknowledged the importance of their shared historical experience. For each of his friends' poems that he wanted to anthologize, Everson writes, "The War lies behind them all— overtly behind Rexroths [sic] and my own, implicitly behind the others—the search for value in the midst of upheaval, the need for redemption, personal absolution, the need to be tried, purified and restored. The need to find Grace."[7] The Jeffers influence can be detected in these poets' attitudes about World War II. Everson and Duncan especially were keen to combine religious belief with their creative practice in their petitions for conscientious objector status. Jeffers's sacramental poetics became the basis, in part, for their war resistance. Everson's pacifism emerged from his pantheism, which was deeply influenced by his reading of Jeffers, and Duncan also cited the elder poet as an influence on his attitude toward the war. In his petition for conscientious objector status, Duncan claimed that his resistance to the war was determined by "1) the teach-ings of Krishnamurti, of Lao-Tze, of Zen Buddhism, of the Tibetan Book of the Dead and 2) the investigation of modern writers D. H. Lawrence, Robinson Jeffers, Sanders Russell and Henry Miller and 3) the work of Sigmund Freud concerning the ego separation."[8]

This petition was filed in 1940. In June of that year, Duncan wrote to Everson from Woodstock, New York: "I have been in New York [City] for two weeks. . . . Now, I am back up here well-dosed with war-jitters which is the entire nature of New York body & spirit at this time. It's clear to all of us that it's our own 'country' that we are afraid of. Our own 'leaders' who are racing away down into hell. Note: reread the shorter poems in SUCH COUNSELS YOU GAVE TO ME."[9] What a young poet with "war jitters" would find in the shorter poems of *Such Counsels You Gave to Me* would be poems that comment on current events in Europe and Russia, such as "Blind Horses," "Thebaid," and "The Answer," lyrics that extend the antiwar statements of "Air-Raid Rehearsals" and "Rearmament," which were discussed in chapter 4.

One of the best indicators of the middle generation's importance as the mediators between the modernist and postwar generations is their resistance to America's entry into World War II. In *Behind the Lines: War Resistance Poetry on the American Homefront since 1941*, Philip Metres examines three major middle-generation poets who were also conscientious objectors: Robert Lowell, William Stafford, and Everson. Metres claims, "The CO poetry of World War II exists in that liminal space between modernism and postmodernism, between the socialist proletarianism of the 1930s and the anticommunist reaction of the 1950s, representing both a departure from, and a continuation of, the radical poetry of the 1930s."[10] For both Everson and Duncan, Jeffers represented a preceding regional voice that they had to absorb and adapt, yet also distinguish themselves from, but he also offered them a poetics that could openly and forcefully respond to the enormity of current events. Metres distorts the impact of Jeffers's antiwar views when he generalizes: "Unlike the elder cynic Jeffers, who could trumpet against 'the mould of [American] vulgarity, heavily thickening into empire' . . . the CO poets struggled to articulate a resistance that neither protested from on-high nor retreated from addressing the nation."[11] Oddly citing "Shine, Perishing Republic," a protest poem written in the early 1920s, Metres misses the more personal and agonizing response Jeffers had to the emerging Second World War. For example, in "Memoir" (*CP* 2:524–25), which Duncan would have read in *Such Counsels You Gave to Me*, Jef-fers compares his own pained and sympathetic response to suffering to the insensitivity of the ranchers who are his neighbors, writing, "These fellows . . . rarely feel pain outside their own skins: whilst I like a dowser go here and there / With skinless pity for the dipping hazel-fork." The speaker reminds himself that his inhumanist perspective, as well as his choice to live in the "sanctuary" of a remote and beautiful place, should inoculate him against such painful empathy, especially considering the current atrocities:

> Here in the sanctuary
> I need not think beyond the west water, that a million
> persons
> Are presently dying of hunger in the provinces of China. I
> need not think of the Russian labor-camps, the German
> Prison-camps, nor any of those other centers
> That make the earth shine like a star with cruelty for light. I
> need not think of the tyrannies, that make the tyrants
> Ignoble and their victims contemptible. I need not think of
> the probable wars, tyranny and pain
> Made world-wide; I need not . . . know that this is our world,
> where only fool or drunkard makes happy songs.

The poem is a kind of rhetorical *occupatio*—the poet need not think of these things, yet he dwells on them in explicit detail, revealing his inability to turn his attention elsewhere. Metres does see the Jeffers influence in Everson's *X War Elegies*—"The poems most keenly echo Robinson Jeffers's antiwar verse, as well as the apocalypticism of modernist poetry"—though he does not point to any specific Jeffers poems echoed by Everson.[12] However, for Duncan and Everson, Jeffers provided not only a possible style but a model of a poetic response to war and world events.

The Jeffers influence was also filtered to Duncan through his friend Sanders Russell, whose work he greatly admired. In the introduction to his collected early poems, *The Years as Catches*, Duncan writes: "Sanders was, when I met him, sometime in 1938 or 1939, already a mature poet. In the small company of poets I have known who remain for me real poets, he was the first one. He had his own language, derived from Jeffers and from Eliot and Auden along another line but having undergone a creative change in Sanders' intense meditations and speculations upon the nature of consciousness and the landscape as an object and mirror of being."[13] In defending Sanders's work against Everson's dismissal of it as uninspired prose, Duncan wrote to his friend, "His work & his life belong to the Tradition of Lawrence, Jeffers, Eliot—men who have had a message among us—more importantly who have tackled the root problems of writing." In the same letter, Duncan addresses the Jeffers influence in Everson's work: "Certainly the one quality I have been aware of in your work is that you have the power to establish contact—I am not going to pull any punches. In writing to you I am at this time totally uninterested in techniques. By being 'influenced' by Jeffers—you have been able to penetrate deep into a life rhythm because you were hypnotised [sic] by a rhythm he had established to make contact. That is what we all do in the beginning."[14] Jeffers was an important figure for these young western poets trying to find their voices, both in style and in message. He provided not just a model of major achievement in their region—of the same stature as Eliot, Lawrence, and Auden—but also an example of a principled stand against the war that threatened to disrupt their lives. In the conversation between Duncan and Everson here, Jeffers is validated as a precursor. After the war, when Kenneth Rexroth enters the conversation, the question of the Jeffers influence becomes more contested.

A Fundamental Disagreement

In the autumn of 1946, Everson asked Rexroth to make a selection of his poetry to be published by New Directions. Rexroth, who had been encouraging him to put together a volume, accepted the job, though he knew it wouldn't be easy. Writing to James Laughlin, the publisher of New Directions, Rexroth complained, "Everson is impossible. I have been trying to get him to send you a book, but he stalls and postures and strikes attitudes. Too much Jeffers in early youth. Then he wanted me to make a selection of his poems for you—about which he struck more attitudes. (NOT antagonistic, would that they were—just Great Strong Inarticulate Poet Against Sunset, Rock and Fog sort of shit.) Afterall [sic], I am in the same grift myself. Let him talk that way to the customers."[15] Rexroth's bluster and sarcasm are doubly revealing. He diagnoses his friend's ailment, suggesting that the influence of California's most prominent poet only "takes" when the recipient is too young to know better, that it is something that should be outgrown or can be remedied with proper discipline in adulthood. Yet he also associates himself with the Jeffersian stance as a swindle or confidence game—it's his "grift," too, he just recognizes that it is a con being pitched to customers. Nevertheless, whether the Jeffersian stance is a weakness acquired in youth or a grift, Rexroth's barbs indicate a sensitivity about being associated with Jeffers. At the midpoint of the twentieth century, these two prominent members of the middle generation of American poets could not agree on the value of being influenced by the major modernist-generation poet who came before them. This could have been the moment when two members of the middle generation confirmed Robinson Jeffers's status as their poetic precursor, acknowledging his place as the modernist-generation figure of their lineage. Instead, Jeffers's distinctive influence was muted or erased from Everson's early work, and a fundamental disagreement about Jeffers took shape, one that Rexroth and Everson would pursue, privately and in print, for the next thirty years.

When Everson asked for Rexroth's help in assembling a collection for New Directions, he had recently been demobilized from a conscientious objector camp in Minersville, California, having spent the years during World War II in the Waldport and Cascade Locks C.O. camps in Oregon. He had been privately publishing small collections—pamphlets, really—since 1935. The poetry was intensely, and openly, autobiographical, not at all in the new critical idiom determined by T. S. Eliot's objective correlative then in fashion among academic poets and critics. Yet, neither was the poetry explicitly political, so it did not participate in the radical tradition that emerged during the economic upheavals of the 1930s. The poems in chapbooks such as *These Are the Ravens* and *San Joaquin* emphasize the agrarian-pantheist life that Everson developed as a laborer and grape grower in California's Central Valley. *The Waldport Poems* and *X War Elegies* derive from his experience in the C.O. camps, portraying the traumas of separation, both from the land and from his wife, precipitated by his pacifism. Everson himself was aware of what was omitted from these collections. In the preface to the volume that Rexroth eventually edited for him, *The Residual Years*, Everson writes, "The earliest of these poems was written in a labor camp for the unemployed in 1934, aftermath of the world's First Great Depression. The latest was written in a labor camp for conscientious objectors in 1946, aftermath of the world's Second Great War. To one more politically conscious or historically acute than myself, it would have been possible to delineate something of the chain of circumstances that yoked those two events historically together . . . [but] those twelve consequential years are not in this book, or not as most people saw them." What was contained there, to Everson, was "the religiousness of Nature" and a political "position . . . so personal and so drastic as to be unintelligible to all but the handful" of fellow conscientious objectors. Of the earliest work, he says, "It has not seemed advisable to include these collections in their entirety, and lacking the objectivity to choose among them I am grateful to Kenneth Rexroth for selecting the poems contained in this section."[16] His friend set about this task with a specific shape in mind for this body of early work.

Rexroth considered Everson a key member of his incipient West Coast poetry renaissance, which also included Robert Duncan and Phillip Lamantia. Everson's biographer, Lee Bartlett, writes, "In 1947, with his poetic movement at stake, Rexroth was taking no chances, and in editing *The Residual Years* he very consciously muted, if not completely expunged, the influence of Jeffers."[17] Earlier, Rexroth had intimated what his intentions were, writing to Everson: "The greatest blemish is the persistent echo of Jeffers in many of the poems in San Joaquin especially. After all—there is no resemblance whatsoever between the demons that possess you and Jeffers. Of course it is hard to write about the overwhelming and dehumanizing California landscape without sounding a little like Jeffers. Even I do—and I dislike him intensely, or anyway, did—I mellow."[18] This last comment is perhaps a bluff to deflect any objection from Everson; as we saw above, Rexroth was less "mellow" explaining the circumstances to James Laughlin.

Rexroth's literary wrangling with his friends and poetic compatriots is well known. One of his early poems, titled "Fundamental Disagreement with Two Contemporaries," stands as his cubist response to the dadaism and surrealism of Tristan Tzara and André Breton.[19] His disagreement with Everson was fundamental because it partly formed the basis of their relationship. According to Bartlett, Rexroth's cajoling and editing achieved the desired effect: "Rexroth's ordering of the poems proved effective—no reviewers mentioned the Jeffers influence."[20] More specifically, Rexroth's omissions and reordering of the poems disrupt the strategy that Everson had developed to claim his status as a California voice distinct from Jeffers. After seeing Tor House, Jeffers's legendary stone cottage on the Carmel coast, and "turn[ing] back to [his] inland town," Everson emerged as the autochthon in the earlier *These Are the Ravens*, finding his source of identity in tending a vineyard in the Central Valley.[21] But the valley-dwelling, peace-loving autochthon was still troubled by the master's voice from the coast. The first poems of *San Joaquin* begin a process of renunciation and affirmation that runs through the collection. Everson renounces Jeffers's tortured and tension-filled sense of place and affirms his choice of a middle landscape that absolves him of the upheavals of spirit of place and blood legacy. Rexroth does not include in the New Directions volume the poems in which Everson is most in dialogue with Jeffers, and, combined with the reverse chronological order of the poems, this editorial decision effectively erases the "Jeffers influence" from the collection, not simply in terms of style or form, but in terms of the originary function that Jeffers as a figure performs in the drama of Everson's early poems.

In his anatomy of the "influence study," Claudio Guillén identifies two phases in its process, the first concerned with the "genetic function," the ascertaining and evaluating of influence, and the second concerned with the "textual function," the analysis of the objective product manifesting the impact of the influence, the poem. He writes, "The genetic function controls the impact, and the textual function the echo or the parallelism."[22] In the account that follows, I want to apply these terms because they clarify the fundamental disagreement between Rexroth and Everson and reveal the tack each one takes when dealing the "Jeffers influence" in the other's work. In short, Rexroth expunges the genetic function in order to obscure the "effectiveness of impact" in Everson's early poetry. Everson, in turn, argues from parallels or echoes of Jeffers in Rexroth's poetry in order to establish a textual function and thus to posit influence.[23]

Jeffers introduced Everson to the sacramental connection to place that is the power of the regional poet, but this left Everson with the problem of defining his unique regional vision in the overshadowing presence of Jeffers's. The pitfalls Everson detected in regionalism were deepened by a masculinist fear of a feminized "local color" aesthetic, so even as he purposefully rooted his life and identity in the San Joaquin Valley, he resisted overtly linking his poetry with his region. Writing to his friend Lawrence Clark Powell in 1938, Everson admitted that his original title for the collection, which Powell had brutally mocked in a previous letter, was inflated and inappropriate—Everson wanted to call the volume "Blue Wind of September," while Clark lobbied for the regional title *San Joaquin.* "You win," Everson writes, willing to give up his title. "But not San Joaquin. You'd have to live here to understand. Every female poet in every town in this Valley entitles her first virginal, hesitant, O so fragile sheaf of po-ems 'San Joaquin.'" About a week later, Everson conceded: "'San Joaquin' it is."[24] Much later in his life, after his years spent in a monastery as a Dominican lay brother, Everson explicitly codified the values of regionalism in a 1976 essay, "The Regional Incentive." There he mounts a three-pronged argument for the primacy of a sacramental connection to place. First, he outlines the rise of modernism, its rejection of regional value, and its subsequent decline as Einsteinian relativity replaced Enlightenment rationality's view of nature as mechanism; he then posits a neoromantic response to the "presence of region" as the solution to existentialist alienation. Second, he draws on Paul Shepard and Mircea Eliade to support his sense of the biological and mystical bases of regional identification in sexuality and sacrality. Third, he offers personal testimony and returns to his early poems and agrarian lifestyle to explain his connection to the land. He writes, "Not only did I see myself in human terms as the native of the San Joaquin, but in religious terms I saw myself as the predestined voice of that region."[25] In *San Joaquin*, Everson's "regional incentive" emerges as he personalizes Jeffers's stance and poetics in an intertextual struggle with the master's dominance.

In the original ordering of *San Joaquin*, Everson begins by renouncing the sublime landscapes of California, the mountains and the coast, and the legacy of passionate violence that he imagines in his Nordic-Celtic lineage. In "Here the Rock Sleeps," he rejects the geological splendor of Yosemite, "the bewildering beauty of stone" that Rexroth was discovering further south in Sequoia National Park at the same time and that Gary Snyder would encounter two decades later in the Yosemite backcountry. After acknowledging its awesome scenery, the speaker resolves to go:

> I think it best to leave this place and not come back;
> To see it once and turn away, the first look scored on the
>   numbed sight,
> The memory kept like a searing coal to startle the nerves in
>   the last thin years
> When the senses lag and the worn mind wavers toward
>   night. (1:17)

The following poem, "Fish-Eaters," finds him turning away from the sea-faring warlords of his distant heritage and their legacy of struggle and violence. The poem concludes:

> O you folk of the farther dark,
> This bone and this blood are nothing of mine,
> But wrung from your flesh and fiercely born in the dimmest
>   days,
> When to live was to lust, to reach for the axe and rise to the
>   fury,
> Wade to the roaring thick of it,
> Shoulders hunched and long arms hacking.
>
> Yet, trying my heart I find no hunger for the sword,
> This blood drowsy and slow, wanting no war,
> Glad for the peace of the hawkless hills,
> Glad for the sleep in the sun. (1:18)

Both poems use renunciation to prepare the way for acceptance and affirmation of his life as a pacifist, pantheist valley dweller, embodied by the agrarian sun worshipper who appears in "August": "He has found the power and come to the glory. / He has turned clean-hearted to the last God, the symbolic sun" (1:25). These poems reveal the "textual function" of Jeffers's influence: long lines that use direct statement; verse paragraphs rather than formal stanzas; hyphenated compounds; a somber, elevated poetic diction. Moreover, Everson draws directly on Jeffers's stance, his expression of the regional impulse, so the gambit of poems such as "Here the Rock Sleeps" and "Fish-Eaters" is intended to distance himself from the older poet by rejecting the "massive mysticism of stone" and the sacrificial violence of Jeffers's cosmic vision. However, he must directly confront the master's voice because it is Jeffers who sanctions the younger poet's arrival "as the predestined voice" of the place. Complicating Everson's self-definition further, Jeffers had already articulated his requirements for a spokesman of the Central Valley.

In "Ascent to the Sierras," a lyric from his 1928 collection *Cawdor*, Jeffers presents his impressions of the Valley, imagining a brief scenario involving mountain raiders coming down from the Sierra foothills to plunder the farms and orchards of the lowlands. Jeffers ponders the Valley's peaceful history, wondering why his fictional episode, which holds true for the relations between valley and mountain dwellers in the Old World, never came to pass in the history of the West. Of course, Jeffers sees such passivity as a liability; according to his theory of place, tragedy—the human passions that take possession of a place through violent and bloody conflict—wards off more ecologically destructive human activity when it is given expression by a poet. So "Ascent to the Sierras" concludes with these lines: "Oh fortunate earth: you must find someone / To make you bitter music; how else will you take bonds of the future, against the wolf in men's hearts?" (*CP* 1:404).

To the budding regional-pantheist Everson such a proclamation both hails and challenges, and in *San Joaquin* he replies with the poem "Oh Fortunate Earth." In this poem, the speaker also surveys the Valley and finds it peaceful. However, rather than inventing a tale of lurking violence to contrast with the georgic scenes of vineyard workers and teams of horses plowing the fields, he rejects the "evil and violence and the tragic splendor of the crashing world" and embraces the tranquillity that the land engenders in its inhabitants: "In islanded calmness, in the deep quiet, spirit nor blood will awake to the drum, / Perfectly tuned to the heavy mood that breeds in the valley" (1:46). In the next verse paragraph, Everson interpolates Jeffers's line about the need for a maker of "bitter music" and, in another gesture of rejection intended as an act of self-definition, concludes: "No chanting of mine lures the talons down. / These places rare, and too dear. / The world is the plunder of hawks." Although Everson's form at this time is more irregular than Jeffers's, especially in its variable line length, the Jeffersian phrasings and diction clearly mark his influence on the younger poet. Singing the praises of the harvest and domestic happiness began Everson's career as a regional pantheist, and positioning himself as the voice of the Great Valley allowed him to adopt and personalize Jeffers's otherwise dominating regional presence. Nonetheless, Everson would later recognize that the master poet had taught more than the apprentice realized—the "bitter music" came when World War II impinged on Everson's agrarian lifestyle and dislocated him from his wife and farm when he was incarcerated as a conscientious objector.

Rexroth's intertextual dialogue with Jeffers is virtually nonexistent. The only explicit reference to Jeffers in his poetry appears in an undated draft typescript in his papers at UCLA.[26] Here Rexroth considers what it means to be a poet in California, a place with grand nature but little culture:

> In California nature is still stronger than man,
> or at least stronger than the rationalist,
> the humanist habitué we think of as specifically
> human. There are those who abandon themselves
> thos[e] whose quarantine succumbs, bit by bit,
> to a corrosion of attrition, like Frost's
> mended wall. Jeffers, distraught, posturing by the sea,
> never a swimmer, Winters, moving from preciuese [sic]
> quatrains of Evelyn's gardens, to meditative elegies
> on the fates that rough hewed the ends of Sutter . . .

After mentioning other minor California writers and "the vast lumpen intelligensia [sic]," Rexroth writes, "This world gives them nothing and they return / still less to it. Maybe Winters, a little, grudgingly, / both the give and the take, the others not at all." It is a measure of Rexroth's animosity toward Jeffers that he grants Yvor Winters, who espoused a conservative classicism in response to romantic irrationalism, more willingness to accept nature's power over humanity. Winters was closer in age to Rexroth, so aligning himself with a fraternal rather than a paternal figure may have diminished any residual Oedipal impulse. In any case, for both Everson and Rexroth, to claim a place as a California poet meant clearing a space of Jeffers in their early work.

Their fundamental disagreement continued into the Cold War and the 1950s. Everson assumed his identity as Brother Antoninus, and the West Coast Beat movement was grafted onto Rexroth's San Francisco

Renaissance. Rexroth made his most public dismissal of Jeffers in this decade, using a review of Radcliffe Squires's *The Loyalties of Robinson Jeffers*, published in the *Saturday Review* on August 10, 1957, to proclaim that "few young poets of my acquaintance, and I know most of them, have ever opened one of his books, and know only the anthology pieces, which, I am afraid, they dislike."[27] Brother Antoninus wrote to Rexroth on August 21:

> One thing about Jeffers: I have never repudiated the old man. He is like a father to me. At a time when I was desperate he showed me God, and prepared me for the true faith. He gave me a body of work I could relate to. He showed me how to write. I have of course long since thrown off his influence, but I still read him with love and excitement. He witnesses to the totality of original sin—man's estrangement from God. I think no one has so shown the disorder at the heart of man.[28]

Privately, then, Everson maintained his position in their disagreement. (And what is most interesting, perhaps, is that he associated influence with technique and style, textual function, more than impact, or genetic function.) In his first critical book on Jeffers, published in 1968, Everson at last wrote publicly about Rexroth's West Coast poetry renaissance: "To me it is a disappointment that my second mentor, Kenneth Rexroth, to whom I am so profoundly indebted in other ways, should scorn my first one, who deserves better. Given Rexroth's origins as an experimentalist it is perhaps only to be expected that he should reject Jeffers. But that Kenneth that could not see his way to centering his West Coast movement around the achievement of Jeffers consigns it, in my view, to insubstantiality and attenuation."[29] Then, in 1976, Everson published *Archetype West*, a Jungian analysis of nineteenth- and twentieth-century West Coast writers. Of course, in Everson's formulation, the West Coast "archetype" reaches its apotheosis in Jeffers. Using the publication of *Archetype West* as another opportunity to take a shot at Jeffers, Rexroth remarked: "I am still amazed to find people who can read Jeffers, and I was not offended but hilariously amused when my friend William Everson wrote a long article, or small book, proving conclusively that the notorious San Francisco Renaissance was all due to the influence of Robinson Jeffers—a writer whom we all, except Everson, detested."[30] What Rexroth failed to mention, or never noticed, was that his friend explicitly addressed the "Jeffers influence" on him in the book. "Although he repudiates Jeffers," Everson wrote, "the stance, the point of view of the isolated consciousness subsumed in the Western landscape is Jeffers' own. But his reduction, or refinement, of the Jeffersian moment of cosmic awareness is efficacious, because in savagely defining himself over against Jeffers he is freed from stylistic imitation even as he refines the point of view."[31] Thus, in their fundamental disagreement, one poet spent considerable energy expunging the influence of Jeffers from his friend's early work, and, in turn, his friend wrote criticism claiming to detect the influence of Jeffers on his mature style and stance. Similarities of style and stance aside, this "fundamental disagreement" between Rexroth and Everson testifies to the presence of a tradition of sacramental poetics and reveals what was at stake for each poet in admitting or denying Jeffers's central place in it.

The Jeffers Legacy

Despite its name, Jeffers's inhumanism instituted a visionary-prophetic mode that was anathema to the New Critical values of impersonalism and formalism that dominated academic criticism at midcentury, the values in which the poets who are recognized as the middle generation were schooled. Sacramental poets such as Jeffers, Rexroth, Duncan, and Everson sought a wholeness through their art—a whole that existed beyond the poem on the page. New Critical practice located the whole in the realm of the aesthetic only, achieved by means of paradox and irony. (Later, in deconstructive readings, paradox and irony became aporias that foreclosed on aesthetic wholes.) Jeffers and these fellow California poets deployed other figurative language in order to bring about the unity of opposites, and they posited that unity in the world outside the text. Despite the stereotype, the New Critics were not ahistorical or apolitical, but they circumscribed the aesthetic object's ability to have effect in the world of politics and history because they insisted on the separation of the individual who created the work from the work itself. Distinct from the return to history that Michael Davidson has identified as postmodern narrative in the work of poets such as Muriel Rukeyser and Charles Reznikoff, sacramental poetics rejects history yet strives to take effect outside the strictly aesthetic realm.[32] The New Critical codification of modernism removed the poem from history to privilege aesthetic order, and the postmodern adaptation of modernist technique returned the poem to history and politics. Sacramental poetics attempts to negotiate this dualism by sacramentalizing the individual subject rather than historicizing it.

Although Jeffers's obsession with the biology of consciousness was not taken up by the next generation of poets, the consequences of this dilemma were inherited by Rexroth and Everson, and their sacramental nature poetry extends and complicates these consequences as they search for their own way of finding spiritual value in a materialist universe. Their body of work constitutes the midcentury benchmark of a poetics that stands in contrast to the skeptical tradition that dominated American nature poetry during the modernist heyday. Elisa New's remark that "an American is one who believes his soul's poetry must first be invented, then discovered" places the bedrock and paradox of sacramental poetics at the heart of the endeavor of American poetry.[33] Invention and discovery produce the constant tension and strain that motivates these poets' search for an absolute in a material world, for spiritual essence embodied in physical matter. Just as the New World was invented by Europeans' dreams and desires and then discovered by their eyes and hands, so sacramental poetics invents sacramentality in language and then discovers the divine in the universe. Although Rexroth's and Everson's disagreement deflected attention from the power of Jeffers's sacramental poetics at a key transitional moment, it also confirmed his central position in American literary history.

Notes

Introduction

1. Jeffers, *Collected Poetry* (hereafter *CP*), 4:552; subsequent citations are given parenthetically in the text by volume and page number. Tim Hunt identifies *The Carmelite* as the source of the questionnaire, which gathered information "for its December 12, 1928, 'Robinson Jeffers Supplement'" (*CP* 5:1048) and prints Jeffers's drafted answers, from which I quote. In Jeffers, *Collected Letters* (hereafter *CL*; subsequent citations are given parenthetically in the text by volume and page number), James Karman includes Una's additional answers to the questionnaire but does not identify the correspondent as *The Carmelite* (*CL* 1:768–80).

2. Gelpi, *Coherent Splendor*, 439.

3. Edmundson, *Literature against Philosophy*, 17. For Edmundson, contextualization privileges history, philosophy, or theory over art: "I have no doubt that texts need, *to a certain degree*, to be read within their historical contexts. . . . But how much one contextualizes a work of art is a matter of some delicacy, an issue of taste. It takes considerable poise and intellectual honesty not to use historical context as another way to engage in the philosophical disenfranchisement of art" (16).

4. Gelpi, foreword to Everson, *Excesses of God*, xi.

5. Everson, introduction to Jeffers, *Cawdor/Medea*, ix, vii–viii.

6. Residing in California for his entire adult life, Jeffers was, of course, very distant from the centers of modernism, and there is good reason to see him as isolated in terms of literary history. Nonetheless, he was aware of the modernist movement through its "little magazines" and his and his wife's correspondents. In a letter to her friend Hazel Pinkham, Una Jeffers refers to reading Sherwood Anderson's serialized novel *Many Marriages* in *The Dial* (*CL* 1:450), and Karman points out that the November 1922 issue, in which one of the novel's chapters

appeared, also contained the first American publication of *The Waste Land* (*CL* 1:452 n. 10).

7. Assmann, "Exorcising the Demon," 14.

8. Ibid., 23.

9. A related discussion of Jeffers and Eliot can be found in John Elder's *Imagining the Earth*. In the first chapter, he observes, "Eliot and Jeffers glimpse reconciliations beyond the apparent logic of human history. But both poets find it hard to relate such visions to the present circumstances of civilization" (20).

10. Surette, *Birth of Modernism*, 218.

11. The prime example of Jeffers's occult interest is his account of a visit to a medium in "Come Little Birds" (*CP* 3:5–9). Though he expresses no skepticism regarding such preternatural phenomena, he describes them in such a matter-of-fact way that one wonders how far his credulity extends. Robert Kafka ("Lighthouse-Keeper's Daughter," 45) notes that critics can read Jeffers either way on this point: Robert Brophy considers Jeffers a scientific rationalist, yet Deborah Fleming presents an equally plausible case for Jeffers as an antirationalist in the mode of Yeats. As Materer observes, "Yeats's mixture of skepticism and naïveté is characteristic of occultists. . . . Depending on their orientation, critics like to emphasize one side or another of [his] vacillation" (*Modernist Alchemy*, 1).

12. Surette, *Birth of Modernism*, 13.

13. Materer, *Modernist Alchemy*, xiv, 4.

14. Ibid., 8, 7.

15. Langbaum, "New Nature Poetry," 331, 324.

16. Scott, *Wild Prayer of Longing*, 9.

17. Ibid., 20–21.

18. Ibid., 51.

19. Ibid., 117.

20. Brophy, *Robinson Jeffers*, 5.

21. Davidson, *San Francisco Renaissance*, 58; Altieri, *Enlarging the Temple*, 129.

22. By this I mean works of environmental history and philosophy that examine environmentalism as a secular faith. A different approach is that of ecotheology, which seeks ways of connecting traditional religions with environmentalist concerns. An example of the latter is Gottlieb's *Greener Faith*.

23. Dunlap, *Faith in Nature*, 13. John Gatta's sense that the American literary tradition both discovers and invents nature as sacred is also relevant to my argument, but he has little to say about Jeffers's contribution. He writes, "I think it most fruitful . . . to imagine 'nature' as something both authentically discovered, or discoverable, *and* humanly constructed. The same is true of our reaction to nature as divine Creation" (*Making Nature Sacred*, 10). Nevertheless, though he acknowledges that this topic is too large and his historical scope too extensive to include every major figure in this tradition (7), Gatta's single comment on Jeffers indicates only a stereotypical view of his work. The "religious ecopoetic of recent nature poetry," he writes, "looks to incorporate, but to pass beyond, Jeffers's misanthropic philosophy of 'inhumanism'" (227).

24. Oelschlaeger, *Idea of Wilderness*, 248–49 (quote on 249).

25. Ibid., 261.

26. Ibid., 279 (emphasis in original).

27. Ibid., 350–51.

28. de Man, *Blindness and Insight*, 29.

29. Harrison, *Forests*, 200.

30. Burke, *Rhetoric of Religion*, 15, 21–22.

31. I am thinking of classic examples of deconstructive interpretation such as de Man's "The Rhetoric of Temporality" (in *Blindness and Insight*, 187–228) and Derrida's "Plato's Pharmacy" (in *Dissemination*, 63–171).

32. Emerson, *Essays and Lectures*, 475. Kerouac, *Dharma Bums*, 206.

33. Abbey, *Desert Solitaire*, 7. The echo is to Jeffers's phrasing in "Credo": "I . . . have found in my blood / Bred west of Caucasus a harder mysticism" (*CP* 1:239).

34. Ibid., x.

1 / Rock, Bark, and Blood

1. Snyder, *Place in Space*, 188.

2. The essay "Performance Is Currency," in Grimes's *Rite out of Place*, 146–59, is an extended meditation on and response to a comment by Snyder on ritual and performance.

3. Grimes, *Rite out of Place*, 134–35.

4. Ibid., 135–45.

5. Ibid., 146.

6. Brophy, *Robinson Jeffers*, 65.

7. Brophy's *Robinson Jeffers* and Everson's *Excesses of God* are the two major works of Jeffers criticism relevant to a discussion of sacramentality and poetics. Another significant book on Jeffers, published between Brophy's and Everson's, is Zaller's *Cliffs of Solitude*, which presents "an Oedipal interpretation" of the narrative poems (xi). More recently, Zaller has considered the entirety of Jeffers's work in light of the "American sublime" in *Robinson Jeffers*.

8. Everson, *Excesses of God*, 104–5.

9. Ibid., 106.

10. Brophy, *Robinson Jeffers*, 36–45.

11. Everson, *Excesses of God*, 108.

12. Ibid., 111.

13. Ibid., 107.

14. Grimes, *Rite out of Place*, 146.

15. Smith, *To Take Place*, 105.

16. The drafts and fragments of an early work called *Point Alma Venus* are unpublished at this time, but Hunt points out that this work "eventually grew into *The Women at Point Sur*" (*CP* 5:55).

17. Buell, *Environmental Imagination*, 7–8. Buell has more recently indicated that he prefers the idea of "environmentality" to his own "more circumscribed definition of 'the environmental text'" (*Future of Environmental Criticism*, 51). Nonetheless, his criteria are a helpful heuristic to get students thinking about texts and their relationship to the environment.

18. Bakker, *Island Called California*, 112.

19. Powers, *Redwood Country*, 100.

20. Hunt indicates that this poem "may derive from an undeveloped narrative" (*CP* 5:422), and the story of Old Escobar's theft is probably the residue of the kind of secondary plot line that often appears in the longer narratives.

21. Powers, *Redwood Country*, 98.

22. Girard, *Violence and the Sacred*, 1.

23. Eliade, *Sacred and the Profane*, 26. For Eliade's discussion of discovering a sacred space as an imitation of the cosmogony, see 20–23 and 63–64.

24. Ibid., 32–33.

25. Smith, "Wobbling Pivot," 138.

26. Brophy, *Robinson Jeffers*, 8–9.

27. Smith, "Wobbling Pivot," 138.

28. Smith, *To Take Place*, 10, 11.

29. Ibid., 105.

30. Karman, introduction to Jeffers, *Stones of the Sur*, 25; Glaser, "Desire, Death, and Domesticity," 147. Discussion of Jeffers and geology are also wide ranging. For example, Nicholas Bradley, in "Men with Guts," discusses Jeffers's interest in geology as a "geopoetic influence" in the work of Canadian poet Al Purdy.

31. Federal Writers' Project, *California*, 25.

32. Robert Kafka reports that Jeffers, his son Garth, and Garth's friend, Lloyd Tevis, made the camping trip in early August 1936. They spent two days and one night in the canyon. Kafka, "Jeffers's 1936 Ventana Creek Hike," 31.

33. James, *Varieties of Religious Experience*, 380–81.

34. For a revised definition of a mystical state in terms of naturalism, which complements James's definition, see Kohák, *Embers and the Stars*, 60–66.

35. Miles, *Pathetic Fallacy*, 51.

36. Rexroth, "In Defense of Jeffers," 30.

37. Evernden, "Beyond Ecology," 101.

38. Quoted in Miles, *Pathetic Fallacy*, 5.

39. Ibid., 6.

40. Ibid., 55.

41. *American Heritage Dictionary*, 3rd ed. Evidence for Jeffers's careful selection of his terms can be found in his correspondence. In a letter from February 1938, not long after "Oh Lovely Rock" was published in *Such Counsels You Gave to Me* (27 September 1937), Jeffers used similar terms to explain his use of the pathetic fallacy: "Why else should a quite neutral thing . . . be somehow lovely and loveworthy" and "The feeling of deep earnestness and nobility in natural objects and in the universe:—these are human qualities, not mineral or vegetable, but it seems to me I would not impute them into the objects unless there were something in not-man that corresponds to these qualities in man" (*CL* 2:815).

42. Rexroth, *Complete Poems*, 278–80.

43. Snyder has acknowledged both Jeffers and Rexroth as influences. Asked by Eliot Weinberger if the elder poets gave Snyder permission to write about the American West in poetry, Snyder replied: "Definitely. Jeffers and Rexroth both, as you say, were the only two poets of any strength who had written about the landscapes of the American West, and it certainly helped give me the courage to start doing the same myself" (Snyder, "Art of Poetry," 96).

44. Snyder, *No Nature*, 6.

45. Ibid., 157–58.

46. The epistemological version of this dialectic can be seen in a pair of Robert Frost's poems, "The Most of It" and "Two Look at Two" (*Collected Poems*, 307, 211). In the former the individual fails to find "original response" in nature, whereas in the latter the love between the couple is reflected in the pair of deer they encounter.

47. Snyder, *Earth House Hold*, 124.

2 / The Strain in the Skull

1. Emerson, *Essays and Lectures*, 447. Robert Richardson observes that "The Poet" has "four main metaphors," but he identifies only fire (*Emerson*, 371). By my reading, the other three are intoxication, liberation, and metamorphosis.

2. In another sense, fire is not only metaphorically linked to consciousness. Anthropologist Richard Wrangham advances "the cooking hypothesis," which proposes that adaptation to cooked food is one of the crucial events in human evolution, that the control of fire literally allowed us to become *Homo sapiens*. Echoing Emerson's figure, he writes, "We are tied to our adapted diet of cooked food, and the results pervade our lives, from our bodies to our minds. We humans are the cooking apes, the creatures of the flame" (*Catching Fire*, 14).

3. Lakoff and Johnson, *Philosophy in the Flesh*, 266.

4. For an examination of the connection between Jeffers's poem and Shelley's play, see Brophy, "'Tamar,' 'The Cenci.'"

5. Kroeber, *Ecological Literary Criticism*, 133–34.

6. Bennett, *Stone Mason*, 41.

7. Coleman, *Biology*, 20–21, 23.

8. Ibid., 30.

9. Ibid., 142.

10. Ibid., 143.

11. The exact date of composition is uncertain; Hunt places it somewhere between spring 1919 and spring 1921 (*CP* 5:57–58).

12. Of his cohort of poets, and also within late nineteenth-century, post-Darwinian poetry in English generally, Jeffers is one of very few who uses the word *cell* in its contemporary, biological sense. For example, on the basis of concordances of their work, we can see that two of his nineteenth-century precursors, Whitman and Tennyson, use it in a limited biological sense ("brain cells"); D. H. Lawrence comes closest to an accurate use of the term in a physiological sense; Wallace Stevens used it only in the sense of a small, enclosed room; Robert Frost never used the word in any of its senses. In 1938, Hyatt Howe Waggoner observed, "Jeffers seems . . . to use more words borrowed from science than any other contemporary American poet" ("Science," 287).

13. "Dead beauty a bird-bright-May-morning" probably refers to the Jefferses' first child, a daughter named Maeve, who lived only one day. She was born on May 5, 1914 (Bennett, *Stone Mason*, 67).

14. Damasio, *Feeling of What Happens*, 4.

15. Ibid., 4.

16. Hunt thinks both poems "are . . . probably spring-summer 1920" (*CP* 5:53).

17. In his anthology of nature poetry *News of the Universe*, Robert Bly proposes that the German romantic tradition, which he calls "the Novalis-Hölderlin-Goethe stream" (126), can be distinguished from the British "stream" of romanticism by the "night-intelligence." Bly's phrase combines two ideas that form the core of the

romantic response to Enlightenment hyper-rationality—the idea that night, darkness, the unconscious have value even though they are dangerous and terrifying, and that the nonhuman is also endowed with a form of consciousness, or intelligence, even though humans may not be able to apprehend it through reason. Philosopher Erazim Kohák offers another version of the night-intelligence when he observes, "Dusk is the time of philosophy. Daylight, with its individuating brightness and its pressing demands, is the time of *technē*.... Nighttime, by contrast, is a time of *poiēsis*.... Night is the time of poetry, when *dichten* overtakes *denken*" (*Embers and the Stars*, 32, 230 n. 1). In other words, night is when the nonrationalizing of poetic consciousness overtakes the philosophic reflection of dusk as well as the instrumental rationality of the day. Jeffers too made this association with night and poetry. During the period in which he was developing his mature poetics, sometime in 1922, Jeffers wrote that poetry "belongs out-doors, it has tides as nature has; while prose is a cultured interior thing, prose is of the house, where lamplight abolishes even the tides of day and night, and human caprice rules" (*CP* 4:375). Not long after this statement, he wrote "Night."

Bly derives the "night-intelligence" primarily from Novalis's *Hymns to the Night*. Certainly, Jeffers was well read in the German "stream," as Bly calls it, but there are numerous examples of romantic and modern poetry—German, British, and American—that variously address, praise, apostrophize, and celebrate night, the trope for death, sleep, dreams, or peace. However, Novalis is the prime example, and throughout "Night," phrases and ideas echo Novalis's "The Second Hymn to the Night," which Bly includes in *News of the Universe*. For example, Novalis writes, "Daylight has got limits and hours, but the hegemony of Night penetrates through space and through time" (*News of the Universe*, 49, Bly's translation). Most important, Novalis's *Hymns to the Night* are classic romantic odes, marked as such by their use of the ode's major trope, the apostrophe.

18. "Night" was written in the later part of the "Roan Stallion" period; Hunt dates it August 1924 (*CP* 5:69). Hawk Tower is mentioned in the poem, so the writing of "Night," as well as "The Tower beyond Tragedy," can be linked to completion of this material symbol of human consciousness. Bennett states that the tower was finished at the end of 1924 (*Stone Mason*, 100). On November 22, 1924, Jeffers wrote to George Sterling that Una's room was being paneled and that he had begun "The Tower beyond Tragedy" (*CL* 1:477). By September 4, 1925, Jeffers reported to Benjamin De Casseres, "The tower is finished, except two little jobs of paving. I laid the last stone in the parapet of the turret yesterday" (*CL* 1:509). So if the line in "Night," "the lamp in my tower," is a literal reference, the poem might have been written slightly later than August 1924. For an examination of the tower as a symbol of antimodernism, see Ziolkowski, *View from the Tower*, especially the chapter "Robinson Jeffers: The Tower beyond Time" (71–95).

19. Everson, *Robinson Jeffers*, 157; Oelschlaeger, *Idea of Wilderness*, 255.

20. Toffler, foreword to Prigogine and Stengers, *Order out of Chaos*, xx, 116.

21. For a valuable discussion of the second law of thermodynamics and the concept of force as they relate to Jeffers's notion of strain, especially with regard to "Prelude," see Zaller, *Robinson Jeffers*, 129–35.

22. Jeffers's choice does not consign him to the irrational or deterministic nihilism that critics such as Yvor Winters, Henry Steele Commager, or, more recently, Lawrence Buell (*Writing for an Endangered World*) accuse him of succumbing to. His allegiance to the night-intelligence came from a reasonable, if somewhat fatalistic, acceptance

of the scientific principles that he knew. Molecular biologists and neuroscientists struggle with this same dilemma today, yet significant advances in the study of the materiality of consciousness have been made. Henry Steele Commager accurately assessed Jeffers's mix of romanticism and science over fifty years ago in *The American Mind*: "The most uncompromisingly scientific of the literary spokesmen of determinism, Jeffers is, at the same time, the most romantic. Trained to medicine, familiar with psychiatry, biology, geology, and physics, living, by choice, close to nature and acknowledging no obligation but to nature, his affluent poetry is a scientific as well as a philosophical commentary on the life of man" (128).

23. Stevens's letters to Monroe regarding her reordering of the stanzas of "Sunday Morning" can be found in Stevens, *Letters*, 183–84.

24. *American Heritage Dictionary*, 3rd ed.

25. Penrose, *Emperor's New Mind*, 309.

26. Edelman, *Remembered Present*, 265.

27. Hunt dates "Credo" late 1926 (*CP* 5:75).

28. Edelman, *Remembered Present*, 264, 265.

29. Everson, *Robinson Jeffers*, 143, 144.

30. Hunt, afterword to Jeffers, *Women at Point Sur*, 196.

31. For a discussion of the young girl and a photo of the oil-tank fire, see Kafka, "Lighthouse-Keeper's Daughter."

32. Emerson, *Essays and Lectures*, 20, 457.

33. Cooke and Turner, *Biopoetics*, 6.

34. Anderson and Kinzie, *Little Magazines*, 493. The dictionary definition of *biopoesis* is "the (hypothetical) origination or evolution of living or lifelike structures from lifeless matter" (*OED*).

35. Another way to think about a biopoetics is Richard Dawkins's theory of the meme. As Daniel Dennett explains: "Meme evolution is not just analogous to biological or genetic evolution, not just a process that can be metaphorically described in evolutionary terms, but a phenomenon that obeys the laws of natural selection exactly" (*Consciousness Explained*, 202).

36. Fenollosa writes that "Chinese notation is something much more than arbitrary symbols. It is based upon a vivid shorthand picture of the operation of nature" (Fenollosa and Pound, *Chinese Written Character*, 45). Both Saussy ("Fenollosa Compounded," 24) and Stalling (*Poetics of Emptiness*, 35–36) observe that characterizing Fenollosa's work as merely an extension of Emerson's transcendentalism to the Chinese written character is a great disservice to him as a cultural theorist of the East-West fusion. However, Pound's denial of what Saussure calls the "arbitrary nature of the sign" is his version of Fenollosa's account of the Chinese written character, which allows him to propound an organic theory of language without reverting to romanticism. Stalling points out that "there is an important interpretive error at the very foundation of both Fenollosa's detractors and supporters: namely, that he, like Pound, says that characters are 'stylized pictures of things.' Pound believed this—Fenollosa did not" (*Poetics of Emptiness*, 36). Even if Fenollosa knew that Chinese written language was somewhat more than pictures of things, his work is the source of what might be called Pound's pictorial fallacy.

37. Edelman, *Remembered Present*, 173.

38. Even for a poet as indebted to Pound as Gary Snyder, sacramentalism leads toward a biopoetic view of language as he absorbs the ideogrammic method. In her

reading of Snyder's metapoem "Riprap," Josephine Nock-Hee Park observes that the "imbrication of the mind within its environment echoes the key concern of environmental literature, which aims to shift the repository of transcendence from the literary mind to the natural environment" (*Apparitions of Asia*, 79). Unlike Emerson and Pound, Snyder sees language's part in this process as systemic rather than ideogrammic: "Snyder, too, eschews the arbitrariness of the signifier by figuring language as a wild system, but his transparent poetics evinces a deep skepticism about the word. For Pound, the word was itself an organic entity, but Snyder ranks the primal world above the secondary word" (80).

39. Jeffers invents Barclay's story to tell of this strain as well, but in Barclay the biopoetic function of a ritualized language is replaced by a messianic delusion: Barclay declares, "I have turned all my lightnings of consciousness / On the one cell; I have turned to love men" (*CP* 1:347).

40. Hunt reaches a similar conclusion, but he believes that the longer narrative offers the reader the opportunity for deeper participation: "The length and excesses of *Point Sur* must be understood as part of Jeffers' strategy to involve himself and his reader in 'discovery.' The poem is not meant to summarize the Inhumanist perspective but to involve the reader in the psychically volatile conflicts of being human and in the world" (afterword to Jeffers, *Women at Point Sur*, 212).

41. Indeed, Jeffers himself referred to his work at this point in terms of experiment and discovery. Describing the failure of the "Point Alma Venus" poem to his publisher Donald Friede, Jeffers writes, "Every story that ever occurred to me had got wound up into this one poem; and it was too long, too complicated, and, from the attempt at compression, neither clear nor true.... One had to try experiments, even costly ones" (*CL* 1:566–67). Then, as the poem began to take shape as "The Women at Point Sur," he wrote to Friede: "I think I've come to terms with my book at last, discovering a form that is quite new, so far as I know, and the only one possible for the subject. It ought to do pretty well now" (*CL* 1:570).

3 / The Whole Mind

1. To be sure, as the decade wore on there were less than "idyllic" aspects of the Jefferses' lives, including increasing development of the Carmel area, marital tensions, and the beginnings of the Second World War. For an overview of life in the Jeffers household during the 1930s, see Karman's preface in *CL* 2:xiii–xx.

2. Coffin, *Robinson Jeffers*, 128–29; Beers, "Telling the Past," 48.

3. Zaller, "Robinson Jeffers, Narrative," 243. Elsewhere, Zaller dubs these middle-period characters "heroes of endurance" to distinguish them from the earlier "heroes of transgression" such as Tamar and Barclay. He writes, "If ... the hero of transgression had served to illustrate the transformative aspect of natural process as embedded in the notion of strain, a very different kind of protagonist might emerge from the contemplation of material *resistance*" (*Robinson Jeffers*, 136).

4. Indeed, the character Cawdor is one of Zaller's "heroes of endurance." "Cawdor" is perhaps best seen as a transitional poem somewhere between the myth-ritual of the 1920s and "Thurso's Landing." However, Jeffers himself saw no distinction between the two poems. Explaining the inclusion of "Thurso's Landing" instead of "Cawdor" in his 1938 *Selected Poetry*, he writes, "The omission of *Cawdor* is purely arbitrary and accidental; I had finally to choose between this and *Thurso's Landing*; and there was no ground for choice; I simply drew lots in my mind" (*CP* 4:390).

5. Edelman, *Wider Than the Sky*, 98, 58–59.

6. Jeffers made this distinction between tragedy and comedy in 1928: "It seems to me that every personal story ends more or less in tragedy; comedy is an unfinished story. The impersonal and universal story . . . never finishes at all" (*CP* 4:555).

7. Waggoner, "Science," 279–80.

8. Indeed, Edelman writes, "In animals without semantic abilities, higher-order consciousness cannot be present. A self derived from primary consciousness is not able to symbolize its memory states, or become truly self-conscious or conscious of being conscious" (*Wider Than the Sky*, 134).

9. Ibid., 136.

10. An intriguing fragment beginning "Great rough-legged hawks" (*CP* 4:515–17), which Hunt believes was drafted in the early 1930s (*CP* 5:1023), expands on the representation of primary versus higher-order consciousness. Jeffers imagines God and Satan, who "is God's contempt of himself," debating the value of humanity; they decide to "go to the hawks for judgment." Endowing a female hawk with human consciousness, they allow her to decide if it is preferable "to her own nobility." Describing the transition to higher-order consciousness in the hawk's mind, Jeffers writes, "Instead of few, sharp, / Single and pure, the motions of her mind were suddenly / Compound, troubled, enormous, (for the set pattern of human emotion and thought is enormous multitude / In the sense of the other animals on earth) but all impure, all unwashed, like a deep dish of colored / Pebbles and mud, in change for a rosary of certain cut flawless gems."

11. Brophy, "Margrave," 11.

12. Hunt's description of the "Margrave" manuscript reveals that Jeffers did consider it related to his poems on consciousness from the early 1920s: "When Jeffers was writing *Margrave*, he was already considering a new collection, even though he had no major narrative to anchor it and was not working on one. . . . A note on one page of the ams. reads, 'Include in the book the sonnets called "Consciousness," and perhaps a few others'" (*CP* 5:498).

13. Brophy, "Margrave," 11.

14. Deacon, *Symbolic Species*, 439.

15. Edelman, *Remembered Present*, 270. Jeffers appears to agree with Edelman's distinction that individual consciousness cannot extend past death, but he still attributes a transpersonal or transhistorical quality to it. In a 1934 letter, Jeffers writes, "I think that death extinguishes personal consciousness. That does not mean annihilation exactly, any more than the extinction of a fire means annihilation. The heat and light of the fire remain, or are changed into other forms of energy; the substances that were burnt and incandescent remain though changed into other forms" (*CL* 2:327–28).

16. Brophy, "Margrave," 11.

17. Jeffers also discussed the poem in a letter to James Rorty, April 1932: "The chief interest of the verses called 'Margrave' was, for me, in the attempt to bring far separated things into affinity, the flight of the nebulae and a crime like the Hickman case, etc. to combine narrative and lyrical passages like the dramatic and lyrical in Greek tragedy" (*CL* 2:84). The details of "the Hickman case" explain the irritation that Jeffers expressed about the valorization of human consciousness. In December 1927, William Edward Hickman kidnapped twelve-year-old Marion Parker from Mount Vernon High School in Los Angeles, intending to extort a $1,500 ransom from her father, a bank teller. He wanted the money to pay college tuition. He strangled Marion

in his apartment and dismembered her body, after first draining it of blood in the bathtub. He then applied makeup to her face, wired her eyes open, and put her torso in a suitcase. When he met the father to obtain the ransom, he raised the torso up in his car to give the appearance she was still alive. As police tracked him through Los Angeles, Hickman escaped in a stolen car and drove north, eventually being captured seven days later in Oregon. The *Los Angeles Times* provided sensationalized coverage throughout the week. Interviews with county jail trustees where Hickman had been held on forgery charges a year before revealed that he had a brilliant mind, talked of collecting insects, was very likable, seemed to know a lot about chemistry, and was greatly interested in the jail hospital's surgical instruments. One Christmas Eve article quotes Hickman as asking, "Do you think they'll hang me for this?" Indeed, his insanity plea was rejected by the jury and the appellate court, and he was hanged on October 19, 1928.

18. Sugihara et al., *Fire in California's Ecosystems*, 538.

19. Snyder, *Practice of the Wild*, 39.

20. Snyder, *Turtle Island*, Introductory Note.

21. Ibid., 112.

22. Sale, *Dwellers in the Land*, 42–43.

23. Berg, *Reinhabiting a Separate Country*.

24. Sugihara et al., *Fire in California's Ecosystems*, 326.

25. Jeffers refers to one of these poems, most likely "All the Little Hoof-Prints," as "a short narrative-descriptive poem" (*CP* 4:555).

26. Una Jeffers reported on various geographical and literary sources for the narratives in a letter to Lawrence Clark Powell from 1932. According to her, the story of "The Dead Men's Child" is derived from the locale of the Tinajas Altas on the Arizona-Mexico border and a legend drawn from Sir Walter Scott (*CL* 2:90).

Jeffers described the poems accompanying "Cawdor" in a note for a publisher's catalogue: "There will be some variety of shorter poems also, narrative and lyrical sketches expressing a state of mind that seems—at least to the writer—neither surprising nor subversive, but the mere commonsense of our predicament as passionate bits of earth and water" (*CL* 1:749).

27. Brophy, *Robinson Jeffers*, 88–89.

28. Ecocritical discussion of Jeffers's work, narrative and lyric, is surprisingly slight. Lawrence Buell, examining determinism in Jeffers and Theodore Dreiser, refers briefly to "Roan Stallion" but otherwise cites only shorter poems (*Writing for an Endangered World*, 149–56). Three prominent books on ecopoetics—John Elder's *Imagining the Earth*, Jed Rasula's *This Compost*, and Bernard Quetchenbach's *Back from the Far Field*—all discuss Jeffers, but none cite any of the longer narratives.

29. Meeker, *Comedy of Survival*, 51. Meeker's "literary ecology" went largely unnoticed when it appeared in the early 1970s, but it was rediscovered by ecocritics in the 1980s and 1990s. Cheryll Glotfelty and Harold Fromm included a selection from *The Comedy of Survival* in their *Ecocriticism Reader* (155–69). However, Meeker has also been rigorously critiqued by later ecocritics. For example, Dana Phillips, although he approves of Meeker's attention to form and genre, finds his ecological and scientific claims dated and metaphorical at best (*Truth of Ecology*, 145–52).

30. Cheney, "Postmodern Environmental Ethics," 132, 133.

31. Frye, *Anatomy of Criticism*, 162, 158.

32. Brophy, *Robinson Jeffers*, 298.

33. Ibid., 298.

34. However, a too rigid application of Frye's theories as schematized here would misrepresent Jeffers's narrative practice. I find it unlikely that we would discover examples of a romantic or satiric mode in the mature work, not only because romance and satire do not seem suited to Jeffers, but also because Frye associates these modes with a dialectical movement that transcends the natural. The "cyclical movement" is "within the order of nature," according to Frye, but "The apocalyptic and demonic worlds, being structures of pure metaphorical identity, suggest the eternally unchanging, and lend themselves very readily to being projected existentially as heaven and hell, where there is continuous life but no *process* of life" (158). This state is in fact not a part of Jeffers's poetry or his view of the cosmos, in which there is no transcendental realm outside natural process. In this sense, the circularity of Brophy's schema naturalizes an artificial aspect of Frye's theory. Whereas tragedy is primarily autumnal and comedy primarily vernal, what matters most is that both are temporal, that both represent an experience of temporality and that the seasonality they manifest is natural rather than archetypal.

35. Preminger, *Encyclopedia of Poetry*, 362.

36. Bennett, *Stone Mason*, 109. Brophy, *Robinson Jeffers*, 275.

37. Of course, Jeffers continued to write the long, tragic poems that provide the title for each volume throughout this period: "Thurso's Landing," "Give Your Heart to the Hawks," "Solstice," and "Such Counsels You Gave to Me" (and the only exception to this rule occurs in this decade; the longest poem in *Be Angry at the Sun*, "Mara," does not give the collection its title). Along with the major poems, midlength narratives of about twenty pages occur regularly: "Resurrection" and "Margrave" in *Thurso's Landing* and "At the Fall of an Age" in *Give Your Heart to the Hawks*, for example.

38. Volume 5 of *The Collected Poetry* contains revealing material from Jeffers's notes for this poem. One reads: "The human norm is a function of geography, and only becomes racial after thousands of years in the same place." Jeffers also seems sensitive to the fancifulness of the story: "Part of the function of poetry is to express things so basically true that in prose they would be ridiculous" (*CP* 5:524). In the published version, the woman is nameless and the man is called "Wolf." Their names in the notes are, respectively, "Dawn" and "Fish-hawk" (*CP* 5:525).

39. Hughey and Hughey, "Jeffers Country Revisited," 23–24.

40. Brophy, *Robinson Jeffers*, 277; Zaller, "Robinson Jeffers, American Poetry," 33; Bedient, "Robinson Jeffers," 160.

41. Bedient, "Robinson Jeffers," 174, 176.

42. Ibid., 177–78.

43. Ibid., 178. Also intriguing is that Clare's final wanderings in this scene take her through the sites of two of the tragic narratives: she comes through "Cawdor's Canyon" on her way back from the ridgetop pastures (*CP* 2:103) and stops at Point Lobos, where Tamar Cauldwell's residence is mentioned (*CP* 2:104). That she finds kind treatment from the current inhabitants perhaps indicates something of a purification of those poems' residual sexual violence.

44. Hunt italicizes the title of the poem as a complete unit, suggesting its status as a narrative; he uses quotation marks when referring to the individual poem by its respective part of the full title. The poem is grouped with the other lyrics from the *Such Counsels* period—a small example of the liminal position the shorter narratives occupy.

45. Everson, foreword to Jeffers, *Double Axe*, xvi.

4 / To Keep One's Own Integrity

1. In *Nature's Economy*, Donald Worster traces the history of holistic organicism in the twentieth century, locating its beginnings in the mid-1920s with Alfred North Whitehead. According to Worster, Whitehead was responding to the Cartesian mechanistic materialism that reduced nature to a senseless, valueless set of quantities that conformed to rigid physical laws. He predicted "an age of organicism" in which "scientists would emphasize process, creativity, indefiniteness, the 'organic unity of a whole,' and 'the realisation of events disposed in an interlocked community'" (317). Nevertheless, even though a concerted movement for reestablishing organicism in scientific ecology emerged in this period, especially among the faculty at the University of Chicago (326), it is paradoxical that when the Age of Ecology dawned after World War II, "the metabiological, idealizing tendencies of organicism had been firmly exorcised" from professional ecology (332). When organic holism reemerged in the 1960s, it took a form that more closely resembled the holism that Jeffers was discovering parallel to the New Ecologists and the University of Chicago group. Rather than emphasizing the benefits to human society of understanding the unity of nature, the new organicism focused on the reconciliation of human and nature through the realization of organic interdependence. Worster writes, "The organicists of the 1960s and -70s go beyond any of their predecessors in promoting what they most often like to call an 'ecological ethic': a science-based sense of relatedness between man and nature. Never has it been so widely acknowledged that humanity is not an island unto itself. For many, that realization defines the Age of Ecology" (333).

2. Worster, *Nature's Economy*, 339; Koestler, *Janus*, 1.

3. Berger, *Forms of Farewell*, 35–36.

4. Stevens, *Letters*, 839.

5. Haas, *Reflection*, 179. For a brief discussion of Stein's "Reflection" compared to William Carlos Williams's later mention of the bomb in "Asphodel, That Greeny Flower," see Gery, *Nuclear Annihilation*, 39–47.

6. Frost, *Collected Poems*, 340, 343.

7. Jeffers's term for this "philosophical attitude," as he called it, is perhaps unfortunate in its similarity to the adjectives *inhumane* and *inhuman,* but he intended it to signify "a shifting of emphasis and significance from man to not-man" (*CP* 4:428). Isaac Cates, who applies the term to Jeffers's poetics, writes, "Some of Jeffers's readers have misunderstood the term to indicate a rejection or negation of one form or another of humanism, but in doing this they take too literally a sort of pun in Jeffers's invented word. He chose this term because the ideology centers on an admiration of the inhuman in the natural world, with *inhuman* here meaning *not human* more than (though not exclusive of) *cruel* or *amoral*" ("Inhumanist Poetics," 113). The *American Heritage Dictionary* defines *inhuman* as "brutal, monstrous" and "unhuman" as "not of human form." Jeffers deployed a variety of terms seemingly interchangeably when using the adjectival form—*inhuman, unhuman, transhuman*—but *unhuman* captures his meaning. He was simply following grammatical convention in changing the prefix from *un-* to *in-* when adding the suffix *-ism* to the term.

8. Zaller points out that the gesture is an allusion to the Roman Caius Mucius Scaevola, who, according to Livy, saved Rome from attack by demonstrating his patriotism and courage by burning his right hand in a fire (*Robinson Jeffers*, 298).

9. Brower, *Not Man Apart*. Interestingly, Jeffers's diction echoes the other classic midcentury formulation of organic holism, Aldo Leopold's "Land Ethic." By 1947, Leopold had arrived at the synthesis of his various lectures on land management from the 1930s, and his succinct expression of the Land Ethic is well known: "A thing is right when it tends to preserve the integrity, stability, and beauty of the biotic community. It is wrong when it tends otherwise" (*Sand County Almanac*, 224–25). Leopold's formula contains two of Jeffers's key terms, *integrity* and *beauty*.

10. Jeffers's terms here, as well as the etymology, echo J. C. Smuts, who coined the term *holism*. Smuts writes, "Wholeness, healing, holiness—all expressions and ideas springing from the same root in language as in experience—lie on the rugged upward path of the universe, are secure of attainment—in part here and now, and eventually more fully and truly. The rise and self-perfection of wholes in the Whole is the slow but unerring process and goal of this Holistic universe" (*Holism and Evolution*, 345).

11. Derrida, "*Geschlecht* II," 178.

12. A late poem returns to the image of the severed hand and connects it with writing: "Fallen in between the tendons and bones / It looks like a dead hand. Poor hand a little longer / Write, and see what comes forth from a dead hand" ("Hand," *CP* 3:469).

13. In another *Double Axe* poem, "Calm and Full the Ocean," Jeffers returns to this connection. He describes the progression of the seasons as "Sane and intact," as opposed to the course of the war, which is "private and mad" (*CP* 3:124). To be "intact," of course, is to be whole, and the word is also etymologically related to the IE *tag-*.

14. Kohák, *Embers and the Stars*, 170.

15. The figure of double consciousness as a circus performer appears in Emerson's late essay "Fate" (*Essays and Lectures*, 966).

16. In the notes for the preface, Jeffers refers to the inhumanist perspective as "new but not untested" (*CP* 5:999).

17. Everson, foreword to Jeffers, *Double Axe*, xvii.

18. Koestler, *Janus*, 61.

19. Morton, *Ecology without Nature*, 117–18.

20. Gelpi, "Robinson Jeffers," 17.

21. Ibid., 14. Cates also believes that by "beauty" Jeffers meant "the sublime" ("Inhumanist Poetics," 114). Sublime nature may in fact be what the Inhumanist witnessed as absolute beauty, but Jeffers's favored term is *beauty*, not *the sublime*. In this sense, his usage comports with Kant, who states, "Sublimity . . . does not reside in anything of nature, but only in our mind" (excerpt from *Critique of Judgment*, 391).

22. Morton, *Ecology without Nature*, 185–86.

23. In "Themes in My Poems," he offered the scientific metaphor of wavelengths rather than the literary metaphor of translation: "Beauty, like color, is subjective. It is not in the object but in the mind that regards it. Nevertheless, I believe it corresponds to a reality, a real excellence and nobility in the world; but as the color red corresponds to a reality: certain wave-lengths, a certain rhythm of vibrations" (*CP* 4:412–13).

24. Everson, foreword to Jeffers, *Double Axe*, xvii, xviii.

25. Snyder, "Without," in *Turtle Island*, 6. In his discussion of Jeffers and Snyder, Oelschlaeger points out that Snyder's "is a poetry more healing than Jeffers's poetry of protest" (*Idea of Wilderness*, 280).

26. Critical reception of this personified axe has been mixed. Patrick Murphy, reading the poem as "a darkly marvelous fantasy," asserts that Jeffers "embed[s] the axe within a complex web of sacred, symbolic, archetypal, and allusive significations"

("Robinson Jeffers' Macabre," 203). Vernon Young, on the other hand, dismisses it as "the ridiculous figure of an animated axe that 'giggles' and sets off the atomic bomb" ("Such Counsels," 182). In *The House of the Double Axe*, anthropologist Agne Carr Vaughan puzzles over the figure of the double axe as a manifestation of the Earth Goddess of Minoan mythology. He comments on the personification of the axe that seems so unprecedented in Jeffers's poem: "This Lady of the Double Axe must be the Mother Goddess herself, capable of appearing to her worshippers in various forms, as a bird or a serpent or even as an axe. The modern mind finds this difficult to understand, but to the Minoan or to the later Greek it was easy enough. Deity, spiritual force, *mana*, call it by whatever name we will, was immanent in all things, animate or inanimate" (172).

27. Four sections of "The Inhumanist" are printed in prose paragraphs rather than verse. For a detailed discussion of this section, see Karman, "End of Prophecy."

28. Eshleman, *Antiphonal Swing*, 237.

29. The phrase *nuclear sublime* is Rob Wilson's. Zaller discusses "The Inhumanist" in relation to this idea (*Robinson Jeffers*, 34–36).

30. Snyder, *Danger on Peaks*, 9.

5 / The Wound in the Brain

1. Michael McClure offers a wonderful example of this first transformation of the memento mori, in which he acknowledges consciousness in a nonhuman being: "I once found a dolphin skull on a beach in Baja, Mexico; I kept the skull and sometimes looked through it, through the eyes, through the foramen magnum, and through the blowhole on the dorsal surface. I thought of Goethe looking at Schiller's skull or Hamlet looking at Yorick's. Perhaps this can be such an instrument—but it is more of a remembrance of life than a memento mori" (*3 Poems*, 71).

2. Hunt believes that the first section of "De Rerum Virtute" "derives from a narrative sketch in which someone finds the skull of a person who has fallen or been pushed into a sinkhole and drowned" (*CP* 5:840).

3. Tobias, "Brain of *Homo habilis*," 748, 765.

4. McClure, a poet who also seeks a biopoetics based in science, describes this shift: "Traditional science of the early twentieth century, before the frontier science of microbiology developed in the 1950s, saw the animal cell as a container—a closed system open to chemical transfers. The cell was seen as an enclosed unit capable of reproducing itself. Now the cell is seen as a complex system that is the center of life, with complements of symbiotic mini-organs and highly complicated life constructs on atomic and molecular levels" (*Scratching the Beat Surface*, 129).

5. For example, major commentators on Jeffers struggle to determine the meaning of these lines from the fourth part of "Apology for Bad Dreams." Brophy, who writes that the meaning of "Apology" has been "a career-long question," believes that the ambiguous pronoun reference indicates the identity of God and poet: "In creating, God and the poet are one (the 'he' refers to both)" ("Jeffers's 'Apology for Bad Dreams,'" 3, 5). Zaller, on the other hand, believes that the syntax indicates a distinction between the poet and God: "It is not entirely clear in the last sentence at which point the voice breaks; 'I think they admit no reason' might still be the poet's musing, but 'they are the ways of my love,' with its sharp syntactical interruption, is surely a distinct, answering voice" (*Robinson Jeffers*, 198). Why the answering voice is not indicated by quotation marks, which Jeffers uses elsewhere in the poem to distinguish between God and his "ape," makes the distinction less sure than Zaller claims. What's

more, in a late fragment Jeffers uses the same phrase ("my love") to refer to the things of nature: "my love: my loved subject: / Mountain and ocean, rock, water and beasts and trees" (*CP* 3:484).

6. Brophy, *Robinson Jeffers*, 272.

7. Bataille, *Erotism*, 40–41.

8. Brophy, *Robinson Jeffers*, 272.

9. At best it reflects a general awareness of contemporary scientific knowledge on Jeffers's part. Although James Baird says that he is "tantalizingly close to describing DNA" here, strictly speaking, it cannot be a reference to DNA ("Robinson Jeffers's Poetry," 8). "De Rerum Virtute" was first published in a special edition in February 1953; Watson and Crick published their findings on the molecular structure of nucleic acids in *Nature*, April 1953.

10. Steven Chapman also notes this shift, from statement of fact to statement of belief, attributing it to Jeffers's awareness that his view runs counter to Darwinian theory ("De Rerum Virtute," 25).

11. Pagel, *Encyclopedia of Evolution*, E-17.

12. It is interesting that Jeffers's plan for this last long poem, which was to tell the story of geogenesis, biogenesis, and the genesis of consciousness, follows the same trajectory as Holmes Rolston III's recent *Three Big Bangs: Matter-Energy, Life, Mind*.

13. An overview of the current understanding of hominid evolution can be found in Robert Foley's entry in the *Encyclopedia of Evolution*, edited by Mark Pagel. For more detailed discussions of the evidence, see Foley's *Humans before Humanity*; on the hominid radiations, see especially 97–103.

14. Burke, *Language as Symbolic Action*, 3.

15. Deacon, *Symbolic Species*, 345.

16. Burke, *Language as Symbolic Action*, 15.

17. Deacon, *Symbolic Species*, 436–37.

18. Ibid., 437.

19. "The Deer Lay Down Their Bones" was a late addition to *Hungerfield*, sent to Random House with "Skunks" in March 1953 after the complete manuscript had been submitted (*CP* 5:849).

20. "Theory of Truth" is discussed above in chapter 4.

21. "Vulture" was posthumously published; Hunt writes that it is "probably from 1957" (*CP* 5:134).

22. Gelpi, "What an Enskyment," 4, 6.

23. Derrida, *Dissemination*, 63.

24. The phrase is Antonio Damasio's (*Feeling of What Happens*, 4).

Conclusion

1. Wyatt, *Fall into Eden*, 174, 185–86.

2. Jeffers's invisibility in histories of American modernism persists. The recent *Cambridge Companion to American Modernism*, edited by Walter Kalaidjian, includes a chapter titled "Regionalism in American Modernism," by John Duvall. The chapter includes a section on regional poetry that discusses Carl Sandburg, Edgar Lee Masters, Edwin Arlington Robinson, and Robert Frost (249–52). Masters, Robinson, and Frost can certainly be considered antimodernist regionalists, a category in which Jeffers should naturally have a prominent place.

3. Snyder, "Art of Poetry," 96.

4. The letter is drafted on University of California Press stationery. For the reflections on this point in his career, see Everson, *Dark God of Eros*, 388.

5. Box 15, William Everson Papers, Bancroft Library, University of California, Berkeley.

6. Hickman, "Theodore Roethke," 183.

7. Box 15, William Everson Papers, Bancroft Library, University of California, Berkeley.

8. Faas, *Young Robert Duncan*, 92.

9. Duncan, "Where as Giant Kings We Gatherd," 140.

10. Metres, *Behind the Lines*, 74.

11. Ibid., 17.

12. Ibid., 79.

13. Duncan, *Years as Catches*, iv.

14. Duncan, "Where as Giant Kings We Gatherd," 141–42, 143.

15. Bartlett, *Kenneth Rexroth and James Laughlin*, 76.

16. Everson, *Residual Years*, [iii], [v].

17. Bartlett, *William Everson*, 102.

18. The letter is quoted in Bartlett, *William Everson*, 103.

19. Rexroth, *Complete Poems*, 83–89.

20. Bartlett, *William Everson*, 103.

21. Everson, *Collected Poems*, 1:12; hereafter cited in the text by volume and page number.

22. Guillén, "Aesthetics of Literary Influence," 62–63.

23. I prefer these terms rather than Bloom's psychoanalytical "anxiety of influence." Everson and Rexroth might have sublimated or repressed reasons for engaging in the Oedipal drama with Jeffers, but Guillén's terms allow for analysis of the conscious choices both poets were making in their dealings with their forerunner. Though Zaller, in "Jeffers, Rexroth," doesn't make any grand claims of influence, his approach retains the unidirectional flow of precursor to latecomer that intertextual theories such as Guillén's avoid. What's more, triangulating Jeffers between Rexroth and Everson allows for consideration of all three poets' decisions about how to be a California poet.

24. Eshelman, *Take Hold*, 29, 39.

25. Everson, *Earth Poetry*, 202.

26. Rexroth papers, Department of Special Collections, Charles E. Young Research Library, UCLA. Material from this typescript is included in lyric XVI of *The Phoenix and the Tortoise*, so it might have been drafted sometime in the late 1930s or early 1940s. The draft concludes:

> Today in California the promise and the problem
> of the world beyond humanism engulphs [*sic*] the humanist
> with silent cogency. Around these islands of
> indommitable [*sic*] will, over the pale and privileges
> of frustration, flows the immense gymnopedia
> of the common people, blissful and ignorant.

When New Directions published his *Collected Shorter Poems*, James Laughlin asked Rexroth to supply titles for the numbered epigrams and lyrics from *The Phoenix and the Tortoise*. He gave it the tongue-in-cheek title "Vitamins and Roughage," Rexroth, *Complete Poems*, 216:

Strong ankled, sun burned, almost naked,
The daughters of California
Educate reluctant humanists;
Drive into their skulls with tennis balls
The unhappy realization
That nature is still stronger than man.
The special Hellenic privilege
Of the special intellect seeps out
At last in this irrigated soil.
Sweat of athletes and juice of lovers
Are stronger than Socrates' hemlock;
And the games of scrupulous Euclid
Vanish in the gymnopedia.

27. Rexroth, "In Defense," 30.

28. Everson to Rexroth, 21 August 1957. Rexroth papers, Department of Special Collections, Charles E. Young Research Library, UCLA.

29. Everson, *Robinson Jeffers*, 7.

30. Rexroth, *Autobiographical Novel*, 386.

31. Everson, *Archetype West*, 103.

32. Davidson, *Ghostlier Demarcations*, 138.

33. New, *Line's Eye*, 2.

Bibliography

Abbey, Edward. *Desert Solitaire: A Season in the Wilderness*. New York: Ballantine, 1971.

Altieri, Charles. *Enlarging the Temple: New Directions in American Poetry during the 1960s*. Lewisberg: Bucknell University Press, 1979.

Anderson, Elliott, and Mary Kinzie, eds. *The Little Magazine in America: A Modern Documentary History*. Yonkers, NY: Pushcart Press, 1978.

Assmann, Aleida. "Exorcising the Demon of Chronology: T. S. Eliot's Reinvention of Tradition." In *T. S. Eliot and the Concept of Tradition*, ed. Giovanni Cianci and Jason Harding, 13–25. Cambridge: Cambridge University Press, 2007.

Baird, James. "Robinson Jeffers's Poetry and Prose and Scientific Theory." *Jeffers Studies* 5, no. 4 (2001): 5–11.

Bakker, Elna. *An Island Called California: An Ecological Introduction to Its Natural Communities*. 2nd rev. ed. Berkeley: University of California Press, 1984.

Bartlett, Lee, ed. *Kenneth Rexroth and James Laughlin: Selected Letters*. New York: Norton, 1991.

———. *William Everson: The Life of Brother Antoninus*. New York: New Directions, 1988.

Bataille, Georges. *Erotism: Death and Sensuality*. Trans. Mary Dalwood. San Francisco: City Lights, 1986.

Bedient, Calvin. "Robinson Jeffers, D. H. Lawrence, and the Erotic Sublime." In *Robinson Jeffers and a Galaxy of Writers*, ed. William B. Thesing, 160–81. Columbia: University of South Carolina Press, 1995.

Beers, Terry. "Telling the Past and Living the Present: 'Thurso's Landing' and the Epic Tradition." In *Robinson Jeffers: Dimensions of a Poet*, ed. Robert Brophy, 48–63. New York: Fordham University Press, 1995.

Bennett, Melba Berry. *The Stone Mason of Tor House: The Life and Work of Robinson Jeffers*. Los Angeles: Ward Ritchie, 1966.

Berg, Peter, ed. *Reinhabiting a Separate Country: A Bioregional Anthology of Northern California*. San Francisco: Planet Drum, 1978.

Berger, Charles. *Forms of Farewell: The Late Poetry of Wallace Stevens*. Madison: University of Wisconsin Press, 1985.

Bly, Robert, ed. *News of the Universe: Poems of Twofold Consciousness*. San Francisco: Sierra Club, 1995.

Bradley, Nicholas. "Men with Guts: Al Purdy, Robinson Jeffers, and Geopoetic Influence." *Canadian Poetry* 62 (2008): 44–63.

Brophy, Robert. "Jeffers's 'Apology for Bad Dreams' Revisited." *Jeffers Studies* 8, no. 2 (2004): 3–19.

———. "'Margrave': Jeffers and the Pathetic Fallacy." *Jeffers Studies* 2, no. 3 (1998): 8–12.

———. *Robinson Jeffers: Myth, Ritual, and Symbol in His Narrative Poems*. Cleveland: Press of Case Western Reserve University, 1973.

———. "'Tamar,' 'The Cenci,' and Incest." *American Literature* 42, no. 2 (1970): 241–44.

Brower, David, ed. *Not Man Apart: Photographs of the Big Sur Coast*. San Francisco: Sierra Club, 1965.

Buell, Lawrence. *The Environmental Imagination: Thoreau, Nature Writing, and the Formation of American Culture*. Cambridge, MA: Harvard University Press, 1995.

———. *The Future of Environmental Criticism: Environmental Crisis and Literary Imagination*. Malden, MA: Blackwell, 2005.

———. *Writing for an Endangered World: Literature, Culture, and Environment in the U.S. and Beyond*. Cambridge, MA: Harvard University Press, 2001.

Burke, Kenneth. *Language as Symbolic Action: Essays on Life, Literature, and Method*. Berkeley: University of California Press, 1966.

———. *The Rhetoric of Religion*. Boston: Beacon, 1961.

Cates, Isaac. "The Inhumanist Poetics of Robinson Jeffers." *Raritan* 30, no. 3 (2011): 110–35.

Chapman, Steven. "'De Rerum Virtute': A Critical Anatomy." *Jeffers Studies* 6, no. 4 (2002): 22–35.

Cheney, Jim. "Postmodern Environmental Ethics: Ethics as Bioregional Narrative." *Environmental Ethics* 11, no. 2 (1989): 117–34.

Coffin, Arthur. *Robinson Jeffers: Poet of Inhumanism*. Madison: University of Wisconsin Press, 1971.

Coleman, William. *Biology in the Nineteenth Century: Problems of Form, Function, and Transformation*. Cambridge: Cambridge University Press, 1977.

Commager, Henry Steele. *The American Mind*. New Haven: Yale University Press, 1950.

Cooke, Brett, and Frederick Turner, eds. *Biopoetics: Evolutionary Explorations in the Arts.* Lexington, KY: ICUS Books, 1999.

Damasio, Antonio. *The Feeling of What Happens: Body and Emotion in the Making of Consciousness.* New York: Harcourt Brace, 1999.

Davidson, Michael. *Ghostlier Demarcations: Modern Poetry and the Material Word.* Berkeley: University of California Press, 1997.

———. *The San Francisco Renaissance: Poetics and Community at Mid-century.* Cambridge: Cambridge University Press, 1989.

Deacon, Terrence W. *The Symbolic Species: The Co-evolution of Language and the Brain.* New York: Norton, 1997.

de Man, Paul. *Blindness and Insight: Essays in the Rhetoric of Contemporary Criticism.* Minneapolis: University of Minnesota Press, 1983.

Dennett, Daniel C. *Consciousness Explained.* Boston: Little, Brown, 1991.

Derrida, Jacques. *Dissemination.* Trans. Barbara Johnson. Chicago: University of Chicago Press, 1981.

———. "*Geschlecht* II: Heidegger's Hand." Trans. John P. Leavey Jr. In *Deconstruction and Philosophy: The Texts of Jacques Derrida*, ed. John Sallis, 161–96. Chicago: University of Chicago Press, 1987.

Duncan, Robert. *Fictive Certainties.* New York: New Directions, 1985.

———. "'Where as Giant Kings We Gatherd': Some Letters from Robert Duncan to William Everson, 1940 and After." Ed. Lee Bartlett. *Sagetrieb* 4, no. 2–3 (1985): 137–74.

———. *The Years as Catches: First Poems (1939–1946).* Berkeley: Oyez, 1966.

Dunlap, Thomas R. *Faith in Nature: Environmentalism as Religious Quest.* Seattle: University of Washington Press, 2004.

Edelman, Gerald M. *The Remembered Present: A Biological Theory of Consciousness.* New York: Basic Books, 1989.

———. *Wider Than the Sky: The Phenomenal Gift of Consciousness.* New Haven: Yale University Press, 2004.

Edmundson, Mark. *Literature against Philosophy: Plato to Derrida.* Cambridge: Cambridge University Press, 1995.

Elder, John. *Imagining the Earth: Poetry and the Vision of Nature.* Urbana: University of Illinois Press, 1985.

Eliade, Mircea. *The Sacred and the Profane: The Nature of Religion.* San Diego: Harcourt, Brace, Jovanovich, 1959.

Emerson, Ralph Waldo. *Essays and Lectures.* New York: Library of America, 1983.

Eshelman, William R., ed. *Take Hold upon the Future: Letters on Writers and Writing.* William Everson and Lawrence Clark Powell. Metuchen, NJ: Scarecrow Press, 1994.

Eshleman, Clayton. *Antiphonal Swing: Selected Prose 1962/1987*, ed. Caryl Eshleman. Kingston, NY: McPherson, 1989.

Evernden, Neil. "Beyond Ecology: Self, Place, and the Pathetic Fallacy." In *The Ecocriticism Reader: Landmarks in Literary Ecology*, ed. Cheryll Glotfelty and Harold Fromm, 92–104. Athens: University of Georgia Press, 1996. Previously published in *North American Review* 263, no. 4 (1978).

Everson, William. *Archetype West: The Pacific Coast as a Literary Region.* Berkeley: Oyez, 1976.

—— [Brother Antoninus]. *The Collected Poems.* Ed. Allan Campo and Bill Hotchkiss. 3 vols. Santa Rosa, CA: Black Sparrow, 1997–2000.

——. *Earth Poetry: Selected Essays and Interviews of William Everson.* Ed. Lee Bartlett. Berkeley: Oyez, 1980.

——. *The Excesses of God: Robinson Jeffers as a Religious Figure.* Stanford: Stanford University Press, 1988.

——. Foreword to *The Double Axe and Other Poems,* by Robinson Jeffers. New York: Random House, 1977.

——. Introduction to *Cawdor/Medea,* by Robinson Jeffers. New York: New Directions, 1970.

——. *The Residual Years.* New York: New Directions, 1948.

—— [Brother Antoninus]. *Robinson Jeffers: Fragments of an Older Fury.* Berkeley: Oyez, 1968.

Federal Writers' Project. Works Progress Administration for the State of California. *California: A Guide to the Golden State.* Rev. ed. New York: Hastings House, 1954.

Fenollosa, Ernest, and Ezra Pound. *The Chinese Written Character as a Medium for Poetry.* Ed. Haun Saussy, Jonathan Stalling, and Lucas Klein. New York: Fordham University Press, 2008.

Foley, Robert. *Humans before Humanity.* Oxford: Blackwell, 1995.

Frost, Robert. *Collected Poems, Prose, and Plays.* Ed. Richard Poirier and Mark Richardson. New York: Library of America, 1995.

Frye, Northrop. *Anatomy of Criticism: Four Essays.* Princeton: Princeton University Press, 1957.

Gatta, John. *Making Nature Sacred: Literature, Religion, and Environment in America from the Puritans to the Present.* New York: Oxford University Press, 2004.

Gelpi, Albert. *A Coherent Splendor: The American Poetic Renaissance, 1910–1950.* Cambridge: Cambridge University Press, 1987.

——. Foreword to *The Excesses of God: Robinson Jeffers as a Religious Figure,* by William Everson. Stanford: Stanford University Press, 1988.

——. "Robinson Jeffers and the Sublime." Introduction to *The Wild God of the World: An Anthology of Robinson Jeffers,* ed. Albert Gelpi. Stanford: Stanford University Press, 2003.

——. "What an Enskyment / What an Enwordment: Robinson Jeffers's 'Vulture.'" *Jeffers Studies* 7, no. 2 (2003): 3–13.

Gery, John. *Nuclear Annihilation and Contemporary American Poetry: Ways of Nothingness.* Gainesville: University of Florida Press, 1996.

Girard, René. *Violence and the Sacred.* Baltimore: Johns Hopkins University Press, 1977.

Glaser, Kirk. "Desire, Death, and Domesticity in Jeffers's Pastorals of Apocalypse." In *Robinson Jeffers: The Dimensions of a Poet*, ed. Robert Brophy, 137–76. New York: Fordham University Press, 1995.

Glotfelty, Cheryll, and Harold Fromm, eds. *The Ecocriticism Reader: Landmarks in Literary Ecology*. Athens: University of Georgia Press, 1996.

Gottlieb, Roger S. *A Greener Faith: Religious Environmentalism and Our Planet's Future*. Oxford: Oxford University Press, 2006.

Grimes, Ronald L. *Rite out of Place: Ritual, Media, and the Arts*. Oxford: Oxford University Press, 2006.

Guillén, Claudio. "The Aesthetics of Literary Influence." In *Influx: Essays on Literary Influence*, ed. Ronald Primeau, 49–73. Port Washington, WA: Kennikat, 1977.

Haas, Robert Bartlett, ed. *Reflection on the Atomic Bomb*. Vol. 1 of *The Previously Uncollected Writings of Gertrude Stein*. Los Angeles: Black Sparrow, 1975.

Haralson, Eric, ed. *Reading the Middle Generation Anew: Culture, Community, and Form in Twentieth-Century American Poetry*. Iowa City: University of Iowa Press, 2006.

Harrison, Robert Pogue. *Forests: The Shadow of Civilization*. Chicago: University of Chicago Press, 1992.

Hughey, Richard Kohlman, and Boon Hughey. "Jeffers Country Revisited: Beauty without Price." *Robinson Jeffers Newsletter* 98 and 99 (1996): 9–84.

Hunt, Tim. Afterword to *The Women at Point Sur and Other Poems*, by Robinson Jeffers, 191–214. New York: Liveright, 1977.

James, William. *The Varieties of Religious Experience: A Study in Human Nature*. New York: Penguin, 1985.

Jeffers, Robinson. *The Collected Letters of Robinson Jeffers*. 2 vols. Ed. James Karman. Stanford: Stanford University Press, 2010–11.

———. *The Collected Poetry of Robinson Jeffers*. Ed. Tim Hunt. 5 vols. Stanford: Stanford University Press, 1988–2001.

Kafka, Robert. "Jeffers's 1936 Ventana Creek Hike: A Miscellany." *Jeffers Studies* 8, no. 1 (2004): 31–50.

———. "The Lighthouse-Keeper's Daughter." *Jeffers Studies* 10, no. 2 (2006), and 11, no. 1–2 (2007): 19–53.

Kalaidjian, Walter, ed. *The Cambridge Companion to American Modernism*. Cambridge: Cambridge University Press, 2005.

Kant, Immanuel. Excerpt from *Critique of Judgment* in *Critical Theory since Plato*, ed. Hazard Adams. Fort Worth, TX: Harcourt Brace Jovanovich, 1992.

Karman, James. "The End of Prophecy: A Response." *Jeffers Studies* 4, no. 4 (2000): 59–63.

———. Introduction to *Stones of the Sur*, by Robinson Jeffers. Stanford: Stanford University Press, 2001.

Kerouac, Jack. *The Dharma Bums*. New York: Penguin, 1976.

Koestler, Arthur. *Janus: A Summing Up*. New York: Random House, 1978.

Kohák, Erazim. *The Embers and the Stars: A Philosophical Inquiry into the Moral Sense of Nature.* Chicago: University of Chicago Press, 1984.

Kroeber, Karl. *Ecological Literary Criticism: Romantic Imagining and the Biology of Mind.* New York: Columbia University Press, 1994.

Lakoff, George, and Mark Johnson. *Philosophy in the Flesh: The Embodied Mind and Its Challenge to Western Thought.* New York: Basic, 1999.

Langbaum, Robert. "The New Nature Poetry." *American Scholar* 28, no. 3 (1959): 323–40.

Leopold, Aldo. *A Sand County Almanac and Sketches Here and There.* New York: Oxford University Press, 1987.

Materer, Timothy. *Modernist Alchemy: Poetry and the Occult.* Ithaca: Cornell University Press, 1995.

McClure, Michael. *3 Poems: Dolphin Skull, Rare Angel, Dark Brown.* New York: Penguin, 1995.

———. *Scratching the Beat Surface.* San Francisco: North Point, 1982.

McGann, Jerome. *The Romantic Ideology: A Critical Investigation.* Chicago: University of Chicago Press, 1983.

Meeker, Joseph W. *The Comedy of Survival: Studies in Literary Ecology.* New York: Scribner's, 1974.

Metres, Philip. *Behind the Lines: War Resistance Poetry on the American Homefront since 1941.* Iowa City: University of Iowa Press, 2007.

Miles, Josephine. *Pathetic Fallacy in the Nineteenth Century: A Study of a Changing Relation between Object and Emotion.* 1942. Reprint, New York: Octagon Books, 1965.

Morton, Timothy. *Ecology without Nature: Rethinking Environmental Aesthetics.* Cambridge, MA: Harvard University Press, 2007.

Murphy, Patrick D. "Robinson Jeffers' Macabre and Darkly Marvelous Double Axe." *Western American Literature* 20 (1985): 195–209.

New, Elisa. *The Line's Eye: Poetic Experience, American Sight.* Cambridge, MA: Harvard University Press, 1998.

Oelschlaeger, Max. *The Idea of Wilderness: From Prehistory to the Age of Ecology.* New Haven: Yale University Press, 1991.

Pagel, Mark, ed. *Encyclopedia of Evolution.* 2 vols. Oxford: Oxford University Press, 2002.

Park, Josephine Nock-Hee. *Apparitions of Asia: Modernist Form and Asian American Poetics.* Oxford: Oxford University Press, 2008.

Penrose, Roger. *The Emperor's New Mind: Concerning Computers, Minds, and the Laws of Physics.* Oxford: Oxford University Press, 1989.

Phillips, Dana. *The Truth of Ecology: Nature, Culture, and Literature in America.* New York: Oxford University Press, 2003.

Powers, Alfred. *Redwood Country: The Lava Region and the Redwoods.* New York: Duell, Sloan, and Pearce, 1949.

Preminger, Alex, ed. *Encyclopedia of Poetry and Poetics.* Princeton: Princeton University Press, 1965.

Quetchenbach, Bernard. *Back from the Far Field: American Nature Poetry in the Late Twentieth Century.* Charlottesville: University of Virginia Press, 2000.

Rasula, Jed. *This Compost: Ecological Imperatives in American Poetry.* Athens: University of Georgia Press, 2002.

Rexroth, Kenneth. *An Autobiographical Novel.* Rev. ed. Ed. Linda Hamalian. New York: New Directions, 1991.

———. *The Complete Poems of Kenneth Rexroth.* Ed. Sam Hamill and Bradford Morrow. Port Townsend, WA: Copper Canyon, 2003.

———. "In Defense of Jeffers." *Saturday Review,* 10 August 1957, 30.

Richardson, Robert D. *Emerson: The Mind on Fire.* Berkeley: University of California Press, 1995.

Rolston, Holmes, III. *Three Big Bangs: Matter-Energy, Life, Mind.* New York: Columbia University Press, 2010.

Rotella, Guy. *Reading and Writing Nature.* Boston: Northeastern University Press, 1991.

Sale, Kirkpatrick. *Dwellers in the Land: The Bioregional Vision.* San Francisco: Sierra Club, 1985.

Saussy, Haun. "Fenollosa Compounded: A Discrimination." In *The Chinese Written Character as a Medium for Poetry,* by Ernest Fenollosa and Ezra Pound, ed. Haun Saussy, Jonathan Stalling, and Lucas Klein, 1–40. New York: Fordham University Press, 2008.

Smith, Jonathan Z. *To Take Place: Toward Theory in Ritual.* Chicago: University of Chicago Press, 1987.

———. "The Wobbling Pivot." *Journal of Religion* 52, no. 2 (1972): 134–49.

Smuts, J. C. *Holism and Evolution.* New York: Macmillan, 1926.

Snyder, Gary. "The Art of Poetry, LXXIV." Interview by Eliot Weinberger. *Paris Review,* no. 141 (Winter 1996): 88–118.

———. *Danger on Peaks.* Washington, DC: Shoemaker and Hoard, 2004.

———. *Earth House Hold.* New York: New Directions, 1969.

———. *No Nature: New and Selected Poems.* New York: Pantheon, 1992.

———. *A Place in Space: Ethics, Aesthetics, and Watersheds.* Washington, DC: Counterpoint, 1995.

———. *The Practice of the Wild.* San Francisco: North Point, 1990.

———. *Turtle Island.* New York: New Directions, 1974.

Stalling, Jonathan. *Poetics of Emptiness: Transformations of Asian Thought in American Poetry.* New York: Fordham University Press, 2010.

Stevens, Wallace. *Letters of Wallace Stevens.* Ed. Holly Stevens. Berkeley: University of California Press, 1996.

Sugihara, Neil G., Jan W. Van Wagtendonk, Kevin Eugene Shaffer, Joann Fites-Kaufman, and Andrea E. Thode, eds. *Fire in California's Ecosystems.* Berkeley: University of California Press, 2006.

Surette, Leon. *The Birth of Modernism: Ezra Pound, T. S. Eliot, W. B. Yeats, and the Occult.* Montreal: McGill-Queen's University Press, 1993.

Tobias, Philip V. "The Brain of *Homo habilis:* A New Level of Organization in Cerebral Evolution." *Journal of Human Evolution* 16 (1987): 741–65.

Toffler, Alvin. Foreword to *Order out of Chaos: Man's New Dialogue with Nature,* by Ilya Prigogine and Isabelle Stengers. New York: Random House, 1984.

Vaughan, Agne Carr. *The House of the Double Axe.* New York: Doubleday, 1959.

Waggoner, Hyatt Howe. "Science and the Poetry of Robinson Jeffers." *American Literature* 10, no. 3 (1938): 275–88.

Whitman, Walt. *Leaves of Grass and Other Writings.* Ed. Michael Moon. New York: Norton, 2002.

Worster, Donald. *Nature's Economy: A History of Ecological Ideas.* Cambridge: Cambridge University Press, 1977.

Wrangham, Richard. *Catching Fire: How Cooking Made Us Human.* New York: Basic Books, 2009.

Wyatt, David. *The Fall into Eden: Landscape and Imagination in California.* Cambridge: Cambridge University Press, 1986.

Young, Vernon. "Such Counsels He Gave to Us: Jeffers Revisited." *Parnassus: Poetry in Review* 6, no. 1 (1977): 178–97.

Zaller, Robert. *The Cliffs of Solitude: A Reading of Robinson Jeffers.* Cambridge: Cambridge University Press, 1983.

———. "Jeffers, Rexroth, and the Trope of Hellenism." *Western American Literature* 36, no. 2 (2001): 153–69.

———. "Robinson Jeffers, American Poetry, and a Thousand Years." In *Centennial Essays for Robinson Jeffers,* ed. Robert Zaller, 29–43. Newark: University of Delaware Press, 1991.

———. *Robinson Jeffers and the American Sublime.* Stanford: Stanford University Press, 2012.

———. "Robinson Jeffers, Narrative, and the Freudian Family Romance." *Journal of Narrative Technique* 27, no. 2 (1997): 234–48.

Ziolkowski, Theodore. *The View from the Tower: Origins of an Antimodernist Image.* Princeton: Princeton University Press, 1998.

Index